Sociological Theory:
Uses and Unities

For Barbara

Sociological Theory

Uses and Unities

Second Edition

Stephen Mennell

Nelson

A Sc + Hum
1982

Thomas Nelson and Sons Ltd
Nelson House Mayfield Road
Walton-on-Thames Surrey KT12 5PL

PO Box 18123 Nairobi Kenya

Watson Estate Block A 13 Floor
Watson Road Causeway Bay Hong Kong

116-D JTC Factory Building
Lorong 3 Geylang Square Singapore 14

Thomas Nelson Australia Pty Ltd
19–39 Jeffcott Street West Melbourne Victoria 3003

Nelson Canada Ltd
81 Curlew Drive Don Mills Ontario M3A 2R1

Thomas Nelson (Nigeria) Ltd
8 Ilupeju Bypass PMB 21303 Ikeja Lagos

© Copyright Stephen Mennell 1974, 1980

First published 1974
Second edition 1980

ISBN 0 17 711131 3 (hardback) NCN 5841/40
ISBN 0 17 712125 4 (limp)   NCN 5842/40

Printed in Hong Kong

301. Q1MEN

Contents

Acknowledgements

I should like to thank the following for permission to quote passages and use diagrams:

Oxford University Press, New York, for passages from Max Weber's *Economy and Society* originally published in *From Max Weber* (translated by H. H. Gerth and C. Wright Mills, 1946) and in *The Theory of Social and Economic Organization* (translated by A. M. Henderson and Talcott Parsons, 1947).

The Linguistic Society of America for the quotation from Noam Chomsky's review of B. F. Skinner's *Verbal Behaviour* in *Language*, 1959.

Juventa Verlag for Table 1, which is based on a table in Norbert Elias's *Was ist Soziologie?* (1970).

The Editor of the *American Journal of Sociology* for Table 2, which is taken from James S. Coleman's article 'Foundations for a Theory of Collective Decisons' in that journal, 1966.

Jeremy Bossevain and Basil Blackwell Ltd for Figure 2, which is from Professor Boissevain's *Friends of Friends* (1974).

Dr Elizabeth Gittus and the Editor of *Human Relations* for Figure 3, which is from Dr Gittus's article' Urban Families: Conjugal Roles and Social Networks' in *Human Relations*, 1955.

Appleton-Century-Crofts for Figure 4, which is from Hubert M. Blalock's article 'The Formalization of Sociological Theory' in *Theoretical Sociology: Perspectives and Developments*, edited by J. C. McKinney and E. A. Tiryakian, 1970.

Claude Lévi-Strauss and the American Folklore Society for Figure 7, which first appeared in Lévi-Strauss's article 'The Structural Study of Myth', in the *Journal of American Folklore*, 78, no. 270, 1955.

Preface to the Second Edition

The first edition of *Sociological Theory: Uses and Unities* seems to have been found useful. The impending exhaustion of the second impression has now offered the opportunity to prepare a new edition. In the event, I found it necessary to re-argue, rewrite and restructure the book rather extensively. The new edition is larger than the first, but apart from adding a good deal of new material I have omitted some of the old. In particular I have cut most of the discussion of old-fashioned 'conflict' and 'consensus' theory and all but a brief reference to exchange theory, which though it provides a nice intellectual puzzle is plainly of no lasting importance to the discipline of sociology.

The words 'uses and unities' perhaps still require justification on grounds other than euphony. 'Uses' alludes to my view that in sociology it is dangerous for the wheels to grind without corn. There has long been a tendency for the grander sort of sociological theorist to fly off into deep conceptual space. But conceptual schemes and theoretical 'approaches' increase our understanding of the social processes in which we are caught up only if they are developed hand in hand with empirical investigation – guiding the investigation but in turn being continuously modified by it. As E. P. Thompson remarks, 'the project of Grand Theory – to find a total systematized conceptualization of all history and human occasions – is the original heresy of metaphysics against knowledge' (Thompson 1978: 303). Yet at present to emphasize the theoretical indispensability of empirical investigation is to expose oneself to the accusation of 'empiricism' and other foul sins of 'positivism'. There is, however, as Thompson has also remarked, a world of difference between 'empiricism' and an '*empirical idiom of discourse*'; the two should not be naïvely confused. I have tried to show that such concepts as 'individual' and 'society', 'conflict' and 'consensus', and 'structure' and 'function', all traditionally important terms in sociological 'theory', can only be meaningfully discussed within an empirical idiom of discourse.

Not surprisingly, then, the word 'unities' does not indicate that I have attempted any final grand conceptual synthesis. But it does signify my dissatisfaction with the pedagogic method which spreads before the student so many 'approaches' to sociology – called 'Marxism', 'functionalism', 'symbolic interactionism', 'phenomenology', 'ethnomethodology' or whatever – and, making no effort to explore how they may be related to each other, invites him to take them or leave them. My dissatisfaction focuses in particular on the view that there are 'two sociologies', one 'individual-centred' and one 'system-centred', which are eternally incompatible with each other. Dawe (1970) may well be right that in the history of sociological thought it is possible to discern one series of writers who depict human beings as free 'acting' agents, 'interacting' with each other to create 'society', 'social structure' or 'social institutions'; and that there is another series of writers who place the emphasis on the durability of 'social structure' from generation to generation, and on its ability to shape and constrain people's actions. But he has to admit that the greatest sociologists of the past usually had a foot in both camps. Which is not unexpected, since the two viewpoints do not contradict each other, although it is true that sociologists have had difficulty in conceptualizing this fact. I have tried to show that any adequate sociological theory will take account not only of the 'subjective' perceptions, motives and intentions of individual people, but also simultaneously of the 'objective' patterns of social interdependence as they stand external to any particular individual. So notable a contemporary figure as Jürgen Habermas has in recent years made this argument at length.

In the Introduction to the first edition of this book, I made the mistake of describing my own position as one of 'methodological individualism'. That remark was – not unreasonably – misinterpreted, though it was true in the sense I intended. I meant, for example, that what we describe as 'social forces' are in fact forces exerted by people over other people. I also meant that social groups or collectivities cannot be said to think, learn or have purposes in the same sense that individual people do. In other words I am suspicious of the kind of teleological reasoning so often evident in functionalist theorizing. But all the same, my self-appellation of 'methodological individualist' was highly misleading. It follows from what I have said about the implications of the word 'unities' that my intention is to reject the false issue of 'individualism' versus 'holism'. Certainly the collectivities we speak of as groups, families, organizations, armies, states, and so on, have an existence just as real as individuals.

The influence of Norbert Elias will be evident in many parts of this book. My conversations over the last few years with Joop Goudsblom have also helped me to focus my arguments more clearly. Neither, of course, would agree with the whole contents.

I should like to thank Rosalind Webber and Susan Langford-Johnson for typing sections of the manuscript. My wife Barbara not only typed another section but read and discussed each chapter as it was written. She reluctantly tolerated my general air of muddle and domestic inefficiency while I was working on this second edition.

Stephen Mennell
Exeter, June 1979

1 'Individual', 'Society' and Social Action

It is frequently said that the central question of sociology is 'why is there order in society?' Like so many commonplaces, this is misleading. The question can be taken two ways. 'Order' can first be taken to mean much the same thing as it does in the popular phrase 'law and order'. The question is then understood to mean 'how do people manage to co-operate with each other so as to achieve a degree of social harmony?' This is often described as the 'Hobbesian problem'. It was Thomas Hobbes (1651) who asked why, if every individual pursues his own self interest, by whatever means – including brute force – that are at hand, is there not a 'war of everyone against everyone'. Why is life in society not in consequence 'solitary, poor, nasty, brutish and short'?

In fact, by the standards of twentieth-century Britain or America, over most of human history and in many different kinds of society, life for a large proportion of people *has* indeed been poor, nasty, brutish and short. If it has not been solitary, that is only because the human animal has never lived other than in societies. But those societies have varied greatly in size. Often only a small band of people have lived in co-operation with each other, while having to face many other similar bands in ruthless conflict. The large-scale societies of millions of people among whom a measure of 'law and order' is maintained, and some control exercised over internal conflicts, are of relatively recent origin. Social order in this sense is thus a very relative matter.

The 'question of order' may, however, take a second form. It is necessary to sociology, as it is to any other discipline pretending to yield reliable and cumulative knowledge, that there be order in its subject-matter. This means only that order in the sense of pattern or regularity can be observed in social processes. It is patterns and regulations which make possible description and explanation, in social science as much as in the natural sciences. Sociologists have been able to find order – pattern or regularity – not only in stable societies and smoothly functioning organizations, but in bitter social conflict, in bloody revolutions, and in periods of rapid, unplanned and superficially chaotic change. Law and order may break down in orderly, patterned and regular ways. Needless to say, order in this sense may be quite imperceptible to the participants, and only become apparent to a sociologist faced with evidence of many similar situations.

On reflection, the 'problem of order' in this second sense resolves itself into the following question: why do individual people, who are apparently acting 'of their own free will', nevertheless interact and intermesh with each other in such a way that their actions form fairly stable patterns, or structured processes of change, of which they themselves may be wholly or partly unaware and which they certainly did not plan? It is these relatively stable collective patterns which sociologists observe and label with such phrases as 'social structure'.

The relationship between 'individual actions' and 'social structure', or simply between the 'Individual' and 'Society' has troubled generations of sociologists, including the greatest. The problem often seems to present itself in this form: should we start from 'the Individual' and try to show how individuals' plans, intentions and actions create 'social structure'? Or should we start from 'Society', from existing 'social structure', and show how it shapes and constrains 'the Individual' to behave in conformity with it?

Posed this way the question is absurd. To debate the priority of 'the Individual' or 'Society' is like asking 'Which came first, the chicken or the egg?' Just as eggs are inconceivable without hens to lay them, and hens inconceivable without eggs from which to hatch, so individuals and societies ought to be inconceivable – impossible to discuss – without each other. For there can be no society without individuals, and no human individual ever existed in total independence of society. Robinson Crusoe, that indispensable figure in the economics textbooks, is only conceivable as a human being in isolation because he had grown up – *become* a human being – in a society. Rare instances of children, like the celebrated Wild Boy of Aveyron, who have apparently survived their first years in isolation from human beings, seem never themselves to become truly human.

It helps if we stop talking abstractly about 'Man' or 'the Individual' in the singular, and instead talk concretely about human beings in the plural. *A fortiori*, we should speak not of 'Society' but of societies. The difficulty disappears as soon as we stop thinking of 'the Individual' and 'Society' as two separate, static entities, and think instead of human beings and societies as interdependent aspects of a continuous process.

Yet the discipline of sociology continues to be plagued by the 'Individual and Society' problem. Two recently fashionable sects offer a revealing contrast. The ethnomethodologists saw their task as identifying the social skills which people constantly employ in face-to-face encounters and conversations. They viewed with scepticism any propositions about large-scale structures within which such encounters take place, and showed little interest in broader questions of how patterns of behaviour and social skills came to develop to be what they are. On the other hand, sociological followers of the French Marxist philosopher Louis Althusser saw human beings merely as *Träger* – carriers or supports – of the structure of society. From the existence of relatively stable collective patterns, Althusser inferred that it was simply an illusion that individual people were capable of thinking and acting freely or independently. Althusser, in fact, makes it clear at last that the misconceived issue of 'the Individual' and 'Society' is a variant of the old metaphysical problem of 'free will' versus 'determinism'. Theologians used to argue whether an individual was responsible for his own actions and for the fate of his own soul, or whether his actions and his fate had already been predestined before birth by God. Since the Enlightenment, 'Society' has gradually replaced God, but the question is still too often framed in a metaphysical way.

Common sense suggests that individual people have some capacity for independent thought and action. Common sense also suggests that people's thoughts, actions and ways of life are powerfully shaped and constrained by what they experience, learn and encounter within established social patterns. In other words 'free will' does not mean that there are *no limits* on action. This common sense insight implies that there are two main requirements for sociology, neither of which can be neglected without distorting the overall enterprise. They are interconnected and neither takes logical priority over the other.

First, sociology needs a plausible social psychology which does justice to the ways in which experience in a society shapes the personality, thinking and behaviour of people enmeshed in it. Such a social psychology must give an account of how people acquire the capacity for *self-control*, without theoretically reducing them to automata whose every last thought and action is pre-programmed by 'Society'. By extension, sociological explanations will have to take due account of the motives, preceptions and purposes of sentient human beings.

But, simultaneously, sociologists must also study the networks of social interdependence within which every human being is caught up. From the standpoint of any single human being, such webs of interdependence are an objective, external fact, setting the limits or constraints on, or at least the cost of, his or her freedom of action. This 'social structure' consists in the last resort of other human beings.

What is experienced as *social control* is in fact control exerted by people over other people. Yet the fact that 'social structure' stands external to and unwilled by any particular individual means that the sociologist must study it as such. No amount of probing into people's perceptions and consciousness will lead to the discovery of the objective contexts within which action takes place.[1] Both the 'subjective' and the 'objective' have to be studied in parallel.

Questions of the relationship between 'Individual' and 'Society', between 'social action, and 'social structure', between 'self-control' and 'social control', are often presented as if they were ones which could be answered for all time entirely by the invention and manipulation of appropriate concepts and categories. But they are also questions to which empirical evidence is relevant. For the patterning of and balance between self-control and social control fluctuate and develop over time, and vary from one type of social group and society to another. This is something to be borne in mind when examining the ways in which sociologists and psychologists have thought about 'social action' and the processes by which people learn patterns of behaviour within society.

Behaviourism: Skinner versus Chomsky

What kind of psychological propositions are necessary for sociological purposes? The simplest but in the end most misleading account of how people acquire their patterns of social behaviour is that given by the proponents of 'behaviourism'. By that is meant the school of psychology which, on the basis of experimental work largely with animals, formulates propositions about how behaviour is shaped by learning or 'operant conditioning'. It is sometimes called learning or S-R (stimulus-response) theory. Human behaviour is extremely malleable, and people learn to behave in very different ways in different social groups or societies. This leads behaviourists, like Althusserians, to take a very deterministic view of the learning process. B. F. Skinner, the most celebrated recent exponent of behaviourism, even wrote a novel depicting how conditioning techniques could be used to create an ideal community (Skinner 1948) – an ideal community which many readers found somewhat sinister. Now, if all behaviour is determined and causally explicable by prior conditioning, then our subjective impressions that we are choosing what we do must be illusory. So it is not surprising that behaviourists also hold evidence of subjective purposes, intentions and mental states to be irrelevant to the explanation of behaviour. A number of sociologists (see for example Homans 1961, and the contributors to Burgess and Bushell, 1969) would accept behavioural psychology as a basis for sociological theory. Many more, variously described as social action theorists, symbolic interactionists and phenomenologists, join in rejecting behaviourism. The issue at stake can best be seen by examining first Skinner's views and then the famous critique of them by the linguist Noam Chomsky.

In a series of elegant books (1953, 1957, 1972), Skinner seeks to give a 'functional' causal explanation of behaviour patterns. For scientific purposes the human organism is to be regarded as differing in no fundamental way from lower organisms. Man must, if necessary, be seen as a machine. To explain behaviour as caused by inner mental states is in Skinner's view to walk up a blind alley. 'The objection to inner states is not that they do not exist, but that they are not relevant in functional analysis.' (1953: 35). Skinner sees any psychology whose primary causes are internal and mental as akin to astrology and alchemy.

> The practice of looking inside an organism for an explanation of behaviour has tended to obscure the variables which are immediately available for scientific analysis. These variables lie outside the organism, in its immediate environment and in its environmental history. They have a physical status to which the usual techniques of science are adapted, and they make it possible to explain behaviour as other subjects are explained in science. (1953: 31)

The kind of explanation acceptable to Skinner can best be illustrated by one of his own experiments in 'operant conditioning' the behaviour of pigeons. A pigeon in a 'Skinner box' is fed by means of an electrically operated retractable tray. Once the pigeon is accustomed to this source of food, its behaviour can be shaped by the scientist. As it moves around the box, the pigeon occasionally and randomly raises its head above the usual height. Whenever its head reaches a predetermined level, the scientist operates the tray and feeds the pigeon. The bird is soon observed to emit the behaviour much more frequently. By manipulating external stimuli, the experimenter changes the bird's normal posture. The change is brought about by the selective reinforcement of one element in an orginally random repertoire of behaviour, and can be explained without any reference to the pigeon's mental process. Skinner soon extends this argument to human behaviour. For instance, by depriving a man of water for a period, or by administering a diuretic drug, we can increase the probability that he will drink a glass of water. His action can then be explained without reference to his internal state of thirst, which we cannot directly observe. The causal chain consists of three links: (1) an operation performed on the organism from without (deprivation of water); (2) an inner condition (thirst); (3) a kind of behaviour (drinking). For the behaviourist, any reference to the middle link is redundant to parsimonious theory building.

It may be objected that quenching a thirst is a very simple example of human behaviour, directly related to physiological need. Our behaviour is typically far more complex and much more remotely linked to biological necessity. Skinner is quite right in replying that complexity in itself is not an adequate objection to his views – complex phenomena merely require a more elaborate theory, which may in practice, it is true, be difficult to construct.

> Self-determination does not follow from complexity. Difficulty in calculating the orbit of a fly does not prove capriciousness, though it may make it impossible to prove anything else. (1953:20)

But the sources of that complexity are relevant. *Control* is essential to Skinner's theory; he predicts and therefore explains behaviour from known and controlled stimuli. He could not explain the behaviour of even a pigeon in the wild, a pigeon whose history is unknown. And human beings in the wild are of course capable of much more complex learning. Sociologists are typically interested in very complex kinds of behaviour resulting from past history and biography of individuals and groups, which is generally unknown and unknowable to the determinedly 'external' observer. Nor is much of human behaviour susceptible to transfer to the controlled situation of the laboratory without being hopelessly distorted.

Where the external stimuli to which the organism has been exposed are unknown, even Skinner admits the desirability of information about inner states.

> Independent information about the second link [inner conditions] would obviously permit us to predict the third [behaviour] without recourse to the first [external stimuli]. It would be a preferable type of variable because it would be non-historic; the first link may be in the past history of the organism, but the second is a current condition. *Direct information about the second link is, however, seldom, if ever, available.* (1953:34, my italics)

What a curious assertion the last sentence contains! Certainly we are unable to talk to pigeons, but we can ask human beings what is going on inside them. They can give us an account of their thoughts and internal states. Their accounts may not be entirely accurate but they are likely to be more so – and more valid – than behavioural explanations based on 'speculative history'. And explanations in terms of external stimuli must be speculative in uncontrolled, non-experimental conditions. (Of course, we could ask them to give an account of their past 'stimulus history', but the logical contradiction there is too obvious to dwell upon.)

The implications of this point became apparent when Skinner

sought to extend his theories to that most human kind of behaviour – verbal behaviour (Skinner 1957). It was this book which was subjected to a devastating critique by Noam Chomsky (1959). The gist of Chomsky's case can be captured in one extended quotation:

> A typical example of 'stimulus control' for Skinner would be the response to a piece of music with the utterance *Mozart* or to a painting with the response *Dutch*. These responses are asserted to be 'under the control of extremely subtle properties' of the physical object or event. Suppose instead of saying *Dutch* we had said *Clashes with the wallpaper, I thought you liked abstract work, Never saw it before, Tilted, Hanging too low, Beautiful, Hideous, Remember our camping trip last summer?*, or whatever else came into our minds when looking at a picture (in Skinnerian translation, whatever other responses exist in sufficient strength). Skinner could only say that each of these responses is under the control of some other stimulus property of the physical object. If we look at a red chair and say *red*, the stimulus is under the control of the stimulus 'redness'; if we say *chair*, it is under the control of the collection of properties (for Skinner, the object) 'chairness', and similarly for any other response. The device is as simple as it is empty. Since properties are free for the asking … we can account for a wide class of responses in terms of Skinnerian functional analysis by identifying the 'controlling stimuli'. But the word 'stimulus' has lost all objectivity in this usage. Stimuli are no longer part of the outside physical world; they are driven back into the organism. We identify the stimulus when we hear the response. (Chomsky 1959: 31–32)

Human language is far more flexible and elaborate than any means of communication used by other animals. Behaviourism, according to Chomsky, is quite unable to explain one of the most striking of all features in language. Why is it that all normal people have the capacity to utter new sentences which have never before been spoken by themselves, nor very likely by anyone else? Why is the listener able to understand sentences never heard before, and why is he able to determine whether they are grammatical and 'make sense'?

> The idea that a person has a 'verbal repertoire' – a stock of utterances that he produces by 'habit' on an appropriate occasion – is a myth, totally at variance with the observed use of language. (Chomsky 1967: 400)

Innovation, not repetition, is the rule.

Chomsky's own explanation of why this is possible is too involved to be adequately explored here.[2] He shows conclusively that language is not learned by anything resembling the simple process of operant conditioning. Obviously the meaning of words has to be learned; children are plainly not born with a propensity to speak one language rather than another. Yet Chomsky points out that the language actually used by parents gives the child who is learning to talk only a relatively limited amount of evidence from which to acquire the normal flexible use of vocabulary and, more especially, of grammar. Furthermore, in the formative years, the child's use of language is simply too different from that of adults to be regarded as a direct reflection of what is heard.[3] Chomsky suggests that the 'deep structure' of every language is much the same, perhaps because the human mind, like the hardware of a computer, performs linguistic operations according to invariant underlying rules. But the child has to 'infer' from the limited evidence available to him, the 'generative grammar' of the language spoken in the society in which he grows up, and can then use this to generate grammatical, comprehensible, but *new* utterances.

Since language is inseparable from social activities, Chomsky's theory of language in itself makes a telling case against the determinism of the behaviourists. But in showing that they are implicitly 'driven back into the organism', Chomsky also demonstrates the falsity of the behaviourists' claim to be able to dispense with 'subjective' notions of the intentions, purposes and meanings constituting actions. For the behaviourists' description of their supposedly external variables depends on their prior, linguistically mediated, understanding of the meaning of the behaviour they seek to explain. Jürgen Habermas, following Chomsky's lead, spells out why this is so:

> Behaviour itself is defined as understandable behaviour; it is only apparently 'objective'. Behaviour is constantly interpreted in the framework of a situation which we interpret from our own experiences. The class of observable events which we call 'modes behaviour' is distinguished from the class of other events through a system of reference which makes explicit an understandable connection. This system of reference establishes a functional connection between the original state of the organism, its environment (including conditions of existence and stimuli) and its final state. The connection is functional from the point of view of a need-satisfaction that is not directly observable – we have already understood in advance what it means to satisfy a need. We should never come to understand it through observation alone....
>
> It is precisely the unacknowledged but unbreakable attachment of the behaviourist approach to a linguistically articulated prior understanding of experience in the everyday world of social life which explains why behaviourist theories of human behaviour are possible. Language cannot be reduced to behaviour, but if we presuppose an initial understanding through linguistic communication of the hidden intentionality of behaviour we can analyse intentional action behaviouristically. (Habermas 1970: 162, 164)[4]

In other words, though behaviourists cannot admit it without contradicting their own premises, behaviourist explanations implicitly rest upon the description and definition of human action in terms which are intersubjectively understood from the outset. An explicit acknowledgement of precisely this point is what principally distinguishes the 'social behaviourism' of George Herbert Mead from behaviourism without the epithet. Mead's work contributes much more powerfully towards a psychological and methodological basis for sociology which recognizes that human behaviour, beliefs and knowledge are learned in society, and yet at the same time does justice to the human capacity for reflection upon and self-modification of behaviour, and makes people's intentions, feelings and purposes available for investigation.

Social Behaviourism, alias Symbolic Interactionism

Many different schools of sociology and psychology have rejected the behaviourist position. The roots of one such school of thought, now generally known as 'symbolic interactionism', run back to late nineteenth-century America and the pragmatist philosophy and psychology of C. S. Pierce (1839–1914), William James (1842–1910) and John Dewey (1859–1952).[5] Pragmatist ideas were first carried into sociology by Charles Horton Cooley (1864–1929), famous for his concepts of 'primary group' and 'looking-glass self', and by William Isaac Thomas (1863–1947).

It was, however, George Herbert Mead (1863–1931) who was to have the most considerable influence on sociology. Mead was professor of philosophy and social psychology at the University of Chicago, where he was a figure in the background during the golden years of the 'Chicago School' of sociology (see Faris 1967). Yet his thought made its main impact in sociology beyond Chicago only after his death, for he published little and the books on which his reputation rests (Mead 1932, 1934, 1936, 1938) were posthumously salvaged from lecture notes.

Mead described his point of view as 'social behaviourism'. The term 'symbolic interactionism' was first applied to it in 1937 by Herbert Blumer, one of Mead's chief disciples (Blumer 1969: 1). Mead took as his starting point the capacity of human beings to understand and communicate with each other, and sought to explain how people acquire within social processes the ability to interpret their own and other people's actions through symbolic thought. Mead's social psychology is, he says, behaviouristic in the sense of starting from the observable activity of the social process.

> But it is not behaviouristic in the sense of ignoring the inner experience of the individual – the inner phase of that process or activity. On the contrary, it is particularly concerned with the rise of such experience within the process as a whole. It simply works from the outside to the inside instead of

from the inside to the outside, so to speak, in its endeavour to determine how such experience does arise within the process. (Mead 1934: 7–8)

The lower animals interact and communicate with each other, but their communication is limited to the *conversation of gestures*. A gesture is part of the social act which serves directly as a stimulus to the other animal. A dog attacks by biting. The initial gesture is the baring of its teeth. This stimulates the other dog to respond by adopting a defensive posture and perhaps baring its teeth too; which in turn acts as a stimulus to the first dog. So the dog-fight begins. But there is no need to assume deliberation and conscious interpretation by the dogs of the other's actions. Skinner could well explain the process as consisting of learned responses. The interaction is non-symbolic. Gestures of this kind remain important in human behaviour. Mead points to boxing and fencing. The boxer or fencer, who has trained and practised, parries a punch or thrust without conscious deliberation. And just as the involuntary tensing of the animal which has sensed danger communicates danger to the rest of the herd, so in human crowds, panic can be communicated by signs expressed involuntarily.

Man's unique ability, however, is the use of symbols. The difference between a gesture and a symbol for Mead is the difference between punching someone and shaking a fist at him. Shaking a fist normally communicates not the possibility of attack, but the *idea* of anger in the shaker's mind. The person at whom the fist is shaken is able to interpret it as meaning hostility; it is the *idea* of anger which has been communicated from one mind to another. Rather than calling forth an appropriate physical, observable response, the *significant symbol* answers to a *meaning* in the second person's experience. But by far the most important category of significant symbols consists of those made vocally, called language.

Sounds, obviously, do not have intrinsic meaning. Their significance, the connection between a sound and its object (whether a physical or 'abstract' object) is learned in social groups: this is how symbols come to have the same (or much the same) meaning for all members of a group. We have to learn the connection between sounds produced on uttering the word 'chair', and that class of objects sharing the minimum characteristics such as are listed under that word in the dictionary. Yet this may be slightly misleading. It should not be taken to imply that words merely serve to express pre-existent inner meanings. In Mead's words:

Language does not simply symbolize a situation or object which is already there in advance; it makes possible the existence or appearance of that situation or object, for it is part of the mechanism whereby that situation or object is created. (1934: 78)

Mead could not have anticipated the recent work on language associated with Chomsky, but he appreciated that the millions of meanings which can be processed in the human brain make possible integrated, precise, differentiated, yet plastic social behaviour far beyond that possible in sub-human animals.

Mead argued that it is only by means of language that thinking can take place. Thought is made possible by the internalization of the symbolic communication of society. Man's unique use of language is the outward manifestation of his unique ability to think about himself as an object. Man is the only self-reflexive animal; the 'I' is able to regard the 'Me' as an object. In consequence we are able to anticipate our future actions, to examine the likely outcome of a number of alternative courses of action, and to determine which of them to implement. From this stems the possibility of purposive action. Mead's social behaviourism is thus seen to be very much at odds with behaviourism as conventionally understood.

Language, thought and reflection thus make possible highly complex behaviour. Verbal communication also makes it possible to learn a vast amount indirectly from other people. At the same time, Mead emphasized that the origins of these capacities in any individual can only be understood by looking at his social experience. The very young child does not have the self-reflexive ability, cannot take himself as the object of his thoughts. The genesis of the self is to be found in the social process.

The child's acquisition of language begins quite early, when cognitive development first permits the discrimination of others' responses.

> The world of the infant is at first a motley confusion of sights, sounds and smells. He becomes able to differentiate a portion of this world only when he is able to designate it to himself by means of a symbol. Initially the infant acts in random fashion, and a socialized other responds to random gestures in a meaningful way, thus giving a social definition to the random gesture of the infant. Once the infant understands the meaning of the gesture (e.g. a cry, a wave of the arm) ... that gesture has become a symbol for him. (Rose 1962: 15)

The development of self-consciousness is, however, not seen clearly until the child begins to understand the set of relationships expressed by the personal pronouns, 'I', 'we', 'you', 'he', 'she' and 'they'. As Elias notes, 'the individual positions in this set of relationships cannot be treated separately.... The function of the pronoun 'I' in human communication can only be understood in the context of all the other positions to which the other terms in the series refer.' (Elias 1978a: 123). When the child demonstrates its understanding of these relationships by using 'I' to refer to that which others address as 'you', it is exhibiting the beginnings of self-consciousness, its ability to think of itself as object, the origins of its 'self'. Close observation of children at play shows that at first they do not really 'play with' each other, but merely in each other's company. Each child's activity is repetitive and solitary, unco-ordinated with that of the other child. Analysis of their 'conversation' reveals it to be not a dialogue but two monologues. A crucial development takes place when the child begins in play to act out the role of 'mother' to its dolls, or 'cowboy' and 'indian'. Mead calls this *taking the role of the other*. It marks a stage on the growth of reflexive self-awareness, but cowboys-and-indians requires minimal co-ordination. The rules can be varied at whim, the role abandoned or changed at will. Only much later does the child become capable of taking part in more elaborate games like football with established rules. In order to play his own part in such a game, the individual has to be able to put himself in place of all the other participants. His role only exists in relation to the roles of others. Each player has to take the role of the *generalized other*; he has to see his own moves as they appear from the perspective of the other participants before carrying them out. The game is a microcosm of social life. Taking the role of the other is involved in all symbolic communication, because in order to communicate we have to anticipate the interpretation the hearer will put on our words. And only thus is organized, co-operative activity possible.

The concept of the generalized other is central to Mead's view of how society shapes the individual's personality and his actions.

> It is the form of the generalized other that the social process influences the behaviour of the individuals involved in it and carrying it on, that is, that the community exercises control over the conduct of its individual members, for it is in this form that the social process or community enters as a determining factor into the individual's thinking. (Mead 1934: 155)

Mead's theories invite empirical exploration through studies of the growth of cognitive processes and moral judgement during the socialization process. In broad outline his views have indeed received substantial support from the work of the great Genevan psychologist, Jean Piaget (b. 1896). Piaget initially formulated his own theories quite independently of Mead's ideas, but they are in many respects remarkably close to them, and he has produced empirical evidence through studies of the psychological development of children in a systematic and detailed way that Mead never contemplated (see for example Piaget 1926, 1932).

In sociology proper, Mead's influence on the symbolic interactionist tradition can be seen clearly in the work of a writer like Erving Goffman. In *The Presentation of Self in Everyday Life* (1959) and subsequent works, Goffman explores the 'arts of impression management' which people employ, largely unconsciously, all the time. Goffman's 'dramaturgical' perspective sometimes leads him to depict people as if they were Ancient Greek actors wearing a fixed mask according to the role they are playing. But he never loses sight of the fact that they are real people, not behaviourist automata. Wearing a mask imposes strains and requires great self-control. Goffman describes how a head waiter 'offstage' in the kitchen, may be loudly cursing the chef seconds before gliding out into the restaurant, 'on stage' in front of the customers, wearing his dignified, deferential mask. Or, when the restaurant or shop is empty, waiters or shop assistants may relieve the tensions their roles impose by caricaturing their absent customers – expressing what Goffman calls 'role-distance' (1961b).

We learn many of these arts of impression management very early. Goffman notes how young children will unselfconsciously enjoy riding on a roundabout, but when they are only a little older will fool around as they ride, showing that the roundabout is really a little below their dignity, and incidentally, that they have acquired the art of expressing role-distance. Sociologists in the symbolic interactionist tradition have however, also emphasized that socialization continues far beyond childhood. Almost every social process – social mobility, emigration, incarceration or just ageing – involves people moving into new social milieux, and has its impact on their self-conceptions and sense of personal identity. One of the earliest classics of Chicago socio-logy, Thomas and Znaniecki's *The Polish Peasant in Europe and America* (1918–20) was a study of the Pole's experience of emigration, the dis-ruption of his stable and traditional way of life, and his struggle to come to terms with his new situation in the U.S.A. Decades later, a similar concern is evident in Howard Becker's discussion (1963) of how people learn to be marijuana users, are inducted into a pot-smoking sub-culture and learn to see themselves as 'outsiders'. Goffman too provides a splendid example of this line of interest in his account of 'total institutions' (1961a). Under the title 'total institu-tions', he groups together mental hospitals, prisons, army barracks and monasteries, and brilliantly brings out their common character-istics. Most basic is that, for the inmates of any of these total insti-tutions, there is no off-stage area to which they can withdraw to remove their mask or change it for a different one. The objectives of incarceration and isolation from the outside world are various – punishment or reform in the case of prisons, discipline in barracks, other-worldliness in monasteries, psychiatric treatment in the case of hospitals. But there are certain common features: the ritual of entering – often a bath, the substitution of uniform for one's own individualistic clothes, sometimes a change of name or the allocation of a number; and large blocks of people are moved around together, doing the same things at the same time. Each total institution constitutes, in Goffman's words, 'a natural experiment on what can be done to the self'. The abnegation of individuality, he suggests, is hardly to the benefit of mental hospital patients at least.

As the term symbolic interaction itself implies, sociologists in this tradition have been mainly interested in studying people interacting face-to-face, and have therefore been at their most impressive when dealing with rather small social units. They have lacked an adequate conception of larger-scale social structures and longer-term social processes.[6] When they have had occasion to turn to the more macroscopic concerns, this has often been accomplished by transforming Mead's 'generalized other' into the concept of 'culture'. By culture, they tend to mean something like 'an elaborate set of meanings and values, shared by members of a society, which guides much of [man's] behaviour'. (Rose 1962:9), and which the individual learns during socialization. To be fair to symbolic interactionists, they have frequently been more uneasy with this conceptual jump than have other sociologists. The blank, undifferentiated conception of culture covers over all suspicion of tension between self-control and social control, and in any case provides a very weak explanation of any particular aspect of behaviour. The difficulties can best be illustrated with reference to a number of sociological explanations for crime and 'deviant' behaviour.

One of the most influential of such explanations has been that advanced by Robert Merton (1968: 185–248, orig. 1938). Merton argued that 'culture' defines certain legitimate objectives for members of society, things 'worth striving for'. Success in America and other industrial societies is largely defined in terms of money and wealth. Commonly accepted rules and norms also define the means which may legitimately be employed to attain these goals. But, Merton pointed out, though in contemporary societies the goals tend to be held out equally as objectives for all members of society, opportunities for pursuing them legitimately are not equally distributed. People receive very different starts in life; educational and career opportunities for example are markedly worse towards the bottom of the social scale. There is always widespread disappointment. Merton identified various ways in which people could adapt to frustrating situations. They could reject conventional goals but continue to accept the conventional means, as in the case of the 'ritualist' clerk at the bottom of some bureaucracy. They could reject ends *and* means, becoming 'retreatist' drop-outs. They could rebel, seeking to change society. Or, most interestingly, they could continue to accept conventional goals such as wealth, but pursue them by illegitimate means such as theft.

Merton recognized, however, that most people, even in unencouraging situations, do none of these things, and continue to conform.

Merton's theory points to some kinds of social pressure which may be conducive to deviance. But why do some people conform and others deviate, though they are equally subject to these pressures? And why does deviance take so many different forms in response to the same pressures? Edwin Sutherland (1947:7–8) expressed his doubts as follows:

> Thieves generally steal in order to secure money, but likewise honest labourers work in order to secure money. The attempts by many scholars to explain criminal behaviour by general drives and values, such as ... striving for social status, the money motive, or frustration, have been and must continue to be futile since they explain lawful behaviour as completely as they explain criminal behaviour.

To explain criminal behaviour, it is clearly necessary to examine the individual in his immediate social context as well as in relation to the general conventional values. For, as Cloward and Ohlin (1960) argued, it is not only opportunities generally considered legitimate which are socially structured and unequally distributed. Opportunities for illegitimate activities are also unequally distributed in society. This aspect of crime was always emphasized by the Chicago school of sociologists, and it was epitomized in the idea of 'subcultures'.

Chicago between the wars was teeming with social and cultural diversity – people of numerous ethnic backgrounds, different religions, contrasting wealth and ways of life. This diversity might serve to make Chicago sociologists cautious of speaking simply of 'culture', but the more limited notion of subculture appeared more defensible. Many ethnic and other social groups could be located quite precisely in the urban structure. Criminality too was apparently concentrated in limited areas of the city. Shaw and his collaborators (1929) identified the principal 'delinquency areas' within Chicago, and Thrasher (1927) located 1,313 gangs among juvenile delinquents in the city. Most acts of delinquency were committed in the company of other delinquents, and gangs and associates gave social support to delinquency. It was a reasonable conclusion that the likelihood of a person becoming delinquent was related to opportunities for learning criminal techniques and patterns of behaviour, and for receiving encouragement from associates. Shaw therefore spoke of the 'cultural transmission' of crime and delinquency. Yet not everyone in even the most crime-ridden area is a criminal. Inner-city Chicago in the 1920s must have been one of the most crime-ridden districts on earth, but nothing like a majority of even its inhabitants were criminals.

How is this to be explained? Rose (1962:13–15) set out some of the conventional defences of cultural and subcultural theories. First, it is argued, many cultural expectations neither prescribe nor proscribe specific behaviour, but permit a *range* of actions. Moreover, many of them are specific to certain roles such as occupations, and the individual has a certain degree of choice in the roles he adopts. Second, cultures and subcultures contain internal contradictions; in some situations the cultural signposts may, so to speak, point in opposite directions. Third, people move from subculture to subculture, and their contradictory standards present further opportunities for choice and innovation. This last point, though, might rather be taken to suggest the difficulties of defining the boundaries of a subculture. The term may have appeared reasonably unambiguous in studies of ethnic groups in Chicago with their own territory and sometimes even their own language. However, Suttles (1972: 21–43) has suggested that the neighbourhoods never were factually so homogeneous as they were depicted, and their boundaries were gradients rather than clear-cut lines. The clear-cut lines, he argues, were imposed by the *simplified* cognitive maps of residents, and accepted as factual by sociologists.

To resolve this difficulty in the notions of subculture and cultural transmission, Sutherland (1947, chapter I) advanced his 'differential association' theory. Though applied to crime, it was intended as a general explanation of how patterns of behaviour are acquired.[7] Such factors known to be associated with crime as poverty, bad homes and personal quirks have, according to Sutherland, 'a causal relation to crime only as they affect the person's associations'. The techniques, motives and rationalizations required for criminal behaviour are learned like other behaviour in immediate face-to-face encounters. But we all experience 'culture conflict in relation to legal codes'. We all encounter situations in which laws are defined as not to be broken and some in which they (or some of them) are defined as breakable. For most of us, the former exceed the latter. The principle of differential association states that 'a person becomes delinquent because of an excess of definitions favourable to violation of law over definitions unfavourable to violation of law'. This sounds remarkably behaviourist, and runs into the same difficulties as Skinner's explanation of verbal behaviour. As Sutherland admits, an 'excess of definitions favourable to violation of law' is not easily quantified. There is a risk of *post hoc* explanation: only when we see the crime can we decide whether favourable or unfavourable definitions were in excess. The difficulty is that in the last resort, every man is his own subculture; he has his own unique past experience and though it may resemble that of his associates closely enough to make generalization possible, it is not identical.

Mead was well aware of this. Although he spoke of the 'generalized

other' as the means by which 'the social process ... enters as a determining factor into the individual's thinking', he certainly did not see
whole cultural or subcultural patterns of meanings, values and behaviour as mere external stimuli which the individual passively absorbed
and replicated *en bloc*. An essential aspect of his theory of the social
genesis of mind was that, through earlier social experience, people
acquired the ability to interpret and select.

> The human animal is an attentive animal ... Our whole intelligent process
> seems to lie in the attention which is selective of certain types of stimuli. ...
> Not only do we open the door to certain stimuli and close it to others, but
> our attention is an organizing as well as a selective process. ... Our atten-
> tion enables us to organize the field in which we are going to act. ... One
> organism picks out one thing and another picks out a different one, since
> each is going to act in a different way. (1934:25)[8]

Mead might be said to have seen the personality as 'sampling the
culture'.[9] One way of representing this is shown in Fig. 1. *For purely
heuristic purposes*, personality development and an individual's acquisition of knowledge and attitudes 'from the culture' could be thought
of as a series of binary decisions between courses of development, each
decision being made by the toss of a coin. The decision at each stage
influences where the person will be, as it were, in the next round.
In other words, what is sampled at one point strongly influences what

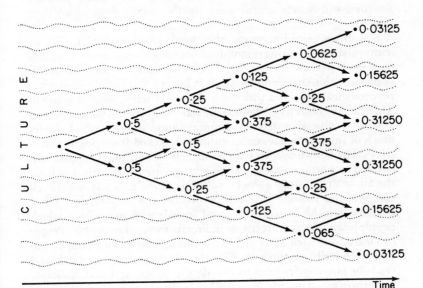

Figure 1

is sampled next. Fig. 1 is drawn so as to show many convergent courses of development as well as divergent ones, so that after only five stages, the probability of attaining a position towards the middle of the cultural stream is ten times that of ending up at one of the 'deviant' poles. Of course, the assumption that sampling decisions are made by the toss of a coin is necessary only to secure mathematical neatness (Fig. 1 actually shows the genesis of a binomial distribution, tending towards a normal curve). In fact, Mead's view would be that such processes are not random: knowledge and attitudes acquired at one point introduce complex selective mechanisms into 'sampling' at later stages.

It cannot be too strongly emphasized that this is a purely heuristic device, not to be interpreted too literally. Nevertheless, it helps to make several things clear. First, in passing, it serves as a reminder that if the social scientist takes a cross section of people in a given community, and collects 'subjective' data about their knowledge and attitudes, the composite picture will be more one of what we speak of as 'the culture' than of individual personalities. If they have 'sampled' from the same population of cultural patterns, their individual samples will differ, but their common features will represent 'the culture' rather adequately and individual quirks will be ironed out. When sociologists present such findings in terms of central tendencies, paying less attention to the variance, they often make people's activities and beliefs appear more rigidly socially determined than they are.

But, much more important, this simple heuristic model, with its 'cultural stream' flowing smoothly in the background draws attention once more to the weakness of the idea of 'culture' as an explanation of people's thinking and behaviour.[10] For it is not merely subjective, psychological processes which structure and select what is learned. There is an 'objective' component too. 'Culture' is not something abstract – 'an elaborate set of meanings and values ... which guides much of [man's] behaviour' – entirely detached from people themselves. The knowledge, techniques, beliefs and attitudes created, discovered and accumulated over generations are not breathed in from the air or drunk from a single 'cultural stream'; they flow through complex and twisting channels, sometimes full of obstacles. These channels are the networks of social interdependence within which people learn, always directly or indirectly from other people. People can learn from each other indirectly, through books for example, but that necessarily presupposes that they have learned to speak and read the language needed to decode the books, and that elaborate patterns of social interdependence have existed for the production and distribution of books. And when we spoke casually of 'the middle of the cultural stream', we begged all sorts of important questions – for example about power in societies.

Mead provided the outline of a valuable social psychology, showing how the human capacity for intersubjective understanding, self-reflexive thought and purposive action is learned within pre-existent intersubjectively understood social relationships. Symbolic inter-actionist sociology, of which Mead's ideas are a principal foundation, is at its most impressive when dealing with rather small-scale social processes. But it has not given much detailed attention to questions of power, of larger-scale social structures and long-term processes of social development. When rather vague notions of culture, subculture and cultural transmission have been introduced as a short-cut to more macroscopic concerns, theoretical shortcomings become evident.

Two sharply contrasting attempts to meet shortcomings of this kind are evident in the work of Emile Durkheim and Alfred Schutz. Durk-heim, writing in the same generation as Mead, started so to speak from the opposite direction, from 'objective social structure', but in trying to show the power this had over individuals, encountered curi-ously similar theoretical problems. Schutz, writing a generation later, used phenomenological philosophy in an attempt to show in much more detail how the 'cultural stream' is structured *in the experience of the individual*. Since the phenomenological approach is more akin to symbolic interactionism, let us cast chronology aside and look at Schutz's work before turning to Durkheim.

Alfred Schutz and Sociological Phenomenology

Phenomenological philosophy, as propounded especially by Edmund Husserl (1859–1938), is so called because it tells us to concern ourselves only with what is directly apprehended by our senses, with things as they appear to our consciousness – in short, with *phenomena*. We cannot determine anything about the *noumenon*, the thing-in-itself which lies, or does not lie, behind the phenomenon, for this remains unknowable. Kant said this much; Husserl went further, and said there was no purpose in speculating about noumena. All experience could be reduced to sense data. All knowledge derives from pheno-mena, and so the programme he proposed consisted of the precise description of phenomena precisely as they appear to our conscious-ness. Put as simply as this, the phenomenological programme may seem naïve. Descriptions and all observation, whether of conscious experience or anything else conceivable, employ the social categories of language. Nevertheless, sociologists influenced by Husserl have carried his programme over from philosophy as a methodological precept for the social sciences.[11]

Phenomenology has had its main impact on sociology through the work of Alfred Schutz (1899–1959). Schutz was principally a philosopher of social science, whose early work, *Der sinnhafte Aufbau der sozialen Welt* (1972, orig. 1932), was a synthesis of Max Weber's approach to the methodology of the social sciences with Husserl's phenomenology.[12] Subsequently, after emigrating to the U.S.A., Schutz incorporated into his later writings (1962, 1964, 1966) many of the main ideas of James, Mead and other American writers. Schutz's views have been popularized by Peter Berger and Thomas Luckmann in their widely read book *The Social Construction of Reality* (1967).[13]

The focus of Schutz's analysis is *intersubjectivity* – how we understand each other and how we come to have similar perceptions and conceptions of the world. Out of his analysis emerge the foundations of a sociology of everyday knowledge. Schutz begins with the Life-World (*Lebenswelt*), also variously referred to as the 'common-sense world', the 'world of daily life' and the 'everyday world'. This is the sphere of physical and social objects within which men live and work, meet each other and pursue their routine activities. Towards it we adopt, in Husserl's term, 'the natural attitude' – we take it for granted, and suspend doubt that things might be otherwise. Our attitude to it is pragmatic – we are concerned not so much to interpret it as to change it, to make our way within it. In short, it is experienced as already organized, for it was there before we were born. Most knowledge of it is handed down to us, and is therefore experienced as being detached from us, as having objective truth and being the same for everyone. Above all, we do not question that we have a being in the world, that there are others like us, and that they make similar assumptions.

Each of us is born into a unique *biographical situation*. We are brought up by adults, usually our parents, from whom we acquire a fundamental part of our knowledge of the world. They, their unique qualities and their location in society leave their imprint upon us. Our biographical situation carried with it a *stock of knowledge* at hand. No two people have precisely the same biographical situation, so they do not have identical stocks of knowledge. Knowledge is socially distributed; no-one knows everything about everything. Therefore they see the world from perspectives to some degree different. Yet the very objectivity and externality which knowledge has for the individual depends on it being to a large extent shared by others. This requirement is met in the case of those whom one is likely to meet within one's everyday world, and so interaction within this sphere proceeds on the assumption of the *reciprocity of perspectives*. Though our perspectives are not precisely the same, we assume that if we changed places, we should perceive as the other does now. In interaction, we assume different points of view are irrelevant and that we each interpret the situation in a similar manner. The assumption of the reciprocity of perspectives is therefore very close to Mead's idea of taking the role of the other. The assumption is only challenged when interaction fails to proceed smoothly, when we fail to anticipate the other's reactions, when perspectives prove not to be reciprocal.

But what is the nature of the knowledge of which everyone has a unique stock? Schutz argues that we experience the external world of things, people and events as *typifications*. Typifications are classifications and categorizations. Schutz appreciates that we have to classify and group in order to organize reality, and that most of these typifications are socially learned and handed down to us. Any unique qualities are seen against a background of typification. And as Schutz remarks:

> The typifying medium *par excellence* by which socially derived knowledge is transmitted is the vocabulary and syntax of everyday language. The vernacular of everyday life is primarily a language of named things and events, and any name includes a typification and generalization referring to the relevance system prevailing in the linguistic in-group which found the named thing significant enough to provide a separate term for it. (1964:14)

We typify other people. Only our own experience is immediate and directly accessible to us, though even that is typified and interpreted in our reflections about ourself. Other people's experience is inferred indirectly. R. D. Laing, a psychiatrist deeply influenced by phenomenology, puts the point vividly:

> ... how can one ever study the experience *of the other*? For the experience *of the other* is not evident to me, as it is not and never can be an experience of mine.
> I cannot avoid trying to understand your experience, because although I do not experience your experience, which is invisible to me (and non-tasteable, non-touchable, non-smellable and inaudible), yet I experience you *as experiencing*.
> I do not experience your experience. But I experience you as experiencing. I experience myself as experienced by you. And I experience you as experiencing yourself as experienced by me. And so on. (1967:16, his italics)[14]

But we experience others in varying degrees of anonymity. Fundamental to our understanding of the social world are our 'consociates' with whom we have 'We-relationships'. In other words, we interact frequently with them face-to-face and they share our social world. We know a great deal, though not everything, of their biography, and more than any others they are seen as unique individuals. Our contemporaries, the countless people we meet fleetingly and impersonally or not at all, are seen as functional ideal-types: shop assistants, bus conductors, bureaucrats. We also typify our predecessors and successors. The dead can be known only through the reports of others, and those yet to be born have an even more shadowy existence in our thoughts.

The corpus of everyday knowledge handed down to us also includes an armoury of practical actions, 'efficient recipes for the use of typical means for bringing about typical ends in typical situations' (Schutz 1964: 14). Not that they always work. For some purposes, the stock of knowledge at hand is quite adequate, while in other situations the individual has to improvise. As the individual's unique biography unfolds, his experience is accumulated. This process is called *sedimentation*; layer upon layer of new knowledge is assimilated into old typifications or forms the nucleus of new typifications.

The everyday, commonsense world is, in Schutz's view, the *paramount reality*, fundamental to our understanding. Within it, taking the natural attitude, we suspend any doubts that things might be other than they seem, that the outer world and other people exist, that they have a past, present and future. This commonsense attitude constantly reasserts itself. However, there do exist *finite provinces of meaning* within the paramount reality, in which we may allow ourselves to doubt, in which our commonsense beliefs about the real world may be suspended. Among the most important of these provinces are those of magic, religion and science. Each of these 'multiple realities' Schutz contends, is experienced as 'real' while it has our attention. But we cannot pass smoothly from one province of meaning to another; they are discontinuous, and we must progress from one to another by a 'leap of consciousness'.

For the sociologist, the most interesting of the finite provinces of meaning is that of social science in which he himself works in his professional capacity. He must work on a plane of reality which offers a sharp contrast to the everyday world. Any individual's stock of everyday knowledge taken as a whole is to a greater or lesser degree incoherent, inconsistent and fragmentary. Perfect clarity is neither attainable nor necessary, for it serves essentially practical purposes. The sheer diversity of practical actions is an obstacle to coherence and, moreover, while the practical recipes 'work', producing the desired and expected results, there is little incentive for conscious pursuit of clarity. Scientific knowledge, on the contrary, serves purely intellectual interests, and clarity, consistency and coherence are a positive requirement of activity in the scientific world. For the social scientist, this poses a paradox. He has to give clear and consistent explanations of a subject matter which itself is often unclear and inconsistent. In order to do so, he has to construct typifications, for his own scientific purposes, of the typifications his subjects make for their practical purposes. He builds 'constructs of the second degree'.

Schutz's discussion of the major dimensions in which the 'life-world', or what we have loosely referred to before as the 'cultural stream', is experienced by individuals seems in many ways convincing if rather obvious. Perhaps a theory about 'commonsense' should be obvious; nevertheless Schutz's sociological followers have produced interesting accounts of the culture of modern societies (see Berger 1973, Luckmann 1967, Zijderveld 1972). On the other hand, Schutz's account of social scientific knowledge, in which the sociologist is a privileged and neutral observer, is less convincing. Can 'everyday reality' and 'commonsense', no matter how incoherent, be considered something quite discontinuous with, or even antithetical to, scientific understanding?

We shall return to that question in Chapter 5. For present purposes, there is a graver limitation to the phenomenological approach. It remains fundamentally egocentric and idealist, concerned to interpret the social world as the product of individual actions guided by subjective meanings and intentions. But probing structures of consciousness cannot reveal everything we need to know about people's interdependence with each other in society. As McCarthy (1978: 160) puts it, summarizing Habermas's views:

> An approach that remains within the confines of an analysis of structures of consciousness is methodologically incapable of grasping the objective context of social action. It is in a sense a sociology without society.

This point is one which Emile Durkheim never lost sight of, even though there are numerous ambiguities in his thought.

Durkheim and 'Social Facts'

Emile Durkheim (1858–1917) might at first appear to be entirely out of sympathy with Mead's approach to the study of society and certainly with any thoroughgoing phenomenology. It is a common-place that one of the central themes of his work was his concern to establish the independence of sociology from psychology. His study of suicide (1951, orig. 1897), seemingly the most individual, 'psychological' of acts, was undertaken for that reason. He sought to demonstrate that individual psychology could not explain why some societies and social groups had higher rates of suicide than others. Suicide rates were an instance of a 'social fact', and social facts were to be explained by reference to other social facts. 'The determining cause of a social fact should be sought among the social facts preceding it and not among the states of the individual consciousness.' (1938: 110, orig. 1895.) Moreover, social facts were to be recognized by their *externality* to the individual and the *constraint* which they exercised over him (1938: 2). Even the *conscience collective*, the common orientation or outlook shared by members of a society, and its constituent *représentations collectives* were properties of the group, not of individual minds. This side of Durkheim's thought is summed up in his dictum 'Consider social facts as things' (1938: 14).

This is, however, only one side of his thought, and highly misleading if considered alone. Durkheim was in fact struggling with exactly the same problem as Mead; unfortunately his mode of expression and perhaps poor English translations often seem to obscure the fact. What Durkheim consistently rejected was any attempt to explain diverse social patterns in terms of psychological constants. Individualistic psychology in the nineteenth century had tended to posit a universal 'human nature' apparently antecedent to society. Durkheim attacked introspectionism which described the contents of the mind without accounting for how they got there (1953: 32), but reserved his greatest scorn for those theories which explained behaviour in terms of biology or innate instincts. Many rival lists of 'basic instincts' have been advanced in the past; they are a very cheap form of explanation. Any item of behaviour, from sexual activity to butterfly collecting can be 'explained' by attributing it to an instinct. If butterfly collecting is considered too specific to merit an instinct of its own, doubt arises as to which other instinct it is to be subsumed under, and how many separate instincts really exist. Durkheim readily saw that any theory involving constants of human nature was an inadequate explanation of the immense variety of human behaviour and social organization. Individualistic psychology could not explain why societies had different kinds of family patterns, or why one social group had higher suicide rates than another: 'the psychological factor is too general to predetermine the course of social phenomena'. (1938:108.)

Durkheim's remarks on the relationship of psychology to sociology need to be interpreted in the light of his perfectly valid criticisms of a good deal of psychology in or immediately prior to his day. They largely explain why he failed to recognize consistently that if individual psychology could not explain differing suicide *rates*, it could help to explain the *incidence* of suicide – why one particular person should commit suicide while others in a very similar social situation did not. Durkheim's problem was that he saw very clearly that individual psychology needed to be explained largely by reference to the individual's experience in society rather than by innate mental properties or innate biological drives. Sometimes this led him to write as if psychological processes were an irrelevant intervening variable between antecedent and succeeding social facts, and that no reference need be made to them. Yet it is important to recognize that Durkheim was never opposed to consideration of inner mental processes as such. He recognized that human beings must be seen as reflecting and reasoning creatures, not as puppets whose actions were utterly predetermined by the social and cultural 'environment'.

> The more this faculty for understanding what happens within ourselves is developed, the more the subject's movements lose that automatism which is characteristic of physical life. The agent endowed with reason does not behave like a thing, the activity of which can be reduced to a system of reflexes. He hesitates, feels his way, deliberates, and by that distinguishing mark he is recognized. External stimulation, instead of resulting immediately in movement, is halted in its progress and is subjected to *sui generis* elaboration; a longer or shorter period of time elapses before the expression in movement appears. This relative indetermination does not occur where there is no thinking mind, and with thought it increases.' (1953: 3)

The pivot of Durkheim's work is his effort to reconcile this 'relative indetermination' with the undoubted power of society over the individual consciousness. In his first major book (1933, orig. 1893), he pointed out that in primitive societies, to which he attributed 'mechanical solidarity', individuality was less developed than in complex societies with 'organic solidarity'. Individualism develops progressively with the division of labour. Mechanical solidarity is the consequence of people sharing very similar activities; they share not only a common way of life but very specific common beliefs and sentiments, the *conscience collective*. In complex societies with an advanced division of labour, people pursue different occupations and have different training and education; the *conscience collective* 'comes increasingly to be made up of highly generalized and indeterminate modes of thought and sentiment which leave room open for an increasing multitude of individual differences' (1933: 172).[15] Even so, Durkheim recognized that there is and can be no total conformity even in societies with mechanical solidarity. 'Crime is present ... in all societies of all types,' he remarked (1938: 65).

What then did Durkheim mean when he defined 'social facts' as externally constraining the individual? *Externality* means something obvious, familiar and uncontroversial. It means that everyone is born into a pre-existent and organized society, and that he is only one element in a larger pattern. Language, religious beliefs, money – none of these are individual creations (1938: 2). As Giddens (1971: 87) comments:

> Durkheim's point here, in other words, is a conceptual one. It is true that this is to some extent obscured by Durkheim's insistence upon talking of

social 'facts'; but it should be obvious that this criterion of 'exteriority' is not an empirical one. If it were it would lead directly to the ludicrous conclusion that society exists externally to *all* individuals ...

The presence of moral *constraint*, on the other hand, is an empirical question. In all societies there are conventions concerning the individual's obligations as father to his children, employer to his employees, priest to congregation, or whatever. If these are supported with legal or informal social sanctions against transgressors, their constraining power is obvious. They can be broken, but at a cost. Durkheim emphasizes, however, that constraint is equally real when the individual accepts them unquestioningly as right and legitimate.

Nevertheless, Durkheim did not find it easy to define exactly the balance between society's undoubted influence in shaping the individual's actions and the individual's scope for autonomous or innovative behaviour. For instance, in a footnote to his preface to the second edition of the *Rules of Sociological Method* (1938: lvi–lvii) he wrote:

> Because beliefs and social practices come to us from without, it does not follow that we receive them passively or without modification. In reflecting on collective institutions and assimilating them for ourselves, we individualize them and impart to them more or less personal characteristics.... It is for this reason that each of us creates, in a measure, his own morality, religion and mode of life. There is no conformity to social convention that does not comprise an entire range of individual shades.

But then he appeared to equivocate:

> It is nevertheless true that this field of variations is a limited one. It verges on nonexistence or is very restricted in that circle of religious and moral affairs where deviation easily becomes a crime. But, sooner or later, even in the latter instance, one encounters the limit that cannot be crossed.

This kind of equivocation and ambiguity has led to numerous conflicting interpretations being put on Durkheim's thought. Parsons (1937) considered that he had swung right over from a position of 'radical positivism' to one of philosophical idealism. Harris (1968: chapter 18) contends, on the contrary, that he was never anything else but idealist. Neither is entirely correct. Durkheim began his work within the intellectual tradition stemming from St Simon and Comte (see Lukes 1937: 66ff.), and in this sense, Parsons is right to use the label 'positivist'. But Harris is right when he points out that positivism is not 'the opposite' of idealism as Parsons implies. Parsons uses 'radical positivism' to mean a crude empiricism or even a behaviourism of the Skinnerian type. Durkheim unwaveringly rejected explanations in terms of any innate, universal psychology, of any 'human nature' prior to society. However, neither Durkheim, nor for that matter Comte, ever had any epistemological objections to the consideration of 'inner mental states'. Though Durkheim never developed as sophisticated a social psychology as Mead's, that he was grappling with the same problem as Mead is especially clear in his last major work, *The Elementary Forms of Religious Life* (1965, orig. 1912). Indeed, Stone and Faberman (1967) have argued that at the end of his life Durkheim was on the verge of adopting a 'symbolic interactionist' stance. In lectures on 'Pragmatism and Sociology' (1960) he examined the work of James and Dewey, but of course he knew nothing of Mead's work. The purpose of *Elementary Forms* had been to investigate the social sources of shared concepts and conceptions of the world, and their part in facilitating in turn the functioning of society. *Représentations collectives* by then fairly clearly resembled Mead's significant symbols.[16] James seemed to Durkheim to leave too much scope for subjectivity; James's individual seemed to construct his own social reality. But it is likely that Mead's approach would have been much more acceptable to Durkheim. For what Mead contributed was a sociologically plausible psychology and an account of how concepts, symbols or *représentations* have their origins in social communications and interaction.

Yet all these interpretations miss the main point. The central reason for Durkheim's equivocation and ambiguity is that he could not escape thinking of 'the individual' and 'society' as two separate and static entities. No-one illustrates more clearly than he the ludicrous chicken-and-egg problems to which that leads. If he had thought instead of people (in the plural) and the social entities they form together as interdependent aspects of continuous developing processes, his main difficulties would have been resolved. In one sense he was right to equivocate in his remarks about the limits on 'individual variations'. For the scope of such variations cannot be established conceptually. It is a matter for empirical investigation, because the limits arise from the nature and patterning of people's interdependence in particular groups, institutions and societies, and the patterning changes over time. For example, it could be argued that less than a century after Durkheim wrote that passage, there are industrial societies today in which 'the limit that cannot be crossed' is encountered in economic life sooner than in religious and moral affairs. Durkheim's tendency to think in static, reified categories led directly to his major problems. It led, for example, to his inability to offer any convincing explanation for the *advance* of the division of labour and the transition from 'mechanical' to 'organic' solidarity. The absence of an adequate developmental perspective is perhaps the greatest single weakness in his thought.

Weber and 'Social Action'

That criticism is not one which can be made of Max Weber (1864–1920). From 1904–5 when he published his essays on *The Protestant Ethic and the Spirit of Capitalism* (English translation 1930), the unifying theme of his amazingly wide-ranging empirical studies was his attempt to explain why rational bourgeois capitalism developed first in the West and not elsewhere. Weber's hypothesis about Protestantism was a complex one; it was certainly not that Protestantism was 'the cause' of capitalism, but he did suggest that what happened in Europe was the outcome of a uniquely favourable conjunction of objective circumstances and subjective motivation. Tracing the rise of rationality in the West led him to study the growth of markets and other economic institutions, law, forms of authority, bureaucracy and even music. His studies of the religions of China and India and ancient Judaism were undertaken to demonstrate that other civilizations at other periods had developed quite favourable social structures, yet had lacked an essential motivational spark. Weber's views have generated great controversy – there is a very extensive literature on the *Protestant Ethic* thesis alone (see Green 1959) – but few sociologists would wish to deny his empirical studies a place among the very greatest achievements in the history of their discipline.[17]

Weber's theoretical views on social action and how it is to be explained are also complex and problematic. Like Durkheim, Weber declared it 'erroneous ... to regard any kind of psychology as the ultimate foundation of the sociological foundation of action' (1968: I, 19), though the context of this remark makes it plain that by 'psychology' he understood explanation in terms of inherent characteristics of 'the individual' independent of the ties of social interdependence within which 'individual' psychology is formed. Weber's argument in *The Protestant Ethic* was plainly 'psychological', but in the contrary sense: he purported to show how, *at a particular period*, a certain development of the Calvinist doctrine of predestination had psychological effects within the personalities of those who adhered to it, and that these psychological effects were conducive to social action of a kind which, *in a particular developmental context*, would have important economic consequences. But Weber produced no general social psychological discussion comparable to Mead's account of the social genesis of self-reflexive thought and how that makes possible purposive social action. All that was largely taken for granted within the German intellectual tradition to which Weber was heir. Yet in some respects, despite their very different substantive interests, Weber and Mead are quite close.

Weber's position was the very antithesis of behaviourism as can be seen from his definition of social action:

> In action is included all human behaviour when and in so far as the acting individual attaches a subjective meaning to it. Action in this sense may be either overt or purely inward and subjective; it may consist of positive intervention in a situation, or of deliberately refraining from such intervention or passively acquiescing in the situation. Action is social in so far as by virtue of the subjective meaning attached to it by the acting individual ... it takes account of the behaviour of others and is thereby oriented in its course. (1968: I. 4)[18]

Action may be orientated not to a single known individual, but to 'collective' concepts like a state, church, class and so on. But not all behaviour is action: the accidental collision of two cyclists is, according to Weber, akin to a natural event, though their attempt to avoid it and any subsequent exchange of insults or friendly concern are action. Nor is all action social action: the response of many members of a crowd in putting up their umbrellas is, Weber says, normally a response to rain, not to each other either singly or collectively. These exclusions of Weber's are, however, perhaps excessively fastidious. After all, bicycles and umbrellas are as much the product of processes of social development as are states, churches, classes or theological doctrines; in that sense collisions between cyclists and crowds putting up umbrellas are very much social actions.

Weber insists that in order to explain an action we must interpret it in terms of its *subjectively intended meaning*, something quite distinct from its objectively valid meaning. That is to say a person's action is to be explained in terms of the consequences he intended it to have – his *purpose* – rather than in terms of its actual effects; the two are sometimes at variance. We have to grasp what ends *he* is pursuing and how *he* perceives that he can achieve them. Cohen (1968: 81) gives a good example: how do we explain why a man is touching his toes by his bedside early in the morning? Does the action have religious or physiotherapeutic significance? We find out by asking him his purpose, or alternatively infer it by generalizing from our previous knowledge of behaviour in his society. This process of interpretation is referred to as *Verstehen* or as 'hermeneutic' understanding. 'Hermeneutics' is a term derived from theology, where it refers to the problems of interpreting scriptural texts. Whatever grand term is used, the process certainly has nothing to do with introspection or any *special* ability of the sociologist to 'empathize' with his subjects. It is the same process of 'taking the role of the other', of interpretation of other people's meanings which is essential to normal social intercourse and even to natural science, and it is no more arbitrary.[19]

Verification of such an explanation is achieved by statistical or comparative analysis of many cases, or very occasionally by laboratory experiment (Weber 1968: 1, 10).

Having established the 'subjectively intended meaning' however, Weber argues, we have a *causal* explanation of the action, in the sense that the end in view is a cause of present actions. Of course, an essential feature of a cause is that it precedes the effect; but the 'cause' of an action is not exactly its intended outcome but the 'mental experiment' of anticipating its consequences in advance before implementing the action. As Alfred Schutz pointed out (1972: 61), the actor pictures the projected act as completed. He sees the situation in the future perfect tense, as it *will have become* if the action has the consequences he expects. Schutz (1972: 86–96) described this as the 'in-order-to motive' of the action distinguishing it (as Weber did not) from the 'genuine because-motive'. The latter refers to some event or experience in the actor's *past* which he views in the pluperfect tense as the cause of his action. We put up an umbrella *in order to* keep dry and *because* we had got unpleasantly wet in the past. In both cases it can be seen that the notion of the self as object, explicit in Mead, is also implicit in Weber.

The simplest actions to explain in terms of subjectively intended meaning are those which involve the fully conscious and rational adaptation of available means to ends in view. Weber had very much in mind the achievements of the British and Austrian economists in analysing economic actions in terms of 'economic rationality'. In building a typology of action, therefore, he thought it best to treat non-rational and emotionally governed actions as deviations from ideal rationality. He distinguished four types of action, beginning with two varieties of rationality, *Zweckrationalität* and *Wertrationalität*.[20]

Zweckrational action is 'determined by expectations as to the behaviour of objects in the environment and of other human beings; these expectations are used as "conditions" or "means" for the attainment of the actor's own rationally pursued and calculated ends' (1968: 1, 24). What this means is that the actor weighs one against the other not only the means available for attaining a given end, but the costs and benefits of using those means for one end or another and finally various ends themselves. Weber has in mind, of course, the models of rational economic action developed in classical economics, involving concepts such as marginal utility, marginal revenue and opportunity cost.

Wertrational action is 'determined by conscious belief in the value for its own sake of some ethical, aesthetic, religious or other form of behaviour, independently of its prospects of success' (1968: 1, 24–25). The various means towards ends may be weighed against each other, but the end itself is not questioned: it is accepted as a binding and absolute good.

The two non-rational (*not* irrational) types of action are *affectual* and *traditional*. Action is affectual when it is directly under the control of the emotions; it may be an uncontrolled response – anger, for instance – but it is meaningful only if orientated towards some social object. Last is a residual category; traditional action is 'determined by ingrained habituation' (1968: I, 25).

Many criticisms have been made of this typology, and Weber anticipated several of them. It may be objected that the actions we actually observe in society are very frequently a mixture of the pure types. For instance, the economic activities and attitudes of capitalist entrepreneurs (as illustrated by Benjamin Franklin's view of time as money – Weber 1930, chapter 2) are prototypically *zweckrational*, and yet in so far as they are an expression of rigid religious and ethical principles, are also *wertrational*. Weber himself was very conscious of this, and emphasized that the four modes of orientation of action were ideal-types. Ideal patterns of action were seen to be embodied in ideal-types of institutions, such as *Zweckrationalität* in rational-legal bureaucracy. Yet any concrete institution might contain characteristics both of, say, rational-length and patrimonial bureaucracy, and comprise elements of all four patterns of action. Weber was most careful not to reify his ideal-types, and consistently spoke in terms of *probabilities* of features being found in concrete examples. And he emphasized that the four-fold typology was only tentative and to be judged in terms of its usefulness.

It has proved useful, and the distinction between *Zweck-* and *Wertrationalität* is often particularly illuminating. Yet there are real difficulties. Even conceptually the boundaries between the four categories become blurred. The emotions are not easily cordoned off in a separate compartment from other actions. This is especially true when the conscious intention conceals even from the actor himself his true subconscious motives, a possibility of which Weber was fully aware (1968: I, 9–10, 25). Nor is the category of traditional action satisfactory. For one who had an encyclopaedic knowledge of other civilizations, Weber was surprisingly and ethnocentrically sceptical about the possibility of understanding action in primitive societies in rational terms (1968: I, 16). Since then, anthropologists have succeeded, by extended fieldwork, in explaining many superficially 'irrational' customs as rational in terms of native cognitive systems. Nor is traditional action necessarily 'habitual'; as Weber himself pointed out (1968: I, 25), when action is more or less consciously justified by the claim 'we have always done it this way', the tradition becomes an absolute value, and the action shades over into *Wertrationalität*.

Furthermore, habit is not associated only with traditional action. We may, for instance, habitually shop at one supermarket but our action is in no sense traditional; if its prices moved far above those of other shops, we should no doubt bestir ourselves to break the habit. As Germani (1968: 149) notes, 'An elective action that has been repeated many times becomes almost habitual, and the whole elective and deliberative process becomes permanently implicit.' To complicate the matter further, original motives for the promulgation of a rule or arrangement may be lost sight of, or the motives may change. There is difficulty in interpreting *any* institutionalized, stable and long established social pattern as purely and consciously rational action.

This draws attention to the main source of weakness in Weber's discussion of rationality in he abstract – its static quality. What a paradox, in view of the richness of Weber's empirical explorations of concrete processes of rationalization! In fact, in the pages of *Economy and Society* devoted to formal definitions, he seems to have at least come close to falling into the same trap as Durkheim. The question of how much of human behaviour can be explained as self-directed purposive action, and how much as determined by established social patterns, is not one which can be resolved conceptually. The balance changes over time and from one social context to another. Weber's preoccupation in this part of his work with the subjective orientation of action also leads him to neglect the objective contexts of action in a way that is not evident elsewhere.

Talcott Parsons and the Voluntaristic Theory of Action

Weber's conception of social action is the ingredient which gives the dominant flavour to the 'voluntaristic theory of action' which Talcott Parsons (1903–1979) first outlined in *The Structure of Social Action* (1973). This book is generally considered his finest. It had a twofold importance. First, more than any other single book, it introduced the work of Weber and Durkheim[21] to the sociologists of the English speaking world. Second, its substantive thesis was that those writers had been converging towards the 'voluntaristic theory of action' which Parsons himself advocated as a general sociological perspective. The 'voluntaristic theory' was not, in outline, so original as Parsons himself seems to have thought. In slightly differing forms, it can be traced back not only to Weber and Durkheim, but to numerous American writers prior to Parsons, including James, Mead, Cooley and Thomas (see Hinkle 1963), none of whom Parsons mentioned.

What, then, was the voluntaristic theory of action? It can be very briefly summarized in the following axioms:

(1) People's actions are directed towards the achievement of *ends*, goals, objectives. (We have already mentioned more than once the relevance of Mead's discussion of how purposive behaviour is possible.)

(2) People select appropriate *means* and procedures from those available, to attain their ends.

(3) Courses of action are constrained by the conditions of the physical environment.

(4) Individuals have emotions and make moral judgements which influence the selection of ends and means, as well as their order of priority.

Parsons emphasized that a person's actions were to be explained from 'the subjective point of view', or, roughly, by his perception and definition of the ends, means and conditions of his situation. Yet there remained a certain residual ambiguity: were constraints or conditions of action only constraining when the actor perceived them as such, or do they have an 'objective' status? Alfred Schutz urged upon Parsons the need for a more radical and consistent, in other words phenomenological, interpretation of the 'subjective point of view', though Parsons did not accept it (see Grathoff, 1978).

The real interest in Parsons's work is not in the 'means-ends schema', but in his treatment of the other side of the equation: how 'society' influences the ends the actor will pursue and the means he will use in attaining them. In *The Structure of Social Action*, he did not himself probe deeply into the psychology of socialization. But he did praise Durkheim and Weber, and the English economist Alfred Marshall, for realizing that the ends of action were neither innate nor random, but deeply influenced by social experience and moral values. The difficulties of Parsons's later work revolve around his efforts to formulate this influence more precisely.

Whatever else it was, *The Structure of Social Action* was a polemic against behaviourism's refusal to consider evidence of inner mental processes as essential data. Yet *Toward a General Theory of Action* and other writings in the 1950s show Parsons flirting with behaviourism, under the particular influence of the behaviourist E. C. Tolman.

> The organization of observational data in terms of the theory of action is quite possible and fruitful in modified behaviouristic terms, and such formulation avoids many of the difficult questions of introspection or empathy. In Tolman's psychology, it is postulated that the rat is orientated to the goal of hunger gratification and that he cognizes the situation in which he pursues the goal. Tolman's concepts of orientation and cognition are ways of generalizing the facts of observation about the rat's

behaviour.... What the actor thinks or feels can be treated as a system of *intervening variables*. (Parsons and Shils, 1951: 64, their italics)

This is one example of the series of 'crucial equivocations' vividly traced by Scott (1963), by which Parsons maintained superficial continuity with his pre-war work. Apart from revealing a misapprehension or at least some ambivalence about the nature of *Verstehen*, it shows that once again Parsons ignored Mead's social behaviourism.

In spite of his equivocations, the salient feature of Parsons's post-war writings is a rather mechanical conception of social norms and their place in the determination of action. Norms and values were increasingly seen as rigid and unambiguous standards. They form patterns of 'institutionalized normative culture' which the individual takes as given and 'internalizes', 'introjects', or just plain learns, thereafter behaving in obedient conformity to them. Once internalized, normative culture seems to have the status of a repertoire of behavioural computer programmes, the appropriate one being called up not by the self-reflexive, thinking individual, but by external stimuli in each situation.

After 1937, Parsons also paid a lot of attention to Freudian psychology, and particularly to the concept of the 'super-ego'.[22] Again, it is interesting that Parsons paid little attention to Mead, though parallels have often been noted between the super-ego and the generalized other. Freud saw the super-ego as the voice within the individual conscience of the demands of social life, perpetually struggling to control the impulses of the ego and id. Socialization was never perfect (see especially Freud 1962). Parsons, however, argued that not only the super-ego but the ego and the id too were products of social experience. In consequence, Dennis Wrong (1961) attacked Parsons for developing an 'oversocialized conception of man'. 'Sociologists', he alleged, 'have appropriated the super-ego concept, but have separated it from any equivalent of Freudian id.' In 'socializing' the ego and the id, Parsons was not out of line with the trend of neo-Freudian thinking, nor with Mead's discussion of the social origins of thought and self-conceptions. Yet Wrong's underlying criticism of Parsons is valid: he sometimes seems to use Freudian terminology to express behaviourist ideas. In his hands, 'internalization' or 'introjection' of moral norms often seems to mean little more than simple learning or habit formation.

During the post-war period, Parsons progressively produced a conceptual scheme of stupefying complexity (for an unstupefying account of it, see Rocher 1975). He claimed to be developing a unifying analytical framework for the social sciences.[23] His passion for synthesis led, however, to numerous ambiguities and obscurities. His decline into something remarkably like behaviourism was of course conditioned by his desire to relate the voluntaristic theory of action to a view of social order dominated by consensus and harmony rather than by coercion and conflict. In still later writings he distinguished between three levels of organization – the personality, the social and the culture – which are 'cybernetically' interdependent and capable of a degree of independent variation.[24] In practice, however, he tended to talk about the same thing at each level: approved patterns of behaviour were institutionalized in patterns of culture and internalized into personalities.

Conclusions

Talcott Parsons was not alone among the sociologists discussed in this chapter in displaying a certain befuddlement with the question of 'the Individual' and 'Society'. As we observed at the outset, that is a misconceived issue – misconceived in the most literal sense of the word, because it is the result of falsely thinking of 'the Individual' and 'Society' as two separate and static entities. The difficulty largely vanishes when we think of human beings in the plural and of the social networks they form together as interdependent aspects of one continuous process. Even so, sociologists still require a social psychological understanding of how learning takes place within that continuous process. Unfortunately, there seems to be a widespread tendency for sociologists greatly to simplify how people learn socially. Notions of 'culture' and 'socialization' are often used in such a way that 'social action' becomes just a matter of the enactment of internalized social norms. The relationship between social control and self-control is certainly more complicated than that. Experience and learning in social relationships from birth onwards may shape people's personalities, impulses and motives. But that does not mean that impulses and motives once acquired can be freely expressed without further constraint in relations of social interdependence.[25]

This tendency to oversimplify the social learning process is at odds with the rejection in principle of behaviourist psychology by most sociologists over a long period. Many of them have taken it for granted that human beings have the capacity for making choices and pursuing purposes. Mead, who did not take it for granted, is important in the history of sociological thought for his account of symbolic communication and how this capacity for purposeful behaviour is possible. A corollary of human beings' ability to interpret each other's meanings and intentions, and to make choices, is that interpretations of people's meanings, purposes and intentions are an indispensable part of sociological explanation. But the process called *Verstehen* should be seen 'not as a technique of investigation peculiar to social scientists, but as generic to all social interaction as such' (Giddens 1976: 52).

To recognize a capacity for self-directed intentional behaviour is, however, by no means to imply either that the sociologist need study *only* subjective perceptives, meanings and intentions, or that 'the agent endowed with reason' (in Durkheim's words) encounters no limits or constraints on his freedom of action. Arguments about the 'freedom' of 'the individual' usually overlook the fact that there are 'always simultaneously many mutually dependent individuals, whose interdependence to a greater or lesser extent limits each one's scope for action' (Elias 1978a: 167). Nor is the patterning of their interdependence created anew in every generation. As Karl Marx put it in a famous passage:

> Men make their own history, but they do not make it just as they please; they do not make it under circumstances chosen by themselves, but under circumstances directly encountered, given and transmitted from the past. (Marx-Engels 1968: 97, orig. 1852)

Conceptual schemes like the 'voluntaristic theory of action' shed no light on the scope for action encountered by particular people in particular patterns of interdependence, which can only be investigated empirically. Nor is the radical subjectivism of Schutz adequate to the explanation of objective (or intersubjective) patterns of interdependence. To cite once more the view of Jürgen Habermas:

> the investigation of individual interpretations of, and orientations to inter-subjective social structures gives us a one-sided picture of social life. It must somehow be integrated with analyses of the 'objective structures' themselves and of the empirical conditions under which both dimensions of the social life-world develop and change. (McCarthy 1978: 161)

In the next chapter we shall examine some of the ways in which sociologists have attempted to do precisely that.

2 Interaction and Interdependence

The notion of *role* has traditionally been seen by sociologists as a conceptual bridge between 'personality' and 'social structure' or between the 'subjective' and 'objective' dimensions of social interaction. Roles are more or less consistent patterns of behaviour. They are in one sense subjective and part of the personality, because the roles people play become part of their self-conceptions, of the way they see themselves and others see them. In another sense they are objective and part of the 'social structure' because many roles in society were handed down from earlier generations. Such roles as farmer, nobleman, capitalist, factory worker, manager, shop-keeper, policeman and countless others have existed for generations – though the length of time varies. All these positions are easily recognizable and well-defined – though the definitions may have undergone considerable changes in the course of time. This kind of role can be said to have an existence independent of any particular person, because if a particular person playing the role stops playing it the part is usually filled by someone else.

The idea of role arises directly out of that of interaction. As Erving Goffmann argued, in social encounters every person tends to act out a 'line'. A 'line' is

> a pattern of verbal and non-verbal acts by which he expresses his view of the situation, and by this, his evaluation of the participants, especially himself. *Regardless of whether a person has consciously taken a line, he does so in effect, because the other people assume he is doing so,* that he is taking a stand. So if he is to cope with their responses to him, he has to allow for the impression he has made on them. And so on. (1955: 213, my italics)

'Lines' can express many qualities: equality, subordination, superiority, friendliness, social distance. But many social encounters are of a stylized, conventional nature, giving little scope for choice of line. In such situations, we assume a great deal on the basis of only a few known attributes of the other person. The course of action is then particularly easy to predict because many similar situations have been observed before. The cursory encounter between customer and shop assistant is an illustration. Frequently repeated between people usually otherwise unknown to each other, it ordinarily comprises little more than an exchange of goods and money accompanied by the common courtesies. Another kind of superficial encounter is conversation at a cocktail party. The main expectation in such a situation, as Georg Simmel noted in his discussion of the 'sociology of sociability' (1950: Part I, chapter 3), is that smooth, pleasant interaction will be an end in itself. The situation is more egalitarian; people are not expected to go beyond certain limits in scoring points off one another. The encounter is somewhat stylized and predictable, but much less so than the anonymous transaction between customer and assistant, and the actor has rather more choice of 'lines'. The chief requirement is that once a line is taken, it is taken consistently, so that it gradually becomes reasonably predictable. If a person has not previously met the others, and particularly if he is unlikely to meet them again, he has more choice of 'line', for the necessity to say and do nothing inconsistent with his past and future actions is diminished.

The idea of consistency is a key one. It is essential to our interpretation and anticipation of others' actions, and equally essential to our anticipation of their interpretations of their actions. What we interpret is not the 'unit act' (Parsons's term) in isolation, but the act as part of a pattern of action. We group acts together into meaningful configurations or *Gestalten*. These configurations have a consistency which may not be in any testable sense logical but which is, or comes to be, recognized as consistent by the participants in a given situation, and often more widely than that. This is the essence of the idea of roles. Placing an action in the context of a role is what makes it possible not only to interpret its meaning and anticipate what will happen next, but also to evaluate it. Ralph Turner notes that

the lie which is an expression of the role of a friend is an altogether different thing from the same lie taken as a manifestation of the role of confidence man. Different actions may be viewed as the same or equivalent; identical actions may be viewed as quite different; placement of the actions in a role context determines such judgments. (1962: 24)

Though the term role has become universal in sociological parlance, agreement on exactly what it denotes has been less than universal. Some writers have tended to emphasize its subjective connotations, some its objective. Underlying many rival definitions have been disagreements about the origins of the standards by which a pattern of action is recognized as consistent role-playing. For Mead a role was a vantage point, and his followers have tended to emphasize that interaction is a tentative process, in which consistent roles are gradually established (see especially Turner 1962). In contrast, for the anthropologist Ralph Linton (1963: chapter 8), a role designated a pattern of behaviour 'defined by the culture' and merely enacted by the individual. Linton distinguished between role and status, although recognizing that empirically they were inseparable.

> A status, as distinct from the individual who may occupy it, is simply a collection of rights and duties.... The relation between any individual and any status he holds is somewhat like that between the driver of an automobile and the driver's place in the machine....
>
> A role represents the dynamic aspect of a status. The individual is socially assigned to a status and occupies it with relation to other statuses. When he puts the rights and duties which constitute the status into effect, he is performing a role. (1936: 113–114)

It can be seen that Linton's view of roles is somewhat mechanistic. As an anthropologist, he seems to have been so impressed by the diversity of human cultures that he came to see roles as pre-existent slots into which the plastic individual could be inserted and trained. Roles were models by which the individual's attitudes and behaviour were made congruent with those of others involved in the pattern of interaction. And the more congruent they were, the more smoothly would the social group or society run. Even in modern societies, most roles were ascribed rather than achieved; Linton placed most emphasis on how people were reared, trained and moulded for given roles, learning to conform to their requirements, rather than on competition for and choice among roles, let alone on the creation of new roles. Obviously this view sheds relatively little light on how roles come to be made, especially within informal and newly-forming groups, the process of innovation in roles, nor on the conditions in which roles become *or do not become* adjusted to each other. Yet it was the Lintonian conception of roles which Parsons and Shils took over into their dyadic model of interaction.

The Parsonian Dyad

The joint monograph 'Values, Motives and Systems of Action' (Parsons and Shils 1951: Part II), written when Parsons was at his most behaviouristic, presents a discussion of roles in the context of dyadic interaction between 'ego' and 'alter'. The whole individual is seen as largely irrelevant to understanding the interaction process; the relevant unit is the role. The role is the segment of his total action which is relevant to the relationship in question. The main ingredient of the role is the 'role expectation'. Role expectations are what ego is expected to do in a given situation, both by himself and by others. Alter, of course, responds to ego's action, and alter's response constitutes a 'sanction' for ego. Sanctions may be for ego either positive, reinforcing and rewarding, or negative and punishing. If alter conforms to ego's expectations, he positively sanctions ego, if he deviates from his expectations, the sanction is negative. The relationship is reciprocal, for ego responds in turn to alter's actions. Ego's actions, in conformity with his role expectations, thus in return constitute sanctions for alter's actions. 'What are sanctions to ego,' write Parsons and Shils, 'are also role expectations to alter, and vice versa.' (1951: 191.) The authors recognize that initially the expectations of ego and alter for each other's behaviour may not be identical. However, they suggest that within a continuing relationship, the interaction of ego and alter will gradually adjust into conformity with each other's role expectations. That is because each experiences the other's conformity as a positive sanction, which in turn is because for each, the other's responses are the means of attaining whatever objectives they seek through the relationship. Underlying the scheme is an implicit assumption that it is always rewarding to conform to established social norms.

The Pattern Variables

That Parsons is concerned almost entirely with socially recognized and established roles, and is too eager to assume that even informal interaction tends towards such roles, is shown by the use he makes of the Pattern Variables in categorizing roles and role expectations. Parsons listed five dichotomous choices of modes of orientation (Parsons 1951: 58ff.; Parsons and Shils 1951: 76ff.). These are said to have had their origins in consideration of Ferdinand Toennies's conceptualization of pre-modern and modern societies as *Gemeinschaft* and *Gesellschaft*. In the course of studying the professions in contemporary America, Parsons realized that many supposedly *gemeinschaftlich* characteristics persist into a fully modern society. Relationships within the family remain intimate. The doctor combines the 'modern' characteristic of professional detachment with a 'pre-modern' rejection of the cash nexus as a basis for the quality of his service. This insight led Parsons to break down the Toennies dichotomy into five independently variable choices. The *Affectivity/Affective Neutrality* choice is concerned with whether the emotions are involved in a relationship or whether detachment is the pattern. (More accurately, since the emotions are always in some sense involved, it is concerned with whether immediate or deferred 'gratification' is sought.) *Diffuseness/Specificity* concerns whether the relationship involves the whole personality (as between husband and wife) or only a limited segment (as between shop assistant and customer). *Particularism/Universalism* poses the question: is a person's performance of a role judged by special criteria (again the husband and wife – 'beauty is in the eye of the beholder') or by generally accepted standards (a secretary's shorthand speed)? The *Ascription/Achievement* variable, borrowed from Linton, is also known as 'Quality/Performance': is a person considered suitable for a position by virtue of some quality, such as being the eldest son of a monarch, or because of some achievement like the acquisition of a degree or a diploma? And, finally, *Collectivity Orientation/Self Orientation* is self explanatory, and closely related to the supposed modern trend to individualism and instrumental relationships.[1]

The primary constituents of role expectations, write Parsons and Shils, 'are analytically derivable from the pattern-variables when these are combined with the specific types of situations' (whatever that might mean). It is difficult to see how it could be possible to substantiate the claim that there are five and only five relevant choices by which all actions may be classified.[2] Many sociologists have also found it more difficult to see the variables as dichotomous than as continua. Nonetheless, it cannot be denied that in a less than systematic way the pattern-variables have been widely used by sociologists for characterizing the innumerable specialized and institutionalized roles found within the advanced division of labour of modern societies. But to describe a doctor's professional role as 'affectively neutral' is not in any way to explain why it is as it is and how the pattern became institutionalized.

Roles vary widely in the degree of their institutionalization. Parsons and Shils explain what this means as follows:

> By institutionalization we mean the integration of the complementary role expectation and sanction patterns with a generalized value system *common* to the members of the more inclusive collectivity, of which the system of complementary role-actions may be a part. Insofar as ego's set of role expectations is institutionalized, the sanctions which express the role expectations of other actors will tend to reinforce his own need-dispositions to conform with these expectations by rewarding it and punishing deviance. (1951: 191, italics in original)

In plainer English, the role of shop assistant is highly institutionalized because everyone knows and accepts the usual patterns of action which constitute the minimum characteristics of the role. Therefore, the assistant and all customers can judge whether the role is adequately and consistently played. Throughout his writings, Parsons is chiefly interested in this kind of role. That is why he adopts the Lintonian conception – 'definitions of the situation' are ready made, and the standards of consistency are brought into the interaction from without. Ralph Turner speaks of this as *external validation* of a role. This happens when:

> the behaviour is judged to constitute a role by others whose judgments are felt to have some claim to correctness or legitimacy. The simplest form of such a criterion is discovery of a name in common use for the role. If the pattern of behaviour can be readily assigned a name, it acquires *ipso facto* the exteriority and constraint of Durkheim's 'collective representation'. (1962: 30)

But with greater caution than Linton or Parsons and Shils, Turner immediately adds that

> Naming does not assure that there will be agreement on the content of the role; *it merely insures that people will do their disagreeing as if there were something real about which to disagree.* (my italics)

For the roles of shop steward and manager are well institutionalized, and specific examples of each may play their parts well. That does not guarantee that everything in the factory will run harmoniously – often quite the opposite. The fact that in the short view at least there is an objective conflict of interest between worker and employer (what is income to one is cost to the other) makes sure that role expectations have a certain obduracy not easily eroded. Parsons would argue that even though the conflict between shop stewards and managers may be very real and sustained, it will usually take place within a matrix of agreement limiting the means by which the conflict is pursued.

Followers of Mead, though recognizing that where statuses are established, named and recognized (as they usually are in formal organizations) the Lintonian-Parsonian conception of roles has a certain superficial plausibility, deny that the actor occupies a position for which 'the culture prescribes' a concise set of rules or norms. The formal organization such as a bureaucracy is a special case. Informal groups, whether in the laboratory or 'in the wild', show the role-taking process in its more general form. Roles correspond to a person's 'me's', which exist in relation to the roles of others, real or imaginary – father and son, leader and follower, 'me now' and posterity. The conceptions others have of their own roles in relation to oneself and of one's role in relation to themselves, have to be discovered in the course of interaction. And the role expectations may change and grow, the boundaries shift during or because of interaction. Even the most familiar roles, such as father and son, change. The roles of father in relation to son, and vice versa, are very different when the son is adult and the father retired to what they were between the young father and the boy. So the process is always tentative.

In task-orientated groups newly formed in the laboratory of people hitherto unknown to each other, the process of role formation and differentiation has repeatedly been observed.[3] Gradually there tend to emerge at least recognizable roles, those of instrumental leader (who guides the group towards its prescribed task) and expressive leader (the guardian of group morale). These roles exist in relation to each other and to other members of the group. Yet they cannot be said to be in any sense culturally prescribed, and members of the group may indeed be largely unconscious of them. It is not easy to predict in advance *who* will assume these roles, though of course members do not enter such groups as *tabulae rasae*. Individuals' past experience, background and personality may increase the likelihood of their assuming the role. Even so, experience and personality count only *relatively* to those of others involved in the interaction – 'in the land of the blind, the one-eyed man is king'. The process of tentative exploration is called by Turner 'internal validation' of role-taking (1962: 29). It is of course supplemented in many situations by external validation – in formal, 'labelled' situations, roles are at least in part pre-defined. Sociologists in the symbolic interactionist tradition, however, would argue that they are never *entirely* externally defined.

Enough has been said to indicate that in part the Lintonian and Meadian conceptions of role draw attention to institutionalized and non-institutionalized roles respectively. This is not a dichotomy but a continuum along which roles vary. Yet this is not the whole story. Used with great care, the Linton view provides a sort of shorthand for what we observe in formal organizations and in the plethora of widely recognized specialities within the social division of labour. It represents a higher level of abstraction than the Meadian concept. What in effect happens is that Linton takes the lowest common denominator of the behaviour of all shop assistants, bus conductors, medicine men or whatever – the minimum qualities by which people in general recognize the role as such. As noted in Chapter One (p. 18 above) the process of describing the common characteristics of a large number of people is unlikely to produce a picture close to the 'cultural norm'. But this procedure poses an acute danger of conceptual reification; it is a very short step from this process of abstraction to reifying the description and arguing that 'the culture prescribes that ...'.

Plainly, external validation plays some part. But around the basic minimum of 'bus-conductor-ness' (the absence of which does draw down on itself sanctions, like the sack) every bus conductor elaborates. The jolly extrovert conductor with a cheery insult for everyone produces quite different interaction patterns among passengers to the efficient but silent conductor. There is no real contradiction here, but the Meadian conception stays closer to interaction as it happens. And this is important, for no role actually observed is ever totally institutionalized. What George Homans calls the sub-institutional or elementary behaviour is never absent.

> [It] does not grow just in the gaps between institutions; it clings to institutions as to a trellis. It grows everywhere – if only because the norms established as institutions and the orders given in institutionalized organizations can never prescribe human behaviour to the last detail, even if they were obeyed to the letter, which they are not. Indeed the elementary behaviour helps to explain how and why they are disobeyed. (Homans 1961: 391)

Blau's famous study of the Federal law enforcement agency (1955), in which agents formally forbidden to consult colleagues other than superiors in deciding whether to take action against firms infringing the law and yet informally did so continually, is a classic illustration of the sub-institutional facilitating the operation of the institution. The equally famous 'bank-wiring group' of the Hawthorne studies (Roethlisberger and Dickson 1939), in which informally evolved norms against 'rate-busting' frustrated formal incentives to greater output, illustrates the possible conflict of the institutional and the sub-institutional.

The Inadequacy of the Dyad

Whether explicitly in the Parsonian model of ego and alter, or implicitly in Mead's discussion of 'taking the role of the other', it has become something of a tradition to use the dyad to explain roles and interaction. Though intended for heuristic purposes, this is in fact seriously misleading, for the most interesting aspects of interaction cannot be explained in dyadic terms.

Role Conflict
Role Conflict is one of the simpler phenomena which appear in situations involving three or more people. It is easy to see how conflict can arise between playing one role with one partner and another role with a second partner. William James commented that it is difficult to be both a philosopher and a philanderer (which shows how misleading it can be to generalize from personal experience!) James was thinking of our limited resources of time and energy, but also of the need for psychic unity. But conflicting role expectations are an everyday phenomenon. Suppose in an examination one student spotted a

friend cheating. He might well disapprove strongly, but it is unlikely (not impossible) that he would take it upon himself to 'betray' the friend to the invigilator. But what would happen if the student were not a fellow examinee, but himself acting as invigilator (a situation apparently not so bizarre in American universities)? To report his friend would still in some sense be a breach of the friendship role, but not to do so would be to breach the role of invigilator. Implicit in the situation is the third party of the university authorities who have employed the invigilator. Taking the role of the other is not so simple – *which* other? Nor does the generalized other help much – the generalized other would be in the same dilemma. What the invigilator-student would do would depend on a number of considerations: his commitment to one role or the other, the risk of discovery by one party or the other, and so on. This situation has in fact been the subject of well-known studies (Stouffer 1949; Stouffer and Toby 1951).

Role-sets
Conflicting role expectations do not arise only through the temporary or accidental conjuncture of two roles such as friend and invigilator in the one person. They are permanent and inherent for the occupants of some positions. Gross, Mason and McEachern (1958) studied the School Superintendent (roughly the American equivalent of Director of Education in Britain). As a public official, the superintendent has to deal with several distinct groups including the elected members of the local School Board who are his employers, with parents as 'customers', and with teachers as subordinates. Each group tends to expect different things of him. For instance School Board members necessarily have to worry about financial control, while teachers are concerned that he obtains for them good pay, conditions and teaching facilities, and the parents make all sorts of demands about the content and quality of their children's education. The superintendent typically cannot 'deliver the goods' entirely to one group's satisfaction without dissatisfying one or more of the others. But it is inherent in his position that he has to seek a *modus vivendi* with each.

It was with this kind of situation in mind that Merton (1957) developed the notion of the role-set. Starting from Linton's definitions, Merton postulated that each status (such as School Superintendent) involves not a single associated role but an array of roles, each relating the occupant of the status to a distinct category of associates. Merton asked what social mechanisms were available to reconcile the conflicting expectations and demands of members of the role-set, at least to the extent that the status in question became a workable proposition. He identified the following as among the most significant. First of all, the relationship may be of relatively less importance for some members of the role-set than others. For parents, membership of the Parent-Teacher Association may be peripheral relative to their occupational and home concerns, so that they may be less concerned to exert pressure on the School Superintendent than are the teachers, whose occupation is a more central part of their lives. Second, some of the members of the role-set may be less powerful than others. The School Superintendent may be able to achieve a degree of autonomy if no one group is sufficiently powerful to impose its will; to the extent that groups form coalitions, his chances are reduced. Third, a useful degree of inconsistency may be possible because it is not observed; members of the role-set do not interact continuously with each other, and so to an obviously limited extent, a person may present a somewhat different face to separate individuals and groups in the role-set – a technique familiar to politicians. Fourth and conversely, if the conflicting demands are recognized by the different parties involved, they may in some circumstances not press their own demands in full but seek some form of compromise. Fifth, if the status is one of many like it (there are many School Superintendents), associations of those similarly placed may develop codes of conduct, thus providing one form of what Galbraith (1952) called 'countervailing power'. Merton gives as an example the American Library Association's code on censorship, an aid to librarians withstanding public campaigns against the theory of evolution, sex, sociology, or whatever. This is a manifestation of increasing institutionalization of the role. Sixth, disconcerted parties may withdraw from the role-set, though this is not easily achieved in a highly institutionalized situation such as that of the School Superintendency which we have taken as our main example. Superintendent, Board members and teachers cannot withdraw (if they resign, someone else has to take their place), and parents can only do so by the drastic expedient of buying private education for their children. Finally though, it has to be said that none of these six mechanisms need inevitably come into action, and conflicting role expectations frequently have to be lived with as a continuing aspect of social interactions.

Numbers, Networks and Interdependence

Underlying discussions of role-theory often seem to be a tacit assumption that even the most complex patterns of social relations can in principle be understood by breaking them down into pairs of people interacting with each other face-to-face. Ideas such as role-conflict and role-set, intended to patch over the assumption, really draw it more closely to attention. Its weakness was partially demonstrated nearly three-quarters of a century ago in the work of Georg Simmel (1858–1918), who perceptively drew attention to the qualitative differences between the dyad and the triad, and more generally to the significance of numbers in social life (1950: Part II). People involved in a dyad, he pointed out, are aware that the relationship has no existence beyond themselves. If either one of them withdraws, there is nothing left. They are jointly responsible for collective actions, and the actions of each are fully known to the other. Therefore they are fully involved in the relationship; in Parsons's terms, it is a diffuse rather than a specific involvement. The introduction of a third party brings changes more decisive than a fourth or subsequent member. A triad survives as a dyad after a third member withdraws. One member can withhold knowledge from the other two, or two from one, and one can hold the other two responsible for collective action. Simmel suggested three kinds of triad in which the role of the third party differs from that of the other two people. The third man may be a conciliator or mediator between the two if he seeks the welfare of the group as a whole. Or he may pursue his own interests in the role of *tertius gaudens*, exploiting their differences. Or he may pursue a strategy of *divide et impera*, not merely exploiting existing disputes, but actively creating them for his own advantage.[4] Compared with the qualitative changes introduced by the third party, Simmel contended, the appearance of fourth and subsequent parties has relatively diminishing impact. It merely complicates and enlarges the possibilities which may emerge, further dispersing knowledge and chances of control.

This last assertion conceals as much as it reveals, and even today it is arguable that a clear understanding of the impact of increasing numbers on social processes is perhaps the single greatest gap in sociological theory. Sociologists still tend to jump from discussing social interaction in the dyad, triad and small groups to 'social systems', 'institutions' and 'societies', gratuitously described as 'very complex'. In sociologists' *argot*, we still lack the ability to link the 'micro' and 'macro' levels of sociological theory, and find it difficult to conceptualize the appearance of 'emergent properties' of large-scale collectivities.

In order to do that, it is best to think not just of people interacting directly with each other in small face-to-face groups, but of sprawling networks in which people are enmeshed in long chains of interdependence. An obvious fact about such networks is that people who comprise them do not even know everyone else personally. Figure 2 shows this diagrammatically, tracing the 'personal network' of one particular individual (inevitably labelled *ego*). *Ego* interacts directly with a number of people in his 'first order zone' (for the sake of simplicity, only three are shown). They have direct relations with three people with whom *ego* does not; these constitute *ego's* 'second order zone'. They in turn have direct relations with people who are still remote from *ego*, and so on indefinitely. In the modern world, everyone's personal network, if traced far enough, inevitably includes many people whom he not only does not know personally, but of whose individual existence he is unaware.[5] But that does not mean that they are of no importance to him. That he does not *interact* with people in his '*n*th order zone' does not prevent him being *interdependent* with them. What they do or what happens to them may

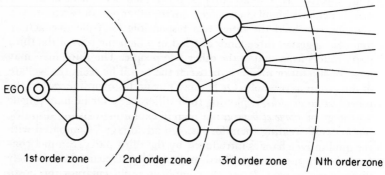

Figure 2 (from Boissevain, 1974)

affect him greatly: repercussions can flow down long chains of interdependence. Many people in Europe and North America found themselves unemployed in the 1970s as a result of the slump caused by the rise in the world price of oil, which followed the Arab-Israeli war of 1973, in which they themselves may have taken little interest – a long and tangled chain of interdependence indeed. The concept of interdependence is more widely serviceable for sociological purposes than that of interaction, because it can be used from the most 'micro' to the most 'macro' level of discussion. The intimate relationships of husbands and wives are relationships of interdependence, and so are the relationships between the industrial states and the 'Third World' states in the modern world-system.

Bonds of interdependence can be patterned into the most elaborate and variable networks. Given the enormous complexity of networks involving more than a few people, it is hardly surprising that network analysis has not been very prominent in sociological investigation of large-scale societies. Fairly typical of the scale on which it has been used is Elizabeth Bott's well-known study (1957) of a few dozen families and their social networks in London. Bott was led to distinguish between highly-connected and dispersed networks. Figure 3 shows in simplified fashion what these terms mean; families replace individuals and only six families are shown in each diagram. Bott's most interesting finding was that the more highly connected a family's social network, the more likely it was that the roles of husband and wife within the family would be highly 'segregated' – that they would have well-defined and separate tasks and activities, the wife cooking and cleaning, the husband holding the purse-strings and so on. Whether this finding is generally valid need not concern us (Bott's

Highly connected network   Dispersed network

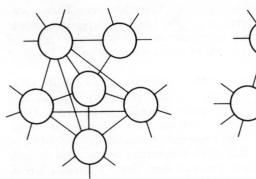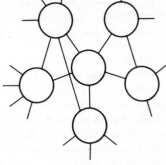

Figure 3 (adapted from Bott, 1955)

study has been extensively debated), but it indicates the likelihood that the quality of face-to-face relationships is not independent of the patterning of the encompassing social networks.

Since Bott's pioneering study, mathematical sociologists have developed several more elaborate measures of the morphology of networks. For example, indices of *density* measure the degree to which members of a person's network are in touch with each other independently of him. Indices of the degree of *connection* in a network measure the average number of relations each person has with others in the same network. Measures of *clustering* identify segments within networks which have a high density relative to the rest of the network. And measures of *centrality* show the degree to which a given person is accessible to all the other people in the network. (For a fuller discussion, see Boissevain, 1974.) The mathematics of these morphological indices becomes very technical, but the ideas underlying them are some of sociology's most longstanding concerns. For example, when Marx made his famous assertion that the French peasantry formed a class 'much as potatoes in a sack form a sack of potatoes' (Marx-Engels 1968: 172), he was saying that their becoming conscious of their common class interests was impeded by the very low density and connectedness of the social networks linking them in the country-side, especially in contrast with the urban proletariat. Measures of density, connection, clustering and centrality all throw light on the potential flows of communication within networks. By extension it is easy to see that a position of centrality within a network may very likely also be a potentially powerful one. And clustering may be a clue to possible patterns of alliance and conflict within networks. For the uninformative lines drawn in network diagrams do not represent simply channels of communication or pairs of role-occupants tending in the Parsonian fashion towards a gratifying harmony. They represent interdependence between people, and interdependent people form alliances and struggle for advantage with each other. Bonds of conflict are just as much bonds of interdependence as are bonds of alliance.

That brings us back to Simmel's problem. Table 1 helps us to explore in more detail how the potential complexity of patterns of relationships increases as the number of people involved rises. Three people can obviously be permutated into three dyads and one triad. Add a fourth person, and the number of possible dyads doubles to six, the number of possible triads quadruples to four, and there is one possible relationship between all four, yielding eleven relationships in all. And so on: by the time there are ten people, the calculations are becoming unwieldy. Ten people, we need hardly add, is only a small social group, yet the structural possibilities within even such a small group are very large indeed.

It is plain that the painstaking mapping out of social interconnec-tions between individual people becomes impractical if the object of interest is the wider society with hundreds, thousands or millions of members. As yet sociologists cannot for many purposes dispense with less precise, unmathematical, concepts like 'organization', 'institu-tion', and 'community'. But the image of a complex network can use-fully remain in mind. The many kinds of social organizations of which sociologists speak, such as families, villages, towns, factories, schools, bureaucracies or classes, can be thought of as various kinds of knots and tangles, more or less highly connected networks strung together by more dispersed networks. These networks within which people are caught up in alliances, conflicts, and fluctuating balances of power, have dynamics of their own, the nature of which is not always easy to

Table 1. Increase in number of possible relationships relative to number of individuals

Number of individuals	Two-person relationships	Increase	All possible relationships	Increase
2	1	—	1	—
3	3	2	4	3
4	6	3	11	7
5	10	4	26	15
6	15	5	57	31
7	21	6	120	63
8	28	7	247	127
9	36	8	502	255
10	45	9	1013	511

'All possible relationships' means all permutations of individuals, in clusters, or alliances, thus:

3 people = AB AC BC ABC = 4 relationships

4 people = AB AC AD BC CD
ABC ABD ACD BCD
ABCD = 11

5 people = AB AC AD AE BC BD BE CD CE DE
ABC ABD ABE ACD ACE ADE BCD BCE BDE CDE
ABCD ABCE ABDE ACDE BCDE
ABCDE = 26

(Simplified from N. Elias, *What is Sociology?*, 1978a: 101)

grasp either by sociologists or by the people actually entangled in them. The interweaving of people's actions leads to the emergence of patternings and processes (or 'emergent social properties') seemingly independent of any individual's actions and beyond his control. Norbert Elias (1978a: chapter 3) has illustrated why this is so through the use of a series of 'game models'.

Game Models

In Elias's game models, the actions and responses of interdependent people in social processes are viewed as moves in games. The game models are used heuristically; they are highly simplified analogies to real social processes.[6] Yet because real games *are* social processes, the analogy is a good deal less dangerous than the biological and mechanical analogies so often used in sociology. The one great danger is that, because real games are played according to rules, the game models may help to give credence to the assumption that rules are essential, the *sine qua non* of any patterning or structure in social life.

Rules are certainly an ingredient in probably the greater proportion of social relationships. But to emphasize that his game models are very different from Parsons's consensual model of dyadic interaction, Elias prefaces them with a model of what he calls the Primal Contest, which is anything but a game. He uses this model as a reminder that social relationships can settle down to a stable pattern without any moral component in expectations, a pattern based entirely on expectations in the probabilistic sense. Consider two tribes, both hunters and gatherers, who repeatedly encounter each other as they search for food in a tract of land. Food is scarce, and for reasons beyond their control and understanding – drought for instance – it is becoming scarcer. Conflict breaks out and deepens between the two tribes pursuing the same scarce resources; one tribe raids the other and kills a few of its members, and shortly afterwards a similar retaliatory raid takes place. Each tribe makes such arrangements as it can to defend its camps, but the war drags on. It may go on until both tribes are wiped out, until only one remains, or until both are so diminished in numbers as to make food supplies adequate once more. Or none of these things may happen, and the war just goes on and on. The tribes are clearly ecologically interdependent. Their interdependence stems from material circumstances, not from shared cognitions, norms or values. Nor do they acquire such shared orientations. They may not even speak each other's languages. Nonetheless, it is impossible to understand the actions, plans, goals or general ways of life of either tribe except by its interdependence with the other. This may be a limiting or rare case, but examples are not unknown. The possibility should be borne in mind as a safeguard against the too ready assumption that relationships tend inevitably towards co-operation, harmony and equilibration.

After this prefatory warning, the game models themselves do assume that games are played according to rules. But they illustrate more emphatically that games are also *contests*, and that is no contradiction. The game models are all based on trials of strength, and the first and simpler ones can be thought of as quite close to a real game like chess. Strength or 'power' in the game is not an absolute quantity, a substance of which each player has a store, but a quality of the relationship in question. In chess, skill is very obviously a relative thing even at the very highest levels.

Two-person Games

(a) Imagine two people playing a game, in which A is a very strong player and B a very weak one. A therefore has a great deal of control and influence over B, and can actually force B to make certain moves. (Think of 'huffing' in draughts.) Yet at the same time, B has a degree of power over A, for A has to take B's moves into account in making his own moves. Both players must have *some* strength or there would be no game. A's power over B is the excess of his strength over B's strength, in this case a considerable excess.

A thus has a high degree of control over his opponent, being able to force him to adopt certain tactics. This also means that A has a good deal of control – though it is not absolute – over the course of the game *as such*, not only over whether he will obtain victory, but how, and how quickly.

(b) Suppose the discrepancy between A's and B's strength in the game diminishes, either because B quickly becomes more skilled, or because A tires or whatever. Two things also diminish: A's ability to use his own moves to force B to make particular moves, and A's ability to determine the course and result of the game. B's chances of control over A increase correspondingly. But as the disparity between the players' strengths is reduced, *the course of the game increasingly passes beyond the control of either.* Elias explains it like this:

> Both players will have correspondingly less chance to control the changing figuration of the game; and the less dependent will be the changing figuration of the game on the aims and plans for the course of the game which each player has formed for himself. The stronger, conversely, becomes the dependence of each of the two players' overall plans and of each of their moves on the changing figuration of the game – on the game process. The more the game comes to resemble a social process, the less it comes to resemble the implementation of an individual plan. In other words, to the extent that the inequality in the strengths of the two players diminishes, there will result from the interweaving of moves of two individual people a game process *which neither of them has planned.* (Elias 1978a: 82, his italics)

Predicting the state of even a two person game like chess, say twelve moves ahead, is extremely difficult. There are numerous possible outcomes with differing degrees of likelihood. What is more, the probabilities change with each successive move.

Multi-person Games on one Level

(a) Imagine a game in which a very strong player A simultaneously plays separate games against a number of less skilled opponents, B, C, D ... N. The weaker players do not co-operate with each other. This is a situation familiar to the chess world in exhibition matches given by Master-class players. A's advantage in each separate game is very great, and each separately resembles model 1(a). The only difference might be that A's superiority could be undermined as the number of separate games increased; there is a limit to the number of separate relationships which can effectively be carried on simultaneously by one person.

(b) Suppose, however, that A plays a single game against a coalition of B, C, D, ... N, each of whom alone is weaker than A. The balance of power is then much more indeterminate. If the weaker players can form a unified and harmonious coalition, their degree of control over A's moves and over the course of the game is likely to be enhanced. If the coalition is beset by inner tensions and disagreements, however, that is likely to reduce the advantages of the coalition and might, just conceivably, put A at a greater advantage than he was in the absence of the coalition.

If the difference in strength between A and the united coalition of B, C, D, ... N should diminish, the course of the game becomes less a direct outcome of either side's plans, just as it did in 1(b).

(c) Imagine a game in which two groups play against each other. The two sides are of roughly equal strength, and the rules favour neither side. With many players, there is a flurry of move and countermove. Neither side can quite determine either the other side's tactics or the course of the game. The moves of one player can be understood neither alone nor solely in relation to those of fellow team members, but only with respect to the whole game. Episodes acquire a certain fleeting structure of their own, and we use distinct terms to describe them. Achieving the overlap in Rugby, for instance, describes the structure and movements of the two lines of forwards, as teams and in relation to each other. The overlap is not a movement of either team alone, but is produced by the interweaving actions of team members as allies and opponents.

Multi-person Games on several Levels

Imagine a game in which there is a very large and growing number of players. We are now thinking of rather elaborate social processes. Perhaps it is inadvisable any longer to try to relate the model to any real-life game, unless it be the medieval village riots from which soccer claims ancestry. It becomes more and more difficult for any single player to put together a mental picture of the state and process of the game in which he is involved. That is very confusing, for every player needs such a picture in order to anticipate what will happen next and plan his next move accordingly. If the web of interdependence becomes too enormous, the individual can no longer make sense of the game nor formulate his strategy.

If the number of interdependent players grows, the figuration, development and direction of the game will become more and more opaque to the individual player. However strong he may be, he will become less and less able to control them. From the point of view of the individual player therefore, an intertwining network of more and more players functions increasingly as though it had a life of its own. (Elias 1978a: 85)

But, emphasizes Elias, just like those in the previous models, this is no more than a game played by many individuals. The difference is merely that as the number of interdependent players grows, and the game becomes more opaque and uncontrollable by any single player, the individual becomes gradually more *aware* of his inability to understand and control it.

If players can no longer map out what is happening overall and plan their moves accordingly, the game is likely to become disorganized, and pressure builds up for the players to reorganize themselves. Several things may happen. The players may segment into several groups, who then continue to play the game independently. This sort of thing tends to happen in hunting and gathering societies, where the hunting bands tend always to remain quite small. Alternatively, the large group may remain but become organized more elaborately in a two-tier (or multi-tier) configuration. (In spite of better intentions, we seem to be making the Football League a model of society!)

In a two-tier game, not all the players any longer play directly with each other. Opposing sides still play against each other and test their relative strengths. But moves are made by specialized functionaries on an upper tier – leaders, delegates, representatives, negotiators, committees, élites, governments. Only these second level players have direct access to the game. Yet they are not independent of the lower level players, and are involved in fact in subsidiary games with the lower tier. Where the discrepancy between the strengths of first and second tier players is very great, we have an oligarchic game.

The distinctive feature of an oligarchic game is that (as the word implies) there is a comparatively small circle of players on the upper tier. So each player at that level is once more able to picture the figuration of players and the course of the game, and to plan a coherent strategy by which to pick his way through the flurry of move and countermove. Yet though the game process may appear relatively transparent, it is in fact much more complex than anything observed in the earlier models; it is far more difficult for one player to steer the game in the direction he desires. For even with only two tiers, several different balances of power have to be taken into account: between the top tier players; between the top tier players and the lower tier players; between the lower tier groupings; and within the lower tier groupings. These are all interdependent. For instance, splits between upper-tier players may enhance the power of lower-tier groups. Or coalitions of upper and lower players against the strongest oligarch may stymie his chances of guiding the game his way. On the other hand, if there are two very evenly balanced coalitions, another upper level player with relatively few allies on either level may be enabled to play the role of *tertius gaudens*.

If power differentials between the two levels diminish, for example as lower-tier groups become better organized, the balances of power and the course of the game become even more indeterminate, fluid and beyond the control of any single individual or group. In an oligarchic game, the lower level players may seem to exist for the benefit of the upper tier. But as the ties of interdependence between the two tiers increase, the opposite may seem closer to the truth. The upper tier players become more overtly spokesmen for the lower groups. For each spokesman, his strategy with respect to lower tier groups becomes as important as strategy towards others on the upper tier. The course of the game becomes still more opaque and still less susceptible to control and influence even by upper level players. The significance of that is re-emphasized when it is realized that a two-tier game is a ludicrously oversimplified model of real societies involving millions of people and innumerable tiers.

People caught up in more and more complex webs of interdependence find themselves subject to ever more complicated and apparently impersonal constraints. The changing patterns of social bonds will be reflected in changing patterns of personality. It will also be reflected in the changing ways people perceive and account for the social processes in which they are enmeshed.

> Instead of players believing that the game takes its shape from the individual moves of individual people, there is a slowly growing tendency for impersonal concepts to be developed. ... These impersonal concepts take into account the relative autonomy of the game process from the intentions of individual players ... as something not immediately controllable even by the players themselves. Metaphors are used which oscillate constantly between the idea that the course of the game can be reduced to the actions of individual players and the other idea that it is of a supra-personal nature. (Elias 1978a: 91)

This oscillation can be traced within most of the great modern political and social belief-systems, and also within the social sciences. The tension between 'individual-centred' and 'system-centred' approaches to sociology is one manifestation of it. The game models help to show why neither approach is adequate without the other, and why neither can be reduced to the other.

An Example: The Civilizing Process

In themselves, the game models provide a rather abstract allegory for sociologists. But long before he sketched them, Elias had undertaken a piece of research which illustrates many of their implications. For that reason it is worth briefly summarizing the argument he presented in *The Civilising Process* (1978b and forthcoming; orig. 1939).

In this long-neglected classic, Elias shows how the development of the nation-state, changing patterns of individual behaviour and personality structure, as well as changing social ideologies, can all be understood as interconnected processes in the long-term development of European society since the Middle Ages.

The process of state-formation is one aspect of the more general process of the weaving of chains of interdependence into more and more extensive webs. Elias traces the emergence of larger and larger territorial units out of the patchwork of tiny feudal fiefs which formed the map of Europe at the end of the first millennium A.D. These small political units were inevitably unequal in power; the fertility of soil, lines of communication and settlement patterns would be among the geographical and economic sources of inequality which affected the balances of power between neighbouring fiefdoms. As they competed amongst each other, some of them grew territorially larger by defeating and absorbing their neighbours. The larger some became, the more easily could they support larger and more effective administrative and military machines, which made it still more probable that bigger units would grow still bigger by absorbing yet more of their smaller neighbours. The logic of this situation led territorial magnates to seek to establish in their own hands three related monopolies: a monopoly of the means of making war or the external use of force; a monopoly of the internal use of force, within their own territory; and a monopoly of the right of taxation, since a fiscal monopoly was necessary to support the first two. Elias's conception of what he calls the 'monopoly mechanism' was clearly based on analogous processes of competition observed by economists.

As the monopoly mechanism concentrated power in the hands of princes, this very concentration soon outstripped the capacity of any individual to exercise all power personally. There began to emerge royal courts with growing administrative staffs, marking the beginning of the depersonalization and institutionalization of power. This was enhanced by the growing complexity of society – itself at least in part made possible by the internal pacification of larger territories – which generated more and more distinct social groups with conflicting interests. Kings were often able to play off these conflicting groups against each other, to the further enhancement of their own functions and power. The process culminated in the absolutist courts of the seventeenth and eighteenth centuries, of which Versailles was the archetype. The aristocrats who lived with the king at that elegant and brilliant court had been stripped of their feudal functions and territorial bases for independent power, being replaced by a royal administrative machine. *L'état, c'est moi*, remarked Louix XIV, and he seemed to dominate the entire society. This is plainly the origin of Elias's Model 3a. But in the middle of the eighteenth century, the costs of maintaining a giant administrative and military machine on an inadequate fiscal system caused growing problems. The story of subsequent events, which took France and later other countries in the direction of Model 3b, characterized by more equal balances of power between social strata, is well-known.

Elias argues that these macroscopic processes of social and political development are essential to understanding changes which took place over several centuries in patterns of individual behaviour, manners and personality structure. He suggests that 'If, over a larger or smaller area the people are forced to live in peace with one another, the moulding of affects ... [is] very gradually changed as well' (1978b: 201). In other words, the increased *social* control or *con*straint which comes from the centralization of political power is also associated with rising standards of *self*-control or *re*straint. Looking back to the medieval period, Elias remarks:

> The expression of feeling by people in the Middle Ages was altogether freer and more spontaneous than in the subsequent period. But it certainly did not lack social patterning and control in any absolute sense. There is, in this sense, no zero point. But the type, the strength and the elaboration of taboos, controls and interdependencies can change in a hundred ways. And as these change, so does the tension and equilibrium of the emotions and, with it, the degree and kind of gratification which the individual seeks and finds. (1978b: 215)[7]

Since internal gratification is a prominent part of the process of state-formation, it is perhaps not very surprising to find, from the Middle Ages onwards, increasing restraint over the expression of agressiveness and the use of violence in private disputes, as well as somewhat less cruelty towards animals and fellow-men. But Elias is also able to demonstrate some less obvious manifestations of increased restraint in many other aspects of social behaviour.

Elias's principal sources of evidence are the numerous 'manners books' which from the thirteenth to the nineteenth century set out the changing standards of acceptable social behaviour. They were, of course, addressed to the literate upper classes. The authors tell their readers how to handle food and conduct themselves at table; how, when and when not to break wind and spit; how to blow their noses; how to behave when passing someone in the act of urinating or defecating; how to behave when sharing a bed (with a person of the same sex) at an inn; and so on. In earlier centuries such matters, which now seem self-evident and mention of which causes embarrassment – or at least mirth – were discussed openly and frankly, without shame. Apparently they needed to be discussed. Then gradually, from the Renaissance, a long-term trend becomes apparent towards higher standards of self-restraint and more elaborate codes of behaviour. The trend is seen in each of the aspects of social behaviour examined by Elias. To take two simple examples, the fork and the handkerchief slowly, very slowly, came into use. These and many other refinements were first adopted in courtly circles, and became *de rigueur* in the courts of the seventeenth and eighteenth centuries. The permanent interdependence of many people living together at court led to pressure 'toward a stricter regulation of impulses, and therefore toward greater restraint' (1978b: 137). As late as the sixteenth century, courts were making regulations against the apparently widespread practice of urinating and defecating in case of urgency in corners, corridors, on staircases or against the tapestries. As time went on, the authors of manners books could take such basic matters for granted, devoting less space to the niceties of how to blow one's nose with the fingers of one hand only, or to use only one hand (the other one!) to take food from the common bowl. On the other hand, other refinements came into use, so that in more recent centuries manners books might more properly be called treatises on etiquette.

To the modern mind it seems obvious that most of the changes Elias describes must have come about for reasons of hygiene. But Elias is able to show that in each case thresholds of shame and embarrassment rose and standards of behaviour changed *first*; only later were reasons of hygiene advanced as *post facto* justifications of the new standard. For instance, when spitting was accepted and frequent, it was said to be unhealthy to retain sputum; only after spitting became socially unacceptable was it declared unhygienic. Controversially, Elias claims that '"Rational understanding" is not the motor of the "civilizing" of eating or of other behaviour.' (1978b: 116.) The justification most frequently given initially for new standards of restraint was that the former unrestricted behaviour shows a lack of respect for associates, particularly social superiors. Reasons of hygiene became prominent only in the later period, when upper-class standards of shame and restraint were spreading to all ranks of society.

Elias's account of the connection between changes in manners and in social stratification and social power is complex. He argues that from the Renaissance onwards, 'feelings and affects are first transformed in the upper class, and the structure of society as a whole permits this changed affect standard to spread slowly throughout society'. (1978b: 115.) This is in marked contrast to the medieval period, when the social figuration was less conducive to the permeation of models of behaviour through society as a whole. A code of behaviour might apply, like knightly chivalry, to one estate, while behaviour in other strata remained quite different. In early modern Europe, transitionally, forms of behaviour were often considered distasteful or disrespectful in social inferiors which the superiors were not ashamed of for themselves. Thus it was disrespectful for a man to appear unclothed before a superior, yet for the superior to do so before an inferior could be a sign of affability. Only later were the same standards of shame and restraint extended to all grades of society, more or less equally, and Elias associates this with the increasing inter-dependence and more equal balances of power between social strata. He also drops some hints about how relations between major social strata were reflected in the development of competing views of society: how, for example, the concepts of 'culture' and 'civilization' came in Germany to express the different ideals of nobility and bourgeoisie. But that is to stray into the sociology of knowledge, a field to which we shall return in a later chapter.

Elias does not claim that the civilizing process proceeded in a straight line with no fluctuations or reversals; nor does he claim it will inevitably continue in the future. Indeed, in the twentieth century, freer and more spontaneous standards of behaviour have in Europe and America replaced many of the rigorous inhibitions of the Victorian era. Elias would argue that the modern 'informalization process' is only possible because of very high standards of self-restraint internalized and taken for granted in the modern personality (see Wouters 1977).

Space, however, prevents us entering into the numerous controversies which Elias's thesis invites. His argument has been summarized here mainly as a provocative example of a sociological investigation of the broadest scope which nevertheless simultaneously concerns itself both with the face-to-face social behaviour of individuals and processes of long-term development in the structure of European societies.

Conclusions

Among the ways in which sociologists have tried to throw a conceptual bridge between their interests in small-scale social interaction and in larger-scale social structures, or in other words between micro- and macro-sociology, role-theory has been the most prominent. Even so, some sociologists have tended to emphasize that roles are facets of personality and are constantly created within interaction, while others have stressed their quality as given, handed-down units of social structure. These differences of emphasis can be reconciled and the concept of role is certainly one which virtually all sociologists find useful as far as it goes. But it does not go very far. Most discussions of roles are couched either explicitly or implicitly in dyadic terms. This is seriously misleading, because most of the interesting dynamic properties of social collectivities arise from the virtually unlimited ways in which social relationships between large numbers of people can be patterned in shifting lines of communication, alliance and conflict within complex networks. For this reason, the concept of interdependence is more generally useful than that of interaction as a bridge between micro- and macro-sociology. Elias's game models provide a valuable aid to understanding how the interweaving actions of numerous people can give rise to social processes which are relatively autonomous from the plans and control of any single person or even alliance within the figuration. One example of a long-term, unplanned, compelling social trend is the 'civilizing-process' hypothesized by Elias. To an unusual extent he brings together in one discussion the objective and subjective dimensions of social life – a concern with the development of objective interdependencies in society, and with correlated developments in personality structure and how people perceive and think about the changing and growing webs of interdependence in which they are entangled.

Several problems have been touched upon towards the end of this chapter without being adequately explored. One is how sociologists conceptualize 'social structures' and explain their development. Another is the nature and dynamics of power, conflict and cohesion is society. A third is the relationship between social development and social belief-systems. These problems will be taken up in the next few chapters.

3 Systems
and Development

That many social processes unfold in an unplanned and uncontrolled way, in apparent autonomy from the actions and intentions of the people who constitute them, is one of the essential insights of sociology. In spite of constantly changing personnel, many 'social structures' persist with recognizable continuity over generations. So, for that matter, do some structured processes of social change and development. But it is the continuity which has most often struck sociologists as problematic, and this helps to explain the traditional popularity of the notion of *social system*.

A system, according to one dictionary definition, is just 'a complex whole, set of connected things or parts, organized body of material or immaterial things'. By implication, a social system can be seen as consisting of interdependent social components. At its simplest, this involves the idea that the presence or the value of one variable in a system imposes a degree of constraint on the range of possible variation in other components of the system. Or it involves the equally simple proposition that a change in one component of a system will be followed by changes in other components. For instance, it has been suggested that if a society has an industrial economy, it is unlikely that it will also have, or long retain, an elaborate pattern of prescriptive kinship relations; among the reasons for this belief is that an industrial economy requires social and geographical mobility of labour, and an extended family would be incompatible with this.[1] It is a short step from this hypothesis of interdependence between the institutions of a society to suggesting that a particular institution (such as the nuclear family unit consisting of husband, wife and offspring) fulfils certain 'functions' (such as the socialization of infants) which are important for the maintenance of the wider social system. This could be equally well expressed by saying that one institution has certain *consequences* for other institutions with which it is interdependent. The word 'function' as used in sociology can in fact usually be translated as 'consequence', which is less ambiguous. But from 'function' comes the name of a controversial school of thought important in the history of sociology, *functionalism*, to which the idea of social systems is central.

Why should the innocuous ideas just outlined be as controversial as they undoubtedly have been?[2] Broadly speaking, there are two reasons. First, functionalism came to be identified with a consensual view of social order; many writers, both in attacking and in defending functionalism, use that word as a synonym for the view that the indispensable foundation of social life is adherence to shared norms and values. Secondly, functionalists have generally not used the idea of system in the very general sense we have just sketched. They have most often conceived of them as self-regulating, goal-directed, self-equilibrating, self-reproducing systems, and this has led to slipshod logic which has earned many functionalist theories well-deserved criticism.

The consensual view of society is not logically inherent in a functional or systemic approach. Analytically they are separate issues, though in the history of sociology there are good reasons for confounding them. For one thing, Talcott Parsons and such influential followers as Kingsley Davis, Wilbert Moore, Marion Levy and Neil Smelser, whom Lockwood (1964) proposes we call 'normative functionalists', combined the systemic approach with an emphasis on consensus, normative integration, shared values and so on. Then it must be admitted that sociologists who believe that all order in society is necessarily derived from interpersonal consensus on values and norms will also find appealing the image of smoothly intermeshing and harmoniously compatible institutions within self-regulating social systems. Lastly, as I shall argue below, to assume that the people who constitute a social system are agreed upon the goals they should pursue together is one possible route of escape (though not a very good one) from the invalidly teleological mode of reasoning which plagues functional explanation.

Yet normative functionalism is not the whole of functionalism. Coser (1956) and Gluckman (1955) discussed conflict within an essentially functional framework. For that matter, what could be more systemic than Marx's discussion of the complex links between economic arrangements and other social institutions, or his view that given certain characteristics of the base or substructure, the range of likely variation in the superstructure of beliefs and political institutions is limited? It could be argued that one reason why Marx and Engels poured such scorn on the 'utopian' socialists (Marx-Engels 1968: 399–434) was precisely that the latter had failed to make a functional analysis of society, and therefore failed to locate the point of maximum leverage for social change, and consequently to show how their new society could be made to grow out of the old.

If even Marx can be enlisted as a systems theorist, it is not surprising that Parsons claimed that 'general agreement exists regarding ... the concept of system' (1961: 33). Kingsley Davis (1959) went even further and announced that functional analysis is merely 'another name for sociological analysis'. But such arguments involve a certain sleight of hand. For, as George Homans (1964) said in reply to Davis, 'if we are all functional analysts, we are certainly not all functional theorists'. In other words, though all sociologists may see the necessity of tracing the interdependencies between social institutions, by no means all of them accept that the development and functioning of the institutions can be *explained* by hypothesizing that social systems are self-regulating and goal-directed. For that is the special sense in which functionalists have historically used the idea of 'social system'. So let us first examine systems analysis in general before looking at the particular form identified with functionalism.

Systems Analysis

'The concept of system is nothing but an application of the criterion of logical integration of generalized propositions.' So said Parsons (1961: 32), and rightly, though it would be unfortunate if we were led to believe that Parsons himself used the concept of social system only in this general, logical sense.

The systemic view is useful – indeed necessary – whenever we are confronted with a situation of other than simple linear causality. Sociology is not often blessed with situations where item A has an effect on item B, which in turn affects item C, with the simplicity of one billiard-ball hitting another. More often than not, a number of variables are causally interrelated with each other in complex ways. A may have an effect on B and C, and C may affect D, but A is itself affected by the reaction of B and D, and so on. In his work on race relations, Blalock (1967, 1970) identifies a large number of variables involved in the patterning of minority group relations. His preliminary identification of the causal links is shown in Figure 4.

These major variables can be further broken down; for example, discrimination can be analysed into educational discrimination, occupational discrimination, political discrimination, residential exclusion, social exclusion, and so on, again all interrelated in far from simple ways (Figure 5). Merely to abstract these variables from the empirical evidence, and to find ways of measuring them is a considerable intellectual achievement in itself.

Yet it is not good enough, faced with such a situation, to put it

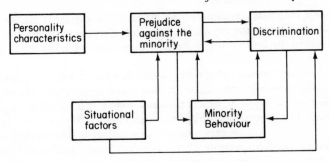

Figure 4 (from Blalock, 1970: 276)

all down to a vague 'reciprocal causality' or to say that 'everything determines everything else'. We must attempt to trace the exact nature of the links between each variable or 'part' of the system. It is no simple matter, under non-experimental conditions where variables cannot be manipulated at will, to disentangle these complex causal systems involving large numbers of variables. The usual approach, however, is to use sets of simultaneous equations called 'structural systems' (Blalock 1964: 52 ff.). Having selected a set of variables as of theoretical interest, each variable must be treated as a possible independent variable, and a separate equation written for each of them. Thus the relationships between the various kinds of discrimination in Blalock's example could be written as follows:

(1) Residential exclusion $R = f_1 (E, O, P)$
(2) Educational discrimination $E = f_2 (R, P)$
(3) Occupational discrimination $O = f_3 (E, P)$
(4) Political discrimination $P = f_4 (E)$
(5) Social exclusion $S = f_5 (R, E, O)$

These relationships are represented in Figure 5.

This is not the place to explore the niceties of how it is possible to test such a structural system against data and to make causal inferences from multiple regression techniques; Blalock has lavished attention on this. It is not, however, merely a matter of esoteric methodology, but a central logical problem of the social sciences. Economists have long struggled with the reciprocal links between macroeconomic aggregates of consumption, saving, investment, income and the demand for money. In a celebrated review of Keynes's *General Theory*, Reddaway set out its basic argument in four simple equations which are now found in every elementary economics textbook, and in form they are not unlike those in the sociological example above. Superficially, however, they presented a puzzle, as Reddaway observed. 'Are we then reasoning in a circle?' he asked. 'The answer is no, we are merely faced with the inevitable difficulty of trying to describe a system where the four variables *mutually* determine each other.' (1964: 106, his italics; orig. 1936.)

The equations used above by way of illustration are of the mathematically simplest kind. They are functional statements only in the mathematical sense in which it is said that x is a function of y, or $x=f(y)$. The object of empirical research must be to give much more precise values to those expressions, but sociologists frequently find it difficult enough to identify all the relevant factors sufficient to construct a logically complete system, let alone to measure them adequately. So it is hardly surprising that they often cannot go beyond

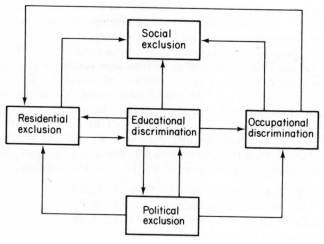

Figure 5

tendency statements of the kind 'x varies directly (or inversely) with y', or that 'x at one point in time is a function of its value in the previous period'. Non-linear relationships are often beyond them. Relationships between social variables are, however, often far from linear. Deutsch (1961) for instance, in constructing a systemic model of communications in political development, points out that a variable such as the volume of mail per capita may be quite unrelated to other factors until it reaches a 'threshold of significance', whereupon it may become a highly sensitive index of modernity related to many other variables. Such 'step functions' are only one of the many possibilities of complex causality in social systems.

There is no point in underestimating the difficulties of making causal inferences from the empirical study of complex social systems. But there is equally little point in baulking the issue, as happened in the past. The sound strategy seems to be to begin from simple models and attempt to make them progressively more consistent with the evidence, using the model of course as a guide to what further evidence is required. Economics has built up an impressive body of theory starting from initially very simple mathematical foundations. The simpler models, incidentally, generally do not assume any tendency to equilibrium, except in the very limited sense that if none of the variables is further disturbed, stasis will set in (see Machlup 1958), and they may even predict explosions or the disintegration of the system. In contrast, sociologists have tended to *assume* from the outset that many social phenomena could only be represented by something altogether more complicated, a *goal-directed* or *teleological system*, the parts of which behave in such a way that certain features of the system are maintained constant. Unfortunately, this kind of model is so complex that it has rarely been rigorously demonstrated to be appropriate to any particular empirical phenomena. So it has remained very much at the level of an assumption. Why the assumption should have been made requires an examination of the history of functionalism and the peculiar place therein of the biological analogy.

The Biological Analogy

The analogy between the groups and institutions within society and the parts of an organism goes back at least to Aristotle, who wrote in the *Politics* that:

> ... every state consists, not of one, but of many parts. If we were going to speak of the different species of animals, we should first of all determine the organs which are indispensable to every animal. ... In like manner the forms of government are composed not of one, but of many elements. (1905: 152–3)

Just as an animal needs certain organs if it is to survive, so the various groups in society each contributed in their own way to its survival. This analogy recurs time and again in social thought. It was very prominent in the work of Herbert Spencer. It was evident in Durkheim's writings, especially perhaps in his discussion of 'normal' and 'pathological' states of society, in *The Rules of Sociological Method* (1938: Chapter 3), even though in the same book he expressed some incisive criticisms of this mode of reasoning. And the biological analogy left its marks on the writings of A. R. Radcliffe-Brown (1881–1955) and Bronislaw Malinowski (1884–1942), the generally acknowledged founders of modern anthropological functionalism.

Radcliffe-Brown and Malinowski were fond of emphasizing their differences from each other. Radcliffe-Brown was more explicitly a follower of Durkheim, and called himself a structural-functionalist; the latter tended increasingly to appeal to psychologistic arguments and called himself a functionalist *tout court* to distinguish himself from the hyphenated school of thought. Nonetheless, the similarities between them are now more striking than their differences. Both were in revolt against evolutionary and diffusionist interests which dominated anthropology in the nineteenth century and persisted into the twentieth. Their revolt was not a total one; both Radcliffe-Brown and Malinowski accepted that, on the whole, societies had tended to evolve from simpler to more elaborate structures, and that customs diffused geographically from one society to another. Historical evidence in literate societies gave ample evidence for these processes. What they did deny was that we were ever likely to have reliable historical evidence about how pre-literate societies had developed. In the absence of reliable historical data, it was possible only to speculate about the past, and such exercises in 'conjectural history' detracted attention from important questions about what actually could currently be observed of pre-literate societies in the field. Why for instance did a society appear to have adopted one custom from a neighbouring tribe, but not another custom equally available for diffusion? Malinowski and Radcliffe-Brown particularly objected to the interpretation of any quaint custom of which the meaning was not immediately apparent as a 'survival' (like the redundant appendix in the human body) from an earlier stage of development. One such case was that of the 'joking relationship' between mother's brother and sister's son among the patrilineal BaThonga (Radcliffe-Brown 1952: 15–31; orig. 1924), which had previously been interpreted as a survival from an earlier stage of matrilineality and matriarchy. But how were customs like this to be explained without reliable information about their origins in the society's past?

In slightly different ways, Radcliffe-Brown and Malinowski gave the same answer. To use a pair of jargonistic terms, *diachronic* analysis was to give way to *synchronic*. Speculation about the past was to be abandoned in favour of analysing the society in its present state, as a unit made up of interrelated parts.[3] Particular customs were to be interpreted in terms of their contribution to the maintenance of the system.

> The function of a particular social usage is the contribution it makes to the *total* social life as the functioning of the *total* social system. Such a view implies that a social system (the total social structure of a society together with the totality of social usages in which that structure appears and on which it depends for its continued existence) has a certain kind of unity

which we may speak of as a *functional unity*.[4] We may define it as a condition in which all parts of the social system work together with a sufficient degree of harmony or internal consistency, i.e. without producing persistent conflicts which can neither be resolved nor regulated. (Radcliffe-Brown 1952: 181; orig. 1935, my italics)

Thus the celebrated joking relationship was interpreted not as a survival from a hypothetical matriarchal stage, but as part of an existing pattern of relationships with mother, father, father's sister, and so on. And it was shown to contribute to the maintenance of the Thonga lineage system. This illustrates the main virtue of the 'postulate of functional unity' as a working hypothesis in field research. It acts as an antidote to excessive ethnocentrism when confronted with some 'quaint' custom, and directs attention to its possible positive role within an existing pattern. Yet what exactly is explained? It is not so much the joking relationship which is explained as the maintenance of lineages. More exactly, Radcliffe-Brown did not explain how the joking relationship originated, and did not claim to, but rather the pattern of continuity once it had been established.

Radcliffe-Brown was quite clear that this 'concept of function applied to human societies is based on an analogy between social life and organic life' (1952: 178). Observing that Durkheim had defined the 'function' of a social institution as the correspondence between it and the *needs* of the social organism, he noted that like all analogies this one had to be handled with care. Can societies have needs? There are a number of striking differences between societies and organisms, notably that if a constituent element no longer functions as it did previously, societies generally change but do not die out. Animals in parallel circumstances tend to keel over. Disparities of this kind caused Radcliffe-Brown some hesitation, but not much, in speaking of social needs.

> ... to avoid possible ambiguity and in particular the possibility of a teleological interpretation, I would like to substitute for the term 'needs' the term 'necessary conditions of existence', or, if the term 'need' is used, it is to be understood only in this sense. It may be here noted ... that any attempt to apply this concept of function in social science involves the assumption that there *are* necessary conditions of existence for human societies just as there are for animal organisms, and that they can be discovered by the proper kind of scientific enquiry. (1952: 178, his italics)

So began the great paper chase for the 'functional prerequisites of a society'. Radcliffe-Brown's own conception of what these were, though shadowy, remained at the structural level – family systems and the like. Certainly he rejected explanations in terms of universal biological or psychological needs. Malinowski (1944), however, late in his life constructed an elaborate set of 'basic needs' of a bio-psychological kind, though allowing that they found expression in very diverse social and cultural arrangements. The details need not concern us, but an interesting aspect of his argument is that every established social pattern must make some contribution to satisfying one or other of these needs. This came to be known as 'the postulate of universal functionalism'.

The great objection to such reasoning is that constants cannot explain variables. We know that the diversity of human societies and cultures is very great. Even if it were conceded that there are some basic similarities in the bio-psychological makeup of all human beings, we should still have to explain how they have become interwoven over countless generations to produce the variety of social patterns which we observe. That has, however, not deterred some sociologists from attempting to draw up short-lists of functional prerequisites, exigencies and whatever.

Among the first to do so was the distinguished group usually abbreviated to Aberle *et al.* (1950). Succinctly, Aberle and his colleagues first defined what they meant by a society, then suggested four circumstances in which a society so defined would cease to exist, and finally produced a long list of the things which were, in their view, necessary to prevent this eventuality. Their definition of a society was 'a group of human beings sharing a self-sufficient system of action which is capable of existing longer than the life-span of an individual, the group being recruited at least in part by the sexual reproduction of the members'. A great deal hinged on this definition, especially on the obscure phrase 'sharing a self-sufficient system of action'.

Given this definition, it does not take any great deductive skill to see that a society will cease to exist in four circumstances: the biological extinction or dispersion of the members; the total apathy of members (disintegration of the 'system of action'); the war of all against all; and the absorption of the society into another society. Ignoring such nagging doubts as whether it is useful to regard Scotland as ceasing to be a society at the Act of Union in 1707, it was then possible to produce a list of nine functional prerequisites which had to be fulfilled if a society was to continue. These were:

(1)   Provision of an adequate relationship to the environment and for sexual recruitment.
(2)   Role differentiation and role assignment.
(3)   Communication, especially through language.
(4)   Shared cognitive orientations.
(5)   A shared, articulated set of goals.
(6)   The normative regulation of means.

(7) The regulation of affective expression.
(8) Socialization.
(9) The effective control of disruptive behaviour.

Most of these points are, of course, banalities. But here is normative functionalism with a vengeance. The scheme shows much more clearly than did Radcliffe-Brown or Malinowski how the biological analogy can be used to prop up a consensual view of society. Of course, if society is defined essentially as consensually integrated, it is scarcely surprising that most of the 'functional prerequisites' are variations on a consensual theme.

Aberle's article antedated Talcott Parcott Parsons's own formulation of a similar set of ideas, which eventually took the form of the four functional exigencies of Adaptation, Goal-Attainment, Integration and Latency-alias-Pattern-Maintenance-and-Tension-Management, first put on public exhibition in *Working Papers in the Theory of Action* (Parsons, Bales and Shils, 1953). These are, in effect, a reworking of Aberle's prerequisites in a more general and abstract form. The main difference is that Parsons said that his apply not just to whole societies but to any social system within a society. The *form* of Parsons's argument is, however, identical with that of Aberle. What Aberle and his colleagues really said was that *if* a set of phenomena meets their definition of a society, and *if* it is surviving, *then* it will contain features that meet their nine prerequisites. And Parsons is saying that *if* a set of social phenomena meets his definition of a social system and is surviving, *then* it will contain features that can be classified into his four functional problems. Unfortunately, over the years he seemed increasingly to assume that virtually anything could be fitted into the schema, and the benefits to be obtained from doing became increasingly obscure.

The 'AGIL' scheme is usually displayed in that best of all possible diagrams, the four-cell box (Figure 6). The Internal/External division separates those activities which are concerned with mediating relationships with the environment from those maintaining its internal structure. The Instrumental/Consummatory distinction points to the difference between ends and means. Some activities are concerned with the achievement of goals either external or internal to the system. Others are concerned with the provision of the means by which these ends can be attained.

The function of *Pattern-Maintenance* refers to the 'imperative' of maintaining the stability of patterns of institutionalized culture which define the structure of the system. The process of socializing children, as the main process by which the shared values of the social system are inculcated, clearly belongs in this box. Also involved are all those

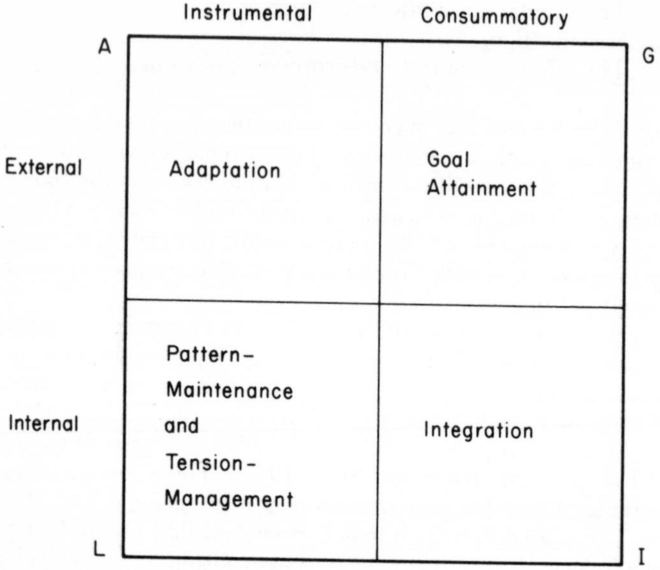

Figure 6

activities from Coronations to reunion dinners by which the sense of common identity is ritually and symbolically reinforced.

Integration is concerned with the mutual adjustments of interrelated units in the system. Socialization merely prepares individuals for participation in groups; integrative mechanisms are still necessary to ensure their co-ordination. Integration involves the 'normative regulation of means', as in patterns of legitimate authority and in mechanisms of social control.

Goal-Attainment is concerned with the allocation of personal and other resources to achieve different goals. Usually there are many goals, so they have to be ranged in a scale of priorities.

Adaptation covers those activities by which the social system adapts to the social and non-social environment. In particular, it is concerned with the provision of disposable facilities independent of their relevance to a particular goal. The difference between adaptation and goal-attainment is relative. The *goal* of a steel firm is the production of steel; but steel is a generalized resource from the point of view of the economy, so the steel firm is adaptive with respect to society's broader goals. This illustrates Parsons's Chinese box conception of social systems. The economy, for instance, can be seen as the adaptive sub-system of society; but it can itself be analysed in AGIL terms, and the capital market then in turn becomes the adaptive sub-system of the economy. And so on *ad infinitum* (see Parsons and Smelser, 1956).[5]

Having dutifully, if rather briefly, outlined the AGIL scheme, I must add that I do not believe it ever contributed to the explanation of anything. Smelser, one of the few people other than Parsons to bother with it, did make some play with AGIL in his *Social Change in the Industrial Revolution* (1959), but as Homans convincingly argued (1964), his Parsonian boxes did not enter at all into his final explanation of the social changes he observed. AGIL might alternatively be regarded as an analytical device potentially useful in facilitating comparisons. Aberle *et al.* remarked that they were 'concerned with *what* must get done in society, not *how* it is done'. The highest aspiration of proponents of functional prerequisites and suchlike would therefore seem to be not to explain why one social system is as it is and different from another, but merely to suggest that different systems may fruitfully be compared because they fulfil equivalent functions. The AGIL scheme, however, is far too vague and elastic sided to serve even for this limited purpose of taxonomy.

Before beginning a critique of functionalism, let us take one conspicuous example of functionalist explanation to illustrate the worst pitfalls of the method. Davis and Moore (1945) propounded what came to be known as the 'functionalist theory of stratification', arguing that 'stratification' was a 'functional necessity' in society. A controversy ensued over the next two decades.[6] Actually, Davis and Moore said nothing about stratification in the sense of strata with discernible boundaries of self-identity. They were in fact concerned with the unequal distribution of rewards which, it is true, is observed in practically every known society. Their argument can be stated very briefly. It was that some positions – doctors and so forth – have greater 'functional importance' for society, and require more talent or training than do others. Society therefore 'has to' reward these positions more than others.

> Social inequality is thus an unconsciously evolved device by which societies insure [sic] that the most important positions are conscientiously filled by the most qualified persons.

Davis and Moore did not explain how the 'functional importance' of jobs was to be assessed empirically, other than by observing how much they were paid which would be tautological. Indeed it is not clear what *is* explained. The focus is mainly on the consequences of inequality for the allocation of labour, and precisely how inequality arises is left implicit. In so far as the theory has a substantial kernel, it is no more than a sociological gloss on the marginal product theory of wages of half a century earlier. However, as we shall shortly see, there is pregnant significance in the remark that stratification (like Topsy?) 'unconsciously evolved'.

Merton's Critique of Functionalism

Though certainly not the last word on this subject, Robert Merton's essay on functionalism (1968: 73–138, orig. 1949) promoted greater clarity and became a classic. Merton focused attention on three assumptions to which we have already alluded, and which are very often implicit and sometimes explicit in functionalist reasoning: the postulates of functional unity universal functionalism and indispensability. Exposing these as unwarranted, he advanced a number of conceptual innovations by which functionalism could be made more defensible.

The influence of the biological analogy is nowhere clearer than in the postulate of functional unity. The image of the whole social structure of society forming a single well-integrated and consistent whole in which 'particular social usages' contribute to the maintenance of the 'total social system' is a very organismic one. Merton wryly notes that the sea anemone, though an organism, is so poorly integrated that when it moves off a rock, it may easily leave a part of its 'foot' behind; how much looser is the integration of most sociocultural systems. 'Functional unity' may have had certain merits as a rough working hypothesis guiding fieldwork in small-scale and fairly static societies,[7] but as a practical matter it simply cannot be assumed that 'everything influences everything else' in society. In complex societies, particular social institutions often have a high degree of 'functional autonomy', and can change without necessarily causing widespread repercussions. The degree of functional integration is itself a variable to be investigated, and that means mapping out the links by which one social pattern has consequences for another.[8] It follows that it is not sufficient simply to say that something is 'functional'; *which* items of social structure it helps to maintain must be specified.

Nor are there any better grounds for upholding the postulate of universal functionalism – the assumption that any and every continuing social pattern or custom must have positive functions, contributing to the maintenance of the established way of life and therefore to the welfare of members of the society. Nineteenth-century anthropologists may have been too ready to dub as 'survivals' any patterns not immediately comprehensible. Yet not to recognize that such *non-functional* patterns may sometimes exist is to fall into the trap which ensnared Clyde Kluckhohn when he tried to explain the retention of the useless buttons on men's jacket sleeves. He said that their function was to maintain tradition, which made people feel comfortable. But what tradition were they maintaining? Only that of having buttons on their sleeves. And if people like the tradition of having buttons on their sleeves, why did they give up the tradition of wearing top hats? This kind of reasoning is plainly specious.

More important, Merton pointed out that established social institutions, far from helping to maintain other institutions, may often undermine them. To take one example at random, in developing countries if the schools and universities turn out educated people faster than the economy can absorb them into suitably satisfying employment, the consequence may be frustration leading to greater political instability. These 'negative' consequences Merton calls *dysfunctions*. Of course, one and the same social process or institution may be functional for one aspect of social structure (serving to maintain it in its established form) and dysfunctional for another (serving to undermine it). Using the concept of dysfunction is, however, very hazardous. The very prefix *dys-*, from the Greek for 'bad', is most unfortunate, carrying with it the implication that any activity which promotes change is to be regretted. Sociology may be able to explain certain kinds of social change, and it may be able to say whether members of the society will consider them bad or good, but it can conjure up no general proof that change is 'a bad thing', like some king in *1066 and All That*. Common sense, nonetheless, suggests that hardly anyone considers all change bad. Freer sexual attitudes, for instance, may undermine traditional patterns of marriage – or at least there are vocal groups who believe they do and consider it a bad thing. The same changes in sexual morality may, however, equally be dysfunctional for the prostitution industry, any reduction in the scale of which is likely to be considered a good thing by the same vocal groups. If the concept of dysfunction is to be used at all, it must be used strictly to refer to consequences which serve to promote change, not, as it too frequently is, as a pompous sociological epithet for anything of which the sociologist disapproves.

Merton's third point of attack was on the 'postulates of indispensability'. The notion of functional prerequisites and system needs has often led to a Panglossian chain of thought. If a social pattern is well established, it must be meeting the needs of the system, and therefore it must be indispensable, and everything is to the best in this best of all possible worlds. This is obviously fallacious. Even if we acknowledge that a social institution fulfils a function and meets a need very satisfactorily, might not the need have been met equally well by a range of different institutions? Given, for instance, a basic 'need' for government, why are some societies totalitarian, some liberal democratic? Merton introduces the complementary concepts of *structural constraints* on the one hand and *functional equivalents* or *alternatives* on the other. Though a fully industrial economy may preclude an elaborate clan system, (structural constraint), it may be quite compatible with a whole range of less rigid patterns (functional alternatives). Kerr *et al.* (1962) argued that in the long term a totalitarian political system is incompatible with a complex industrial economy, essentially because the rational allocation of resources requires individual freedom of initiative in the economic field, and that this must spread to the political. Others, on the contrary, have argued that there are functionally equivalent ways of achieving rational allocation in a command economy, or that economic freedom can exist alongside political regimentation.

Merton claims that the idea of functional equivalents 'unfreezes the identity of the existent and the inevitable'. This is true. Yet it does not entirely dispense with the troublesome notion of functional 'needs', and this remains the central problem of functionalism.

The Problem of Teleology

Durkheim's work is by no means free from all functionalist fallacies but he did express very clearly the dangers of reasoning from 'needs'.

> To show how a fact is useful is not to explain how it originated or why it is what it is. The uses which it serves presuppose the specific properties characterizing it, but do not create them. The need we have of things cannot give them existence, nor can it confer their specific nature upon them. It is to causes of another sort that they owe their existence.[9] ... We must seek separately the efficient cause which produces it and the function it fulfils. (1938: 90, 95)

If social customs and institutions are to be explained as arising in response to some need, the implication is that they are goal-directed or purposive. In other words, the explanation is teleological. Now, as was argued in Chapter 2, individuals are capable of purposive action, and teleological accounts of individuals' behaviour may be quite legitimate. So there is no difficulty if we can point to individuals who have recognized a social need and taken action to meet it. For instance, it is arguable that in late-nineteenth-century England there was a social and economic 'need' for mass elementary education. How did it come to result in the 1870 Education Act? The question could perhaps be answered by establishing in what ways the 'need' became obvious, who recognized it, what power resources were at their disposal, and how they overcame opposition.

But it cannot be seriously argued that all, or even most, social customs and institutions have been consciously and deliberately created in full knowledge of all their consequences. There is often a discrepancy between the subjective motive and objective consequence. The conscious intention which leads participants to act in the way they do may not entirely coincide with what the sociologist can observe to be its consequences. As an example, Merton discusses the effects of the political machines and bosses in the big cities of America in the late nineteenth and early twentieth centuries. Organizations like Tammany Hall, the famous New York Democratic Party machine, and its counterparts in other cities, are chiefly remembered as the foundation-stones of corrupt municipal governments. But Merton points to a number of less widely recognized effects. The bosses provided necessary but unofficial political co-ordination where power was constitutionally very much fragmented and dispersed. In return for bribes and payoffs they in effect regulated uncomfortable competition between legitimate businessmen; and they protected illegal businesses like prostitution and gambling for which there was nevertheless widespread public demand or 'need'. Most interesting, though, were their functions for the poorest sections of the population, for whom they provided both opportunities for social mobility (through advancement in the machine itself) and a sort of welfare service. The poor needed housing, jobs and assistance of all kinds. The political machines gave them help, without asking too many questions. The motive uppermost in the minds of the bosses and precinct captains was that those they helped would out of a sense of obligation vote for the machine's candidates. That indeed was one result. But the machines also played an important part in the integration of American society. That is perhaps especially true of their part in helping the millions of poor immigrants then arriving from Europe, who were assimilated into American society with surprising rapidity. The machines helped to stoke the great American melting-pot. But it is doubtful whether that was something of which the bosses were much aware. Merton therefore draws a distinction between *manifest* functions or dysfunctions (those intended and recognized by the participants) and *latent* functions or dysfunctions (those neither intended nor recognized). The welfare activities of the political machines had both manifest consequences (building up the vote which maintained corrupt government) and latent consequences (the integration effects).

The distinction between the manifest and the latent consequences of an institutional pattern or social custom is of great significance in sociological analysis, and has passed into general use. But it in no way resolves the problem of teleological explanation – it merely defines it more narrowly. As one sociologist noted '... if all functions that actually tend to maintain the system are manifest functions (i.e. recognized by the participants) there ceases to be any real difference between functional and causal analysis' (Catton, 1964: 919). In other words, explaining the persistence of a pattern the consequences of which are manifest to all involved is *relatively* unproblematic. If they are all agreed that those consequences are desirable, we can infer that people are acting purposefully, so that the manifest effects are also the end-in-view and therefore also the cause. (In Schutz's terminology, the in-order-to motive is also the because motive.) Things are more difficult if the consequences are manifest only to a minority, or if there is disagreement about their desirability. It may be possible to show that a minority has the power to impose what it wants on others. But the Game Models sketched in the previous chapter serve to remind us of the hazards of interpreting any social pattern as the implementation of the plans and intentions of any single person or group of people.

In any case, none of this helps in the least to explain why a *latent* need, recognized by no-one, should give rise to any social pattern. At this point it would be useful to be able to hypothesize something like a Jungian collective unconscious, but such metaphysical entities are by general assent out of court. Yet to explain a social institution as an unconscious response to a social need, as Davis and Moore did with social inequality, is to adopt an almost equally illegitimate form of teleology. Collectivities have no group mind, and therefore cannot merely be assumed to be capable, like individual human beings, of learning from experience, recognizing needs, and acting in a purposeful way to achieve goals.

Three Escapes from Teleology

There are, however, three possible ways in which teleological explanation of collective social patterns, organizations or institutions may be justified if there is sufficient empirical evidence. Not surprisingly Talcott Parsons made use of all three arguments, which became very entangled in his work. They are: consensus on common goals; cybernetic mechanisms in society analogous to the common thermostat; and evolutionary processes akin to natural selection.

Consensus

Though, as we have noted, systems analysis and consensual images of society do not logically entail each other, the association between functionalism and consensus theories has been extremely close. The implicit connection between them is that the more nearly people think alike and share common values, the more nearly it is possible to treat them as equivalent to a single individual acting purposively in pursuit of goals. Alfred Schutz put it more exactly:

> The concept of functionalism – at least in the modern social sciences – is
> not derived from the biological concept of the functioning of the organ-

ism.... It refers to the socially distributed constructs of patterns of typical motives, goals, attitudes, personalities, which are supposed to be invariant and are then interpreted as the function or structure of the social system itself. The more these interlocked behaviour patterns are standardized and institutionalized, that is, the more their typicality is socially approved by laws, folkways, mores, and habits, the greater is their usefulness in common-sense and scientific thinking as a scheme for the interpretation of human behaviour. (1962: 61–62)

Schutz was wrong, I think, to play down the influence of the biological analogy on modern functionalism, but in other respects this is an accurate and succinct statement of the logic of the Parsonian kind of functionalism. Two very important reservations about that logic must be entered. First, the extent of social consensus has to be established empirically; it cannot be merely assumed for the convenience of being able to treat social systems as goal-directed. Parsons himself tended to build consensus into his definition of a social system, so that if there is no consensus on goals there is no social system. But he applied the idea of system very freely, often without much empirical justification of its applicability in a particular context. Secondly, if a set of people *are* shown to be pursuing some common goal, to have some common purpose, this is some sort of explanation of their activities. Yet if these activities have latent functions, to demonstrate that there is consensus in no way establishes why a pattern of behaviour with such happy consequences should so fortuitously have been hit upon.

To demonstrate that there was an omnipotent dictator or a highly unified élite with clear objectives of its own and the power to achieve them would equally justify treating a social entity as goal directed. However, as was argued in Chapter 2, social networks of any complexity are more difficult to control than the would-be Machiavellis involved in them often imagine. That is because complexity makes them opaque and the consequences of actions are difficult to anticipate. Yet many sociologists who are hostile to consensus theories are ready and eager to detect guiding élites in equally dubious circumstances. Merely to assume that a collectivity is goal directed by a powerful élite is to make exactly the same mistake as merely to assume that it is goal directed by virtue of value-consensus. In either case the assumption has to be justified by empirical evidence, a task which is never likely to be easy. This difficulty prompted Jürgen Habermas to look at functional analysis from a novel angle. He suggests that instead of trying to identify empirical goals, desirable objectives might simply be specified and the functional approach then used to analyse the conditions necessary for the stated goals to be achieved (Habermas 1970: 176–80; McCarthy 1978: 219–22). That would, however, turn functionalism away from its pretensions to being an empirical science and transform it into a kind of decision-theory, a useful tool for policy-makers. But proponents of functionalism have not traditionally seen it that way.[10]

Cybernetics

Cybernetics is the study of communication and control mechanisms in machines and living creatures. The most familiar example of a cybernetic mechanism is a simple thermostat, a heat-sensitive device which through an electrical circuit controls a central heating boiler. The thermostat is set to a desired temperature, and the boiler then heats the house to the point where the thermostat responds by break-ing the circuit and cutting out the boiler. The temperature then falls until the thermostat switches the boiler back on again. The house tem-perature therefore fluctuates about the desired level, its amplitude and frequency of oscillation depending on the sensitivity of the thermostat, the thermal properties of the heating system, and so on. This system constitutes a simple kind of feedback loop, by which the results of each stage of the cycle become the causes of the next. The system therefore stimulates a simple kind of purposeful behaviour, seeming steadily to pursue the goal of the desired temperature, as if it were turned on and off by an individual reading a thermometer. Indeed, according to Mead's account (see p. 11 above), the purpose-ful behaviour of individuals *is* a kind of cybernetic phenomenon, made possible by the symbolic anticipation of the outcome of actions feeding back into the decision-making process.

In the body, there are similar self-regulating, 'homeostatic' mechanisms by which, for example, the body temperature is main-tained despite quite wide variation in atmospheric temperature, and the constituents of the blood are also maintained within narrow limits. Analogies drawn between these biological mechanisms and social pro-cesses by the physiologists L. J. Henderson and W. B. Cannon had a strong influence in the 1930s on sociologists including Talcott Par-sons. So it is not surprising that Parsons sought to make functionalist teleology respectable by looking for cybernetic processes in society. However, he tended to overlook some of the demanding logical re-quirements of this kind of explanation.

Philosophers such as Hempel (1959), Nagel (1956) and Rudner (1966) who have examined the logic of functional explanation in sociology have identified it with the implicit use of a 'directively organized' or 'goal-seeking' system model. This is 'appropriate in connection with systems possessing self-maintaining mechanisms for certain traits, but seem pointless and even misleading when used with reference to systems lacking such self-regulating devices' (Nagel 1956: 251–2). That a set of social phenomena is directively organized has to be demonstrated. The phenomena must be analysable into two kinds of components: 'goal-states', which are maintained more or less as constants (like the temperature of a house); and 'state co-ordinates' which change in such a way as to maintain the existence of the goal-states (like the boiler switching on and off). The existence of such cybernetic feedback mechanisms has to be shown through appeal to empirical evidence, and Rudner (1966: 109) doubts whether the stringent logical requirements for this kind of explanation have been met in many (if any) of the works in which, to date, social scientists purport to be giving functional explanations.

Simple illustrative examples can, however, be suggested, though convincing ones are easier to find in economics than in sociology. Some markets, though not all, are self-equilibrating. Or consider an arrangement in which pensions are pegged to a cost-of-living index. If the prices of some important goods rise, the pensioners' purchasing power falls slightly until the cost of living index responds, whereupon the pension increases again to restore its former value. That would be very much a consciously created feedback mechanism, in which the cost of living index serves as little more than an aide-mémoire to those responsible for paying pensions. As a more questionable and sociological example, small task-orientated groups like the 'bank-wiring group' in the celebrated Hawthorne studies (reported in Roethlisberger and Dickson 1939: 379–548) might be seen in similar light. An average output can be seen as the goal to be maintained. The actual rate of output fluctuated. As the group worked hard, tempers frayed. So a period of relaxation and joking followed, in which the conditions conducive to production were re-established. Studies of small groups in fact show that this kind of oscillating process is common (for example in discussion groups in social psychological laboratories). But why should this self-regulating, goal-directed pattern emerge? People may not be fully conscious of alternating the types of activity, but the changes of mood are seemingly unconscious or semi-conscious responses to maintain the goal-state (production, reaching a conclusion in a discussion, etc.). On the other hand, using a cybernetic model to explain the behaviour of the bank-wiring group is like taking a sledge-hammer to crack a nut: ensuring that output did not rise so far that their piece-rates were cut seems to have been a perfectly rational strategy for its members to follow.

Rudner is probably right that valid teleological explanations of the cybernetic kind are few and far between in sociology. Probably the most sophisticated (and certainly the most abstruse) use of cybernetic ideas has been made by Niklas Luhmann, who has engaged Habermas in a controversy about social systems theories (Habermas and Luhmann, 1971).[11] Other sociologists seem to have borrowed the imagery of cybernetics but little of its substance. Parsons made extensive use of cybernetic jargon, speaking of 'input-output' and 'cybernetic hierarchies of control'. He saw Pattern-Maintenance as the highest level of control in AGIL, and cultural systems as the highest level of control over social, personality and organismic systems, each level being linked to the others by feedback loops. Walter Buckley (1967) ruminated on cybernetics and General Systems Theory, but seemed to achieve little more than a translation of old ideas into new jargon, and much the same can be said about Etzioni (1968).

Evolution

A third way in which social organization may appear to respond and adapt unconsciously to latent 'social needs' is through some process of evolution. There may be social processes equivalent to Darwinian natural selection, and this can give the appearance of purposeful, even planned, change.

Consider the case of the moths who changed their colour. Certain species of hitherto light-coloured British moths have been observed to be becoming darker in industrial areas of the country. Formerly their habitat may have been silver birch trees, on which they would be inconspicuous. On sooty buildings (or sooty birch trees) they would, however, be very conspicuous, and be eaten by the birds. So they become darker. But it is not plausible that they held a council of war and decided to change colour. Rather, natural selection must have been at work. By some random process, a proportion of darker moths must always have been bred; but on silver birches, they would tend to be spotted and eaten more quickly than the lighter members of their species, so bred less, ensuring the preponderance of lighter moths over darker. On black buildings, of course, the opposite happens: the darker moths survive longer and breed more, so the strain gradually becomes darker.

Social analogies to this process have been implicit in functionalist sociology all the time. Evolution was very much explicit in Spencer, and though Radcliffe-Brown and Malinowski rebelled against Spencer and their evolutionist precursors in anthropology, they did not reject evolutionism wholly. Though they rejected speculative reconstructions of the past of non-literate societies, their assumptions of functional unity and universal functionalism depended absolutely on their belief that natural selection of social customs and institutions was at work. Synchronic analysis of social institutions as a unified, well-integrated, well-adapted system made sense only if natural selection could be assumed to have eliminated the poorly integrated and ill-adapted. This too is the significance at which we previously hinted of the assertion by Davis and Moore that social inequality is 'an unconsciously *evolved* device by which societies insure ...'. Though badly expressed, what this implies is that unequal societies, like dark moths on sooty buildings, thrive better than egalitarian ones. The suggestion is not altogether implausible. It is easy to believe, for example, that hunting bands with the degree of inequality involved in having a recognized chain of command in battle might have an advantage in the struggle for survival over more egalitarian bands. But as an explanation of the appropriateness or inappropriateness of all known patterns of social inequality to their particular social contexts, the Davis and Moore 'theory' is entirely inadequate.

More modest and precise parallels to evolutionary reasoning can, however, be found in sociology. Take for example Joan Woodward's research (1958) on the relationship between management structure and commercial success in a sample of English manufacturing firms. Commercial success was broadly defined, and several different measures were used, including profitability, share of market, rate of growth, labour relations record and rate of labour turnover. Preliminary analysis of the results showed that there was no straightforward correlation between organization and any of these measures of success. There was an enormous range of differences in organizational structure. The number of tiers in the organizational tree ranged from two to twelve, and spans of control from two to nineteen. These differences were not related in any simple way even to the size of the firm – the variations seemed random.

The crucial insight which produced order out of this chaos was that technology and the nature of production objectives had to be taken into account. It appeared that the type of production – whether single units to a customer's individual specification, or mass production of cars on an assembly line, or flow production in an oil refinery or paper works – placed rather different constraints on management structure. Grouping the firms in terms of the technology they employed – broadly into unit and small batch production, mass production, and continuous flow production – produced some order in the data on management structure, irrespective of size. The median number of tiers and the median span of control differed markedly for each technological class. But more interestingly, the commercially more successful firms tended to have management structures which approximated to the median values *for their technological class*, and the least successful firms diverged most from these medians. How is this finding to be interpreted?

In this specific context, it does seem possible to speak meaningfully of the 'demands of the technical situation' or organizational needs. It seems likely that in unit production, where the product is being made to the customer's requirements, there has to be close consultation between the customer, the designer, and those who design and cost the product. So a relatively fluid organization without remote and inflexible chains of command is an advantage. In mass production on assembly lines, and still more in process production, routine production decisions can in contrast be delegated far down the line. Once production is started, the main objective is to keep it going; after the design stage, there is probably little need for consultation between designers, sales and production staff. These differing 'situational demands' are consistent with Woodward's finding that the median number of tiers in the administrative chart was least in the case of unit production, more in mass production, and greatest in process production.

Now, asks Woodward:

> Are those responsible for building the organization in successful firms consciously aware of the demands of the technical situation, and does this affect their decisions? The findings suggest it is unlikely. In only three firms was there any definite evidence that organization was determined by a systematic analysis of 'situational demands'. (1958: 38)

Fortunately, in this particular situation, it is easy to point to an analogy to natural selection in market forces. One reason why the most successful firms approximated to the median organizational patterns for their technological type was presumably that these by chance produced the best commercial results; the market 'encouraged' those forms whose structure most closely met the latent 'needs' of the situation. Yet it would be unwise to assume that market discipline was perfect, or to rely entirely on unconscious adaptation to the economic environment in explaining these findings. Managers may not have been fully aware of the relationship between technology, organization and commercial success. But they were striving for success, and it is probable that successful organization was in part intentional creation, part a latent consequence of trial and error. In studying complex figurations of human actions, the simple dichotomy between latent and manifest consequences becomes a little blurred. It should be remembered that people, unlike moths, can think about their situation and even if they perceive only part of it, their actions may not be entirely inappropriate.

It is paradoxical that nowhere in her study does Woodward explicitly refer to the theory of evolution or even functionalism. Her argument about management structure and technology clearly resembles Darwin's perception that species which survive and thrive in a particular environment must be well adapted to it. But Woodward's study also helps to show that the analogy with natural selection does not give unambiguous justification to synchronic systems analysis in sociology. Woodward was still left wondering how it was that appropriate management structures were hit upon in the first place. This question corresponds to the other aspect of evolutionary theory, which deals with the *development* of species. What so shocked the religiously orthodox of his time was Darwin's rejection of the belief that species had been fixed and immutable since the Creation. In fact Darwin himself had no idea of the exact mechanisms by which mutations came about. His theory was made more complete and plausible later, with the growth of the modern knowledge of genetics out of the work of Mendel. If there is a message for sociology in this side of evolutionary theory, it is that synchronic analysis has to be complemented by diachronic study of the development of social patterns. Synchronic systems analysis on its own was a useful second-best for anthropologists studying pre-literate societies which possessed little or no firm evidence about their past development. For most of human society there is a great deal of such evidence, and to find an analogy to genetics we have to study how social patterns came to develop. Whether we are studying limited sociological problems like Woodward's, or concerning ourselves with global history, it is relevant to know how individuals or groups of people hit upon innovations which proved to be solutions to problems – problems which they had not necessarily previously perceived.

It is significant that in response to criticisms that his earlier theory of social systems was static and unable to account for social change, in later work (1964, 1977b) Talcott Parsons turned to evolutionism to dynamize his functionalism. From Herbert Spencer he borrowed the ideas of structural differentiation and of increasing complexity of social organization through evolutionary processes. He particularly emphasized the importance of certain crucial social and cultural innovations which have constituted 'adaptive upgrading' for the societies which spawned them or subsequently adopted them, and which gave these societies an evolutionary advantage. Among these critical breakthroughs in social organization, he particularly listed social stratification, bureaucratic administration, money and markets, and democratic associations. He played down technological developments, the significance of which would be stressed by Marxist theorists, but paid especial attention to cultural innovations like literacy, monotheistic religion and rational philosophy. The last two were invented in 'seedbed societies', ancient Israel and Greece, which did not themselves long survive as independent political units but from which the innovations subsequently spread widely.

Parsons's evolutionary theory has many weaknesses, but his emphasis on cultural innovations has the merit of drawing attention to a significant difference between biological and social evolution. Organisms do not *genetically* pass onto their offspring behaviour which they have learned during their lifetime to be useful in their particular environment. Biologically, the 'inheritance of acquired characteristics' is not possible. But, as Konrad Lorenz (1966: 205) notes, 'Conceptual thought and speech changed all man's evolution by achieving something which is equivalent to the inheritance of acquired characters.' Conceptual thought and speech do not grant men perfect knowledge and foresight; people still have to solve problems, and their actions often have unforeseen or latent consequences. What conceptual thought, speech and literacy do is to speed up the process of innovation and the transmission of acquired knowledge.

It should now be clear that functionalism does not provide a way of studying social 'wholes' independent of the actions of the people who constitute them. To resurrect the conclusions of previous chapters, we can again say that it is the interweaving actions of people entangled in complex webs of interdependence which unintentionally creates social processes relatively autonomous from individuals' plans and purposes. In the past, the use of the concept of social system has actually impeded understanding of such processes by encouraging sociologists to think of 'individual' and 'social system' as static, unchanging entities, and thereby creating a false difficulty in accounting for the origins of change and development. This is demonstrated very vividly in the Marxist functionalism of Louis Althusser, which has enjoyed a certain vogue among sociologists.

Marxist Functionalism, or Symptomatically Reading Althusser

We have already noted in passing that the correlation between the material 'basis' and the social, political, legal and ideological 'superstructure' of societies, which plays so prominent a part in the Marxist theoretical tradition, embodies the essential systemic idea of interdependence between aspects of social organization. Harris (1968: 4) states the gist of the principle of materialism most succinctly:

> This principle holds that similar technologies applied to similar environments tend to produce similar arrangements of labour in production and distribution, and that these in turn call forth similar kinds of social groupings, which justify and co-ordinate their activities by means of similar systems of values and beliefs.

That statement has the merit of brevity, but most Marxists and non-marxists alike would now agree that it oversimplifies the relationship between technology, economic organization, social arrangements and social beliefs. It implies that the causal arrows point all one way, from technology upwards through several storeys of the social edifice to modes of social consciousness. In that, it is reminiscent of the rather mechanistic versions of Marx's thought which emerged in the period of the Second International and were dominant in the era of Stalin. This 'vulgar Marxism' was never the whole of Marxist theory; the diverse strands of what Anderson (1976) calls 'Western Marxism' are altogether more lively. Even vulgar Marxism contains a most important insight though, pointing social scientists towards covariation of economic, political, legal and ideological facets of social organization. But the hypothesis that if one thing changes, other changes are likely to follow is not very close to the functionalist idea of self-regulating, goal-seeking systems. Marxist thought traditionally stressed the inevitability of change generated by forces inherent within societies, rather than the capacity of societies to maintain their existing patterns of organization indefinitely. Nevertheless, in recent decades sociologists in the officially Marxist states of eastern Europe have shown distinct signs of a predilection for functionalism. For instance, the Polish sociologist Sztompka (1974) has made an explicit attempt to integrate Marxist theory and functionalism. The explanation for this tendency may be simply that Marxist governments, like other regimes, have a necessary interest in social stability (see Friedrichs 1970: 259–87; Gouldner 1971: 447–77).

The most complete parallel within the Marxist tradition to a full-blown functionalism of the pre-evolutionary Parsonian kind is, however, to be found in the work of Louis Althusser.[12] The two most extensive statements of his views are in the books *Reading Capital* (Althusser and Balibar 1970) and *For Marx* (Althusser 1969), but one of his best-known essays, 'Ideology and Ideological State Apparatuses' (1971) contains a revealingly simple exposition of some of his main ideas. Insofar as Althusser's philosophy is about anything more than the interrelationships of concepts, it is about the means by which social formations *reproduce* themselves. Althusser derives the imperative for the reproduction of social formations from Marx's economic theory (1971: 123–8), but it plays a part in his work analogous to system problems, exigencies or prerequisites in functionalism. The term social formation is used in a sense very close to that of social system, to designate social 'wholes'. Althusser retains the metaphor of society as a two- or three-storey building with economics on the ground floor, politics and law on the mezzanine, and ideology and culture on top, but in common with other Western Marxist theorists he no longer depicts the causal arrows all pointing the same way. Althusser's architecture is of the advanced modern kind where some of the lower parts of the building are suspended from the cantilevered roof. The mode

of production may still 'in the last instance' determine social organization and social consciousness, but Althusser's emphasis is on the 'over-
determination' of the social formation through the complex mutual
reinforcement of mode of production, political structure and ideology.
(There is a parallel here to Parsons's 'cybernetic hierarchy' though
with opposite bias: Althusser expects changes emanating from the in-
frastructure to have greater 'efficacy' than those originating in the
cultural superstructure.) Ideology, in particular, serves to stabilize
the social edifice. As Anderson (1976: 84) explains:

> Ideology, for Althusser, was a set of mythical or illusory representations
> of reality, expressing the imaginary relationship of men to their real condi-
> tions of existence, and inherent in their immediate experience: as such,
> it was an unconscious system of determinations, rather than a form of con-
> sciousness as ordinarily conceived. The permanence of ideology as a lived
> medium of delusion was, in turn, a necessary consequence of its social func-
> tion, which was to *bind* men together into society, by adapting them to
> the objective positions allocated to them by the dominant mode of produc-
> tion. Ideology was thus the indispensable cement of social cohesion, in every
> period of history. For Althusser, the reason why it was inescapable as an
> ensemble of false beliefs and representations was that all social structures
> were by definition opaque to the individuals occupying posts within them.

Though Althusser plainly dislikes the capitalist society which is thus
conserved, while Parsons rather approved of it, it can be seen that
the function they assign to ideology and to values in their respective
theories is logically rather similar. Althusser's well-justified belief that
all social structures are inevitably opaque also points the same way
as the distinction between manifest and latent functions.

Ideology, according to Althusser, plays its part in the reproduction
of the conditions of production, including the reproduction of an
amenable labour-force, through 'ideological State apparatuses'
(ISAs), which he distinguishes from the 'repressive State apparatus'
(RSA). The RSA comprises the State apparatus as it is more traditionally conceived – the government, administration, army, police,
courts and prisons – and it 'functions massively and predominantly
by repression', ultimately by violence (1971: 138, 136). The ISAs,
on the other hand, 'function massively and predominantly by ideology', that is by the propagation and inculcation of beliefs favourable
to the reproduction of the mode of production. Among the many ISAs
to be found in mature capitalist societies, Althusser lists the religious
ISA, the educational ISA, the family ISA, the legal ISA, the political
ISA (including political parties), the trade union ISA, the communications ISA and the cultural ISA. It is striking that many of these
institutions coincide with those which Talcott Parsons tended to
identify with his functional exigency of pattern-maintenance. Many

of them, including churches, trade unions, families, most newspapers and cultural ventures, are not within the public domain as conventionally understood, but Althusser maintains that

> What matters is how they function. Private institutions can perfectly well 'function' as Ideological State Apparatuses. (1971: 138)

In other words, an ISA is to be identified by its *function* in maintaining the status quo – by its functions as opposed to dysfunctions in exactly Merton's sense.

Under feudalism, the dominant ISA was the Church; it 'accumulated a number of functions which have today devolved on to several distinct ideological State apparatuses' (1971: 143). The plurality of ISAs found under modern capitalism are the outcome of what Parsons would call functional differentiation. Some ISAs are more important than others. Althusser considers that 'the ideological State apparatus which has been installed in the *dominant* position in mature capitalist social formations ... is the *educational ideological apparatus*. (1971: 144–5, his italics.)

The high degree of durability with which he credits social formations leaves Althusser, like Parsons before him, facing a serious problem of how to explain change and development. Each of Marx's great historical modes of production – those of antiquity, feudalism and capitalism – apparently constitutes a 'structure-in-dominance' – a coherent system with an internal logic of its own and capacity for self-maintenance or reproduction. The immanent contradictions between the economic forces of production and the social relations of production, which for Marx provided the engine of history, for Althusser appear mysteriously to produce not continuous processes of development varying in pace, but a number of abrupt and discontinuous historical ruptures. Transformations from one self-maintaining mode of production to another apparently occur in cataclysmic structural 'breaks'. That does not conform with most historians' reading of the empirical evidence, but Althusser has no great respect for history or historians. What is quite clear is that Althusser, for once unlike Parsons, does not take the evolutionary road out of teleology.

Althusser in fact compounds his difficulty in explaining social change by taking an extremely deterministic view of the actions of individual human beings. He rightly criticized Jean-Paul Sartre, among others, for exaggerating the extent of the 'free will' people enjoy within society (Althusser 1976: 94–98), and for justifying it by wrenching out of context Marx's observation that 'men make their own history' (see p. 36 above). But Althusser then proceeds to use the rest of Marx's remark – 'but they do not make it just as they please ... under circumstances chosen by themselves ...' – to justify an equally absurd and extreme contrary view. He sees people as mere *Träger*, 'supports' or 'carriers' of the social formation, whose actions and motives are determined by their location within the formation. The notion of human *subjectivity* is dismissed as a consequence of human *subjection*.

> There are no subjects except by and for their subjection. That is why they 'work all by themselves'. (Althusser 1971: 169)

In other words, people's apparent ability to choose and pursue goals of their own is an ideological delusion made possible by their subjection to, and shaping by, social forces.

> The structure of the relations of production determines the *places* and *functions* occupied and adopted by the agents of production, who are never anything more than the occupants of these places, insofar as they are the 'supports' (*Träger*) of these functions. The true 'subjects' (in the sense of constitutive subjects of the process) are therefore not these occupants or functionaries, are not, despite all appearances, the 'obviousness' of the 'given' of naïve anthropology, 'concrete individuals', 'real men' – but *the definition and distribution of these places and functions. The true 'subjects' are these definers and distributors: the relations of production* (and political and ideological social relations). But since these are 'relations', they cannot be thought within the category subject. (Althusser and Balibar, 1970: 180)

Except that it is more extreme and somewhat less clear stylistically, this passage is reminiscent of Linton's view of roles as fixed slots to which people are 'allocated', and of Parsons's insistence that only roles, not whole 'concrete individuals', are relevant for understanding patterns of interaction (see pp. 39ff above).

As a philosopher, Althusser is intent upon purging Marxist thought of all Hegelian taint. He rejects 'historicism', not seeing history as teleological, but as a 'Process without a Subject or Goal(s)' (1976: 94–99). At first glance, that might suggest that he has reached the same insight as we discussed in Chapter 2 (see pp. 51–56 above), that social processes may unfold through a dynamic of their own relatively autonomous from the goals of the individual people whose interweaving actions generate that dynamic. But that is not what Althusser is saying: his view of men as *Träger* is simply a denial of the ability of individuals to choose and pursue goals of their own within any kind of social figuration. As a philosopher, Althusser tries to resolve conceptually what are questions for empirical investigation: the *degree* to which particular social figurations constrain individual people, and the *degree* to which individuals' actions can have effects upon the particular figurations in which they are caught up. Althusser's writings lack all the subtlety of the conception of the relationship between acting, thinking individuals and structured processes of change which we tried to illustrate through the series of game models, or of Elias's account of the relationship between social control and self-control in the civilizing process (see pp. 57–60 above). As Thompson (1978: 290) comments:

> Althusser's structuralism is, like all structuralisms, a system of *closure*. It fails to effect the distinction between [on the one hand] structured process, which, while subject to determinate pressures, remains open-ended and only partially determined, and [on the other hand] a structured whole, within which process is encapsulated. It opts for the latter, and goes on to construct something much more splendid than a clock. We may call it Althusser's orrery, a complex mechanism in which all the bodies revolve around the dominant sun.... So inexorable is this mechanism, in the relation of the parts to the whole within any mode of production, that it is only by means of the most acrobatic formulations that we can envisage the possibility of transition from one mode of production to another.

Conclusions

Functionalism in all its forms, from Radcliffe-Brown and Malinowski via Parsons and Merton to Althusser, contains a useful but very general injunction for sociologists: look for the ways in which institutions are related to each other within societies. Look, in other words, for the connections between economic organization, kinship systems, political arrangements, religious and ideological beliefs, and so on. But when it comes to *explaining* the ways in which social patterns persist and change, the interdependence of institutions is an idea at an over-abstract level. The facets of social organization which we refer to as institutions are already abstractions, disentangled by sociologists, anthropologists, historians or by the people involved in them, from the flux of social life. When these abstractions are then brought together within the further conceptual abstraction of a 'social system' or a 'social formation', the whole social process is too easily reified as something closed and static, standing outside and separate from people. It is not just the words system or formation which produce this effect. New words like 'figuration' with more dynamic connotations can be introduced. But new words too would rapidly become polluted unless a whole mode of thought is abandoned, a mode of thought which reduces open, partially determined, social processes to closed, self-maintaining, unchanging systems. 'In the last analysis,' comments Thompson (1978: 276), 'the logic of process can only be described in terms of historical analysis; no analogy derived from any other area can have more than a limited illustrative, metaphoric value (and often, as with basis and superstructure, a static and damaging one); "history" may only be theorized in terms of its own properties.'

And not just history but social life in general. What matters in explaining processes of development and persistence is, *pace* Althusser, interdependence between *real people*. The development of patterns of interdependence can be studied on every scale from the smallest to the largest. One might, for instance, be interested to observe the development of patterns of co-operation and conflict among children in a single school class. At the other extreme, 'dependency theorists' like André Gunder Frank (1967, 1971) and Immanuel Wallerstein (1974) work at the global level in analysing the growth of interdependence between the industrial nations and non-industrial countries of the Third World. The account of world capitalist development given by Frank and Wallerstein, deeply rooted as it is in historical evidence, offers a notable contrast with the theories of their fellow Marxist, Althusser. Their work illustrates a number of aspects of the explanation of developmental processes in the wider sense. The thrust of their 'dependency theory' is that the so-called 'underdevelopment' found in the present-day Third World is not to be understood, as functionalist writers (see for example Hoselitz and Moore, 1963) represented it, in terms of properties or deficiencies internal to the non-industrialized countries themselves.[13] Rather, their 'underdevelopment' is a consequence of their connection with the capitalist world.

> Economic development and underdevelopment are not just relative and quantitative, in that one represents more economic development than the other; economic development and underdevelopment are relational and qualitative, in that each is structurally different from, yet caused by, its relation with the other. (Frank 1967: 9)

A similar and striking point is made by Wallerstein (1974: 94–99), who asks why industrialization happened so much earlier in Western Europe than in countries like Poland where circumstances were initially not much less favourable. His answer is that though the process may have originated in Western Europe by little more than chance, that chance or conjuncture created interdependencies which effectively 'peripheralized' Eastern Europe.

> Either eastern Europe would become the 'breadbasket' of western Europe or vice versa. Either solution would have served the 'needs of the situation' in the conjuncture. The *slight* edge [enjoyed by western Europe in the Middle Ages] determined which of the two alternatives would prevail. At which point, the *slight* edge of the fifteenth century became the great disparity of the seventeenth and the monumental difference of the nineteenth. (1974: 99)

This, then, is an example of a relatively open, partially undetermined process (though the degree of determination increased as the disparity widened). It is a conception quite different from the functionalist models of goal-seeking systems with functional prerequisites and so forth. Most of the baggage of functionalism can be discarded, though a few functionalist ideas, suitably adapted, remain useful. There is no theoretical problem in explaining processes of social development on whatever scale if we see them as happening through the interweaving actions of real people. But that involves hard empirical research, one essential element of which is to trace the foreseen and unforeseen, intended and unintended consequences of people's actions through the long and entangled chains of interdependence of which complex social figurations are composed. That reminds us of Merton's distinction between manifest and latent functions and dysfunctions. The idea of functional autonomy or reciprocity is also a reminder of something important: not all social processes are equally open or relatively undetermined to the same degree. Changes emanating in some parts of a figuration will certainly have wider consequences than others; some figurations will have greater potential for transformation than others, and this potential may change over time.[14]

4 Power, Social Order and Social Interests

In their attempts to generalize about why social patterns persist or change, sociologists have in the past been strongly influenced by the great political philosophers, among them Hobbes, Locke, Rousseau, Hegel and Bentham. From them have been derived some extremely general ideas, about which sociologists have proceeded to disagree vehemently. Some, 'consensus theorists', argued that social order rested on general agreement or 'common values' among the members of society. Others, 'conflict theorists', countered that it was the result of some people having the power to coerce others into obedience, and that change stemmed from conflicts within society. A third tradition, 'exchange theory' rooted in utilitarianism, saw social cohesion as the outcome of people striking bargains with each other which were to everyone's advantage as well as the collective advantage.

Each of the old philosophical views has a grain of empirical insight in it, for each comes near to describing what is observed in some societies, or parts of societies, of different types, at different periods of history, in particular circumstances. But each, as a universally valid 'theory' of social persistence or change, is laughable. The actual state of relative stability and change in a particular social figuration is the outcome of complex forces of dependence and interdependence, of co-operation and conflict, of strength and weakness, of alliances and cleavages between people and groups. All the old philosophically-derived views are agreed that central to any understanding of these forces is that aspect of the structure of societies called the division of labour.

Specialization, or the Division of Labour

In *The Wealth of Nations*, the most celebrated of all discussions of the division of labour, Adam Smith described the advantages of specialization in human activities. Consider the pin-makers' shop, said Smith

(1970: 109–10; orig. 1776). About eighteen separate operations were involved in making each pin. A single worker carrying out each and every operation – drawing and cutting the wire, sharpening the point, forming and attaching the head, and so forth – could make no more than twenty pins in a day. Yet ten men working together in one of the primitive 'manufactories' of Smith's day, each specializing in one or two operations, could between them produce perhaps forty-eight thousand pins a day. Together, they could produce at least two hundred and forty times as many pins as if they each worked separately. Little wonder that Smith considered the division of labour a chief cause of 'the wealth of nations', and that it has been carried forward without apparent limit in industrial societies. Nor is the division of labour of only economic significance. The less elegant terms 'role differentiation' and 'structural differentiation' signify sociology's recognition that increasing specialization of activities is not confined only to the sphere of production.

For the economist, the chief interest of the division of labour is the vast multiplication of output of goods and services it makes possible. Even if the increased output is distributed very unequally, it is quite likely that in factual economic terms – discounting any speculation about whether the general 'quality of life' is better or worse – everyone will be better off. Nor should the sociologist lose sight of the great incentives there are to specialization. Herbert Spencer (1893), with Victorian confidence in progress, followed the economists in explaining the increasing differentiation of industrial society by the incentive to specialize offered to individuals through the increasing standard of living it made possible. Durkheim was too ready, in his discussion of the division of labour (1933), to dismiss Spencer's thesis; he argued that the prospect of individual gain could not be the moving force of the advancing division of labour, since it was only in societies of certain types that people would be able to conceive of the benefits of pursuing individual advantage. This is another illustration of Durkheim's rigid 'two-sector model' of 'individual' and 'society', which made it difficult for him to explain social innovation and the advance of the division of labour. It is certainly true that societies are known, like the Bushmen of the Kalahari existing on the margins of survival, where individual innovation is dangerous and inconceivable. Innovation may mean not evolutionary advance but extinction. But more generally it is reasonable to suppose that human beings are capable of making innovations and learning from experience whether or not such innovations have advantageous consequences. Of course, Durkheim was right that 'social structure' will determine the acceptability of an innovation and what its consequences will be, and advances in the division of labour usually prove to the benefit of some people and to the detriment of others. The famous innovations of the early industrial age, such as flying shuttles, spinning frames and power looms, were to the economic advantage of some – perhaps all in the long-term. In the short-term, though, their adoption resulted in some people suffering (hand-loom weavers thrown out of work, for instance), and provoked a good deal of social conflict.

For the problem of social order, however, increasing specialization as such is of less significance than its inevitable corollary, the growing web of interdependence which it spins through society. A person's position in the division of labour both makes others dependent on him, and simultaneously makes him dependent on others; it is a source both of power and of constraint. The degree of power and dependence varies widely. On the one hand, everyone who performs some specialized task on which others depend has some resources for power. The resources are obvious in the case of the owner of a factory producing some general necessity, especially if he has a degree of monopoly power in the product market and monopoly power in the labour market. They are least obvious in the case of the unskilled labourer, whose labour power is a drop in the ocean, whose place may readily be taken by someone else, and who is not even organized into a union with some degree of monopoly power.

On the other hand, in an industrial society, the overwhelming majority of the population directly produce for themselves no more than an infinitely small fraction of their individual needs. Even the most powerful are dependent on countless others. Concomitant with an advancing division of labour, then, is a great lengthening of chains of interdependence. Now what constitutes 'social order' in complex networks of interdependence? Essentially it is *calculability*. People have to rely for many of their needs on people who are anonymous to them; their trust cannot be based on personal knowledge of everyone involved. If the network does not prove reliable, people may cease to contribute to it and become more self-reliant, and certainly fall into contention with each other. Chains of interdependence may break and the division of labour regress, as they did in Europe during the decline of the Roman Empire. A rapidly advancing division of labour may be equally disruptive. Rapid structural differentiation often outstrips the process of social integration, and brisk social change is often accompanied by marked social conflict. This brings into focus the twofold significance of the division of labour for social order. Advanced specialization raises the question of how the activities of countless individuals are to be co-ordinated sufficiently to maintain the web of interdependence. The corollary is that the interdependence which specialization entails is a powerful source of constraint on individuals' activities. We shall examine first the problem of collective action, then that of constraint.

Collective Action

Why collective action is theoretically problematic can be seen if we consider a group in which each member is a free agent and has his own scale of preferences for collective objectives. Suppose every member's participation is essential to the attainment of any objective. Now it is easy to see that if a particular objective is desired by no-one, no action will be taken to achieve it; and if it is equally desired by everyone, collective action will not be very problematic. But consider the much more probable situation in which some want one thing, others another. Suppose members face three possible alternative objectives of collective action, A, B and C, and are asked to rank them in order of preference. Person *x* ranks them A, B, C; person *y* ranks them B, C, A. It can then be seen that with only two people involved, it is already impossible to construct a *collective* ordinal scale of preference (A, C, B, or C, B, A, etc.) which satisfactorily aggregates and reflects the two individual scales. Next let us introduce a third person, *z*, with preferences C, A, B (Table 2). It may then appear that the deadlock can be broken by a simple voting rule. But still more paradoxical effects then appear. Suppose the alternatives are offered in pairs. The first choice is between A and B; A wins with two votes. Then the choice lies between A and C; C wins with two votes. The paradox is that had the initial choice lain between B and C, B would have been chosen; then B would have been chosen in preference to A. It seems unreasonable that collective decisions should hinge on the order in which alternatives are offered – though anyone with experience of the deliberation of committees will know that the sequence and timing of proposals is precisely what often determines the outcome.

Table 2 (from Coleman, 1966)

Rank	Actor *x*	Actor *y*	Actor *z*
1	A	B	C
2	B	C	A
3	C	A	B

This is only to touch on an old problem in welfare economics and a growing body of work in mathematical sociology.[1] Even this simple heuristic model, however, makes it possible to characterize (or perhaps slightly to caricature) the ways in which the traditional 'theories' of social order tried to solve the problem of collective action. The so-called 'consensus' view denies, in effect, that people's preferences are independent of each other; socialization tends to produce similar scales of preference. Or socialization inculcates an acceptance either that some people's views *should* take precedence over others', or of a voting or decision rule which in spite of imperfections is accepted as binding. The 'exchange' perspective takes a broader view; there are numerous collective decisions and actions, and no-one can expect to be satisfied every time. But people are prepared to participate in one action to which they are relatively indifferent or even anti-pathetic, in order that when it comes to matters about which they care more, others will assist them in turn. The activities of Con-gressmen in log-rolling – exchanging support for each other's measures in order that each can build up an alliance to push through his own pet legislation – are a good example. The exchange view is in effect a sub-species of the consensus view, for it implies some degree of agreement underlying the exchange process. It is striking that not even in the consensus and exchange traditions is much account taken of the possibility of resolving deadlock through rational discussion. Habermas (1974: 271) observes:

> Revealingly enough, according to [this kind of decision-model], agreement on a collective value system can never be achieved by means of enlightened discussion carried on in public politics, thus by way of consensus rationally arrived at, but only by summation or compromise – values are in principle beyond discussion.

That assumption is even plainer in the so-called 'conflict' view, which is that conflicts over collective objectives are endemic and continuous, and that collective action takes place chiefly because some people have the *power* to impose their preferences on others.

Power and Constraint

Though they use the term often enough, sociologists do not find it easy to define exactly what they mean by power and to agree upon it. Max Weber's definition must be the most frequently quoted. 'Power,' wrote Weber (1968: i, 53), 'is the probability that one actor within a social relationship will be in a position to carry out his will despite resistance, regardless of the basis on which this probability rests.' This definition has certain merits. It locates power firmly within social relationships, or more exactly within relationships of social interdependence. Power cannot be measured as an absolute quantity; it is always relational. Using the word according to Weber's defini-tion, it is meaningless to say that a person or group 'has power' without specifying in relation to which other people or groups they have it, and what it enables them to do.[2] Weber also saw that power must be discussed in terms of probabilities, not certainties. In a whole series of matches, it is highly likely that a First Division football team would establish itself as more 'powerful' than a Fourth Division opponent; but in a single decisive encounter in a knockout competition, it occasionally happens that the 'weaker' side wins. Furthermore, since social relationships are never static, neither are the balances of power which they always involve. Power should be seen as a process, always shifting, changing and developing. All this was implied in the game models discussed in Chapter 2.

On the other hand, though Weber certainly does not treat power as if it were a quality or possession of an individual, his definition does perhaps make it too personal and intentional, too much a matter of people pursuing conscious strategies against other people.[3] Certainly that is an important aspect of the process of power. But the concept of power also shades gradually into the more impersonal one of constraint, the limits on people's freedom of action which derive simply from their mutual interdependence within a social figuration. Of course, 'social forces' are always in the final analysis forces exerted by people over each other. But conceptually it ought to be possible to distinguish between, on the one hand, the constraint which would stem merely from people's mutual interdependence even if they were all *equally* interdependent within the social division of labour (an admittedly almost inconceivable state), and, on the other hand, the constraint which stems from *unequal* interdependence, from some people and groups having greater power resources than others. In practice, it is extremely difficult to make this distinction empirically. All the same, the idea of impersonal constraint is an important one which sociologists have often associated with the concepts of alienation and anomie, derived from Marx and Durkheim respectively.

Alienation and Anomie

The Marxist and Durkheimian traditions of thought are associated with very different views of the constraint which the division of labour imposes on individuals. The two traditions are agreed that social relations and institutions constrain and shape the individual's activities, and that the division of labour is especially significant in this context. But they evaluate the fact very differently and draw opposite conclusions. Sociologists have used the concepts both of alienation and anomie extensively in research. In trying to use them in a reasonably value-free way, however, they have noticeably transformed both in a similar direction, so that in some usages, the two words are almost synonyms.

Both 'alienation' and 'anomie' have come to be used rather loosely.[4]

This is especially true of alienation, which some writers have used quite indiscriminately. Schacht (1971:139) remarks that Erich Fromm

> seems to refer to almost everything of which he disapproves as an instance of 'alienation'. He disapproves of a great deal; so it is not surprising that he finds alienation to be 'all-pervasive'.

In Marx and Durkheim, alienation and anomie both refer primarily to characteristics of social structure, not to subjective feelings of the people enmeshed in it. Anomie essentially means the absence of norms or *common* standards of behaviour and aspiration, and in this sense is a quality observable only in the group, not in the individual. Durkheim first used the term to describe a situation in which the division of labour is ill-co-ordinated, and where people's roles and responsibilities are poorly defined. A situation of general disorganization and conflict results (1933: 353–73). Later he used it to describe one of the situations to which suicide was a potential response. For Marx similarly, alienation was an objective property of certain patterns of social organization. Labour in a broad sense ought to be a basic form of self-expression and self-fulfilment. But the progressive division of labour in capitalist society prevented this. It fragmented skills, and more and more of a worker's time and energy was absorbed in narrower and narrower activities. What obscure phrases like 'the worker is alienated from the product of his labour' really boil down to is that labour is not performed for its own sake as an end in itself, but only as a means of subsistence. This is so because within the division of labour opportunities for alternative action are structured and restricted. The mere fact of employment is not essential for alienation; a self-employed farmer forced by economic circumstances to toil long hours and unable to do the things he would really like to do, would be as alienated as a factory worker.

> A man's labour is truly 'his own labour' for Marx only when it is 'spontaneous', 'free and self-directed activity'. It is his own only when it reflects his own personality and is prompted by his own need to build or create or do something of his own choosing. It must, in short, be precisely what he wants to do. (Schacht 1971: 90–91)

That is why Marx made his famous remark that in communist society it would be 'possible for me to do one thing today and another tomorrow, to hunt in the morning, fish in the afternoon, rear cattle in the evening, criticize after dinner, *just as I have a mind*, without ever becoming hunter, fisherman, shepherd or critic'. (1947: 22, my italics.)[5]

Though alienation and anomie are to be seen as objective properties of social structure, both clearly also have social psychological implications (Lukes, 1967). And these implications reveal antithetical views of social constraint. Although no-one was more conscious than Marx of the power of social institutions to shape men, his discussion of alienation implies that he had some conception of human needs and potential existing independently of social influences. Capitalist society interferes with the free development of this potential. But why should men raised in capitalist society not *choose* to do the kind of jobs which exist in it, and find them satisfying? Surely all societies shape their members' behaviour and personalities, and even if there is an infinite variety of social patternings, all of them impose constraint? Durkheim's discussion of anomie represents a continuation of precisely this line of thought. The implication here is that the individual becomes psychologically disorientated and disrupted in the absence of firm social guidance. The anomic suicide illustrates this most clearly; one of Durkheim's most inspired suggestions was that sudden good fortune (for example windfall wealth) is as effective as bad fortune in shattering accustomed standards of behaviour and aspiration, and it could equally drive some people to suicide. So although, as Horton (1964) argues, alienation and anomie express Marx's and Durkheim's common condemnation of rampant economic individualism, they also express opposing views of human needs. To put it a little too simplistically, Marx concluded that less, and Durkheim that more, social control and constraint were desirable for human well-being.[6]

In trying to make practical use of the concepts of alienation and anomie in their research, sociologists have tended to make them more exclusively psychological, and to play down the structural implications. To distinguish the psychological from the structural or 'sociological' sense of anomie, McClosky and Schaar (1965) speak of 'anomy', and Srole (1956) chose the term 'anomia'. These are subjective feelings to be measured by responses to attitude-scale items. Similarly, Nettler (1957) and Blauner (1964) assess the extent of 'alienation' by individuals' attitudes. In consequence the two ideas have increasingly converged. Inspecting the attitude-scale items used by Srole to measure 'anomia' and by Nettler to measure 'alienation', the difference between what they purport to measure is not immediately striking. Thus the psychological interpretation makes it possible to amalgamate anomie and alienation and merely distinguish several varieties of some generalized psychological *Angst*. The best-known attempt to do so is that of Seeman (1959). Seeman identifies five distinct dimensions of 'alienation' – powerlessness, meaninglessness, normlessness, isolation and self-estrangement. Normlessness is superficially closest to Durkheimian anomie, but in fact all five of Seeman's dimensions refer to the subjective feelings of the individual, not to any external conditions of his social existence. Yet powerlessness for one certainly should not be conceived of as only a subjective state. Nor for that matter should powerfulness. And the mention of power-lessness and powerfulness brings us back to the problem of the nature and unequal distribution of power in society.

The Deployment and Distribution of Power Resources

When is it appropriate to speak of 'power' and when not? Even if we accept Weber's definition, there remain certain difficulties in circumscribing the boundaries of the concept. Suppose one person suggests to another that it would be a good thing if the latter did so-and-so. Suppose further that the suggestion is well received, that it is willingly, even eagerly carried out, not to please the person who suggested it, but because it was a good idea in itself. We should be reluctant to describe this case of willing compliance as an exercise of power. But what if it required some persuasion and rational discussion to convince the second person that the course of action were desirable? He might at first resist, but change his own evaluation of its desirability. Should we describe this as an instance of the exercise of power, as the phrase 'the power of persuasion' might suggest, or should we call it something else, such as 'influence'? At the other extreme, to meet Weber's requirement of resistance, some sociologists have been inclined to define the exercise of power as involving the use or threat of negative sanctions – 'You may not want to do this, but I can make things unpleasant for you if you don't.' To add to the confusion, some sociologists would not count an unsuccessful attempt to exercise power as an example of power itself. Thus Bierstedt (1950: 733) writes that 'power is always successful; when it is not successful it is not, or ceases to be, power'.

To avoid these problems of demarcation, power is best viewed broadly as the process by which some actors in social relationships are able to carry out their will by changing the balance of advantage of alternative courses of action for others in the relationship. To exercise power it is necessary to have some control over whatever it is that others desire, to be able to withhold what they need. Yet control is always a matter of degree; it consists merely of the ability to alter the balance of costs and benefits of two or more courses of action *as they are perceived by the other person*. Even physical coercion merely alters the probabilities of various outcomes (from the observer's point of view) or their relative costs and benefits (from the point of view of the person subjected to coercion). So there is little point in defining power entirely in terms of the deployment of negative sanctions. That would mean that while blackmail was seen as an exercise of power, bribery was not – for bribery involves positive sanctions. Positive sanctions suffice as well as negative ones in altering the balance of advantage between courses of action. Nor does it make much sense to exclude unsuccessful attempts at exercising power. Bierstedt would unnecessarily restrict our attention only to certain outcomes of a wider social process – the deployment of inducements and deterrents to bend others to our will, successfully or unsuccessfully.[7]

What resources can be used in the exercise of power? Weber's definition is explicitly and deliberately unspecific. *Any* resources can be used which alter the balance of advantage of another person's action in the direction desired by whoever deploys the resources. The resources which may be deployed in this way are of infinite kinds – whatever constitute inducements and deterrents *to those subject to them*. Among resources discussed by sociologists are income, property, sacramental and magical capacities, scarce skills and charisma. Listing possible power resources would be a purely taxonomic exercise, were it not that sociologists have asked two related types of probing question about them. First, they have asked what kinds of society engender what kinds of interests, goals and wants among members, realizing that this is of crucial importance in determining what kind of resources will enable their controller to exercise most power in each kind of society. The relationship between wants and power is seen particularly clearly in Riesman's *The Lonely Crowd*. Tracing the evolution of American 'social character' from 'inner-directed' to 'other-directed' in an age of high mass consumption, Riesman seeks to show that changes in what Americans value had consequences for the types of power resource to which they respond, and therefore for the distribution of power in American society (1950: part II). With greater historical sweep, Weber shows the intimate connection between the prevailing values and interests of a society and the forms of domination found in it. One of the themes of his sociology of religion, for instance, is the link between the structure of society, its beliefs, its members' conception of their interests, and its type of leadership.

Second, some writers have not contented themselves with a taxonomy of power-resources but have sought to show that some resources are 'more basic' than others, which are in some way reducible to the basic forms. Marxists have always paid particular attention to the control of economic resources, of the means of subsistence and the means of production. The ownership of capital, the means of large-scale industrial production, concentrated in the hands of a comparatively few entrepreneurs, gave them overwhelming power over workers, any of whom alone had control only over his labour power, an insignificant fraction of total labour resources. It is still a matter of controversy whether the growth of organized labour and the proliferation of scarce skills among workers has significantly shifted the balance of economic power. Many Marxists would be inclined to argue that these factors are somehow superficial and that ownership of capital still remains the decisive power resource in capitalist economies.

Authority and social organization are best seen as two more kinds of power resource, though this is perhaps not a conventional view. They occupy a special position because they cross-cut other power resources – they can reinforce the exercise of power, no matter what its other bases. So far, the exercise of power has been depicted as the deployment of resources as inducements and deterrents, and compliance with power as a calculation of costs and benefits. Not that calculation need be rational in any sense of the term. Nor need it even be conscious; as economists point out, it is not necessary that people think in terms of marginal utility for the theory to predict the outcome of their actions. This view of power can take us quite a long way. Legitimacy, however, is a new element in the situation. Resources can yield domination to which people comply for their own advantage, without considering it legitimate (Weber 1968: 1, 212–13). Domination which the dominated regard as legitimate, as morally justified in terms of their values, is usually called *authority*. Legitimacy can be thought of as an element in the minds of those who comply, which alters their evaluation of the costs and benefits of compliance or non-compliance. People are very likely to comply with the orders of a man with a gun; they are perhaps still more likely to do so if they think he has a legitimate reason for having the gun and for giving orders. But legitimacy and means of coercion are functional alternatives which can be traded off against each other; the more the police have *authority*, the more their powers are regarded as legitimate in a given community, the less frequently are they likely (*ceteris paribus*) to have to brandish guns there. The dominator may also, of course, consider his power legitimate, though this does not enhance his power one jot. What does enhance his power is his success in promoting his legitimacy in the eyes of those over whom he would exercise power.

Weber distinguished three pure types of authority by the grounds upon which they claimed legitimacy (1968: 1, 215). They were rational-legal authority, traditional authority and charismatic authority. Rational-legal authority rested upon 'a belief in the legality of enacted rules and the right of those elevated to authority under such rules to issue commands'. Traditional authority rested on 'an established belief in the sanctity of immemorial traditions and the legitimacy of those exercising authority under them'. Finally, charismatic authority rested on 'devotion to the exceptional sanctity, heroism or exemplary character of an individual person, and of the normative patterns or order revealed or ordained by him'. It will be seen that these three types of authority are related to Weber's four ideal-types of action (see pp. 30–32 above); in fact the distinction between traditional and rational authority runs into the same difficulties at the margin as did that between traditional and rational action. The boundaries of charismatic authority, which is related to affectual action, are also susceptible to blurring, so that it becomes a dustbin for whatever refuses to fit into the other categories. Nevertheless, it cannot be denied that when Weber explores how these three kinds of claims to legitimacy are embodied in typical institutions, the result is highly illuminating. Out of the notion of authority flow some of Weber's most celebrated discussions. Bureaucracy is the exemplar of rational authority. Patriarchalism, patrimonialism and feudalism are among its traditional precursors. Charismatic authority has repeatedly created social movements through history; it is a revolutionary force in state and church, but inevitably becomes transformed and 'routinized' into one of the other forms of administration with the departure of the charismatic leader. Discussion of all this occupies the whole of the third volume of *Economy and Society*.

Yet it is less important to categorize the forms of legitimacy than to appreciate the effect of any form – which is to amplify, even to multiply, the potential of other power resources, whether guns, money, property or magical gifts. Certain resources for power exist only in a legitimate form. For example, high social status may in some circumstances be a power resource. Status situation, however, 'is determined by a specific, positive or negative, social estimation of honour' (Weber, 1968: ii, 932), and clearly 'positive estimation of honour' implies legitimacy by definition. Similarly, a religious leader can only bring supernatural sanctions (like the threat of damnation) to bear on a believer, for they do not constitute sanctions to the atheist. On the other hand, these necessarily legitimate forms of domination need not be considered legitimate by the *entire* community in order to be felt by the entire community. The priest may not be able to cow the atheist by threat of damnation, but if many do accept his authority, he may be able to incite them to ostracize or even to lynch the atheist.

Which brings us to social organization. For a leader or ruler to dominate a large number of people permanently, he normally needs a special inner group, a trusted and disciplined staff, to carry out his orders (Weber, 1968: i, 212). Such henchmen may adhere to the leader purely out of self-interest; but if so, domination is likely to be unstable and periodically prone to Byzantine intrigues and squabbles. Greater stability will result if the staff at least accept the leader's dominance as legitimate, whether on rational, traditional or charismatic grounds. Whether or not they themselves are based on legitimate authority, such administrative groups constitute a power resource conceptually distinct from the legitimacy of domination in the eyes of *all* those subject to it. But they act upon other power resources in the same way as legitimacy, enlarging the span over which power may be exercised. Organization formalizes chains of command and improves co-ordination, stabilizing power resources as plant roots fix sand dunes, and increasing the predictability and probability of success in the exercise of power.

Group Interests, Group Consciousness and the Structure of Conflict

There is, however, something unreal about discussing resources and bases for power in this formal and timeless way. The distribution of power resources is a process, something which *happens* in the course of social development. The study of power is necessarily closely related to the study of social stratification, and that too is a process. In all societies, save perhaps the smallest and most egalitarian hunting bands, categories of people can be distinguished which have greater or lesser control of resources of various kinds. They may or may not, and to a greater or lesser extent, be aware of sharing common interests vis-à-vis other categories of people. Through the conflict of interests, through trials of strength, control over resources and balances of power between social groups shifts over time. To discuss stratification as if it were something static, like the ancient rocks to which geologists first applied the word, is to distort the social reality. E. P. Thompson makes the point with characteristic pointed humour:

> Sociologists, who have stopped the time machine and, with a good deal of conceptual huffing and puffing, have gone down into the engine room to look, tell us that nowhere at all have they been able to locate and classify a class. They can only find a multitude of people with different occupations, incomes, status-hierarchies, and the rest. Of course, they are right. Since class is not this or that part of the machine, but *the way the machine works* once it is set in motion – not this interest and that interest, but the *friction* of interests – the movement itself, the heat, the thundering noise. Class is a social and cultural formation (often finding institutional expression) which cannot be defined abstractly, or in isolation, but only in terms of relationship with other classes; and, ultimately, the definition can only be made in the medium of time – that is, action and reaction, change and conflict. When we speak of a class we are thinking of a very loosely defined body of people who share the same categories of interests, social experiences, traditions and value-system, who have a *disposition* to *behave* as a class, to define themselves in their actions and in their consciousness in relation to other groups of people in class ways. But class itself is not a thing, it is a happening. (1978:85)

It is beyond the scope of this book to survey the vast and intricate sociological literature on social stratification.[8] However, it is certainly necessary to say something about the area in which discussions of power, conflict and stratification merge, and in particular about the seminal writings of Marx and Weber.

Marx

To say anything about Marx is to step into a minefield of academic and ideological controversy, and to say anything briefly is especially difficult. With that warning let us nonetheless proceed. Marx is usually thought of as one of the greatest writers on social conflict. So he was, yet he was equally concerned with the conditions which promote consensus as those which lead to conflict. It is true that he saw little prospect of society-wide harmony, except in the communist society of the future, about which he said precious little. But he was much concerned with the circumstances in which men in similar social situations would recognize their common interests and unite in groups capable of collective action in pursuit of their interests. As a first approximation, Marx's essential insight was that a society's mode of production and division of labour generates a finite number of social groupings, the members of each of which share a similar social situation and therefore have interests in common. These groupings, however, are mere categories – Dahrendorf (1959) was later to call them 'quasi-groups' – and their members are by no means necessarily *conscious* of their common situation and interests. There may therefore be considerable conflict between segments of the same grouping. Marx asked how social categories could become conscious of a common identity and unite against other groups.

There are numerous difficulties with the Marxist model of 'base' and 'superstructure'. Radically different versions of it are advocated even among those theorists who would identify themselves as Marxists. In the mechanistic versions which arose in the late nineteenth and early twentieth centuries and have broadly been adopted by contemporary Marxist states, the technological forces of production and the social relations of the productive sphere together form an economic base which in the final analysis 'determines' a society's superstructure of politics, law, ideas and culture. Late in his life, Marx himself showed dissatisfaction with this mechanistic or 'economistic' (as Althusser terms it) oversimplification, in which all change flows in a single direction from technology to ideas. It raises all sorts of problems. Plainly, 'ideas' enter in a big way into technological innovation; are they to be interpreted simply as an inevitable response to technological 'needs'? If so, we return to all the questions raised in Chapter 3. In any case, 'ideas' are an integral aspect of economic relations, as of all social organization; is the distinction between base and super-structure an artificial one which serves only to mystify? Structuralist versions of the base-superstructure model go some way to meet these objections: technological innovation through learning sets up con-tradictions between the forces and the relations of production, and it is these contradictions which power the conflict of classes and interests which transform other social relations. A more radical amendment to the 'economistic' model is the view that specifically *economic* forces do not determine relations of production in all kinds of society. Productive relations, and therefore the distribution of power and wealth, may be seen as determined in primitive societies by kinship and in pre-modern societies by the political system (see Habermas, 1976a, Part I, Chapter 1).

But there is little doubt that Marx saw the economic system as the leading sector in capitalist society, to the genesis and dynamics of which he paid most attention. The structure of interests had changed during its growth. Marx did not have a romantic utopian image of the past; he saw that the proletarian and bourgeois classes had a com-mon interest in the overthrow of the remnants of feudalism, and wrote glowingly of the vigour with which the bourgeois entrepreneurs trans-formed the economy (Marx-Engels 1968: 36 ff). As industrialization proceeded, however, the interests of the two classes came to be at odds. The workers might fail to perceive this, and retain a false conception of their true interests, but economic forces gradually drew them into conflict with the bourgeoisie. In the early capitalist economy, many groups persisted whose class affiliation was ambiguous – the artisan whose special skills were in short supply, the self-employed craftsman, the small factory-owner who worked alongside his men. Marx, how-ever, predicted the increasing polarization of society into two camps. The petty bourgeois would disappear, prosperity making him a true bourgeois or lack of it a wage-slave; with him would disappear the ambiguities of interest and the cross-cutting ties between the classes. Why was this to happen? Marx's argument is essentially economic. The logic of machine production and economies of scale would dictate larger and larger productive units, driving out the self-employed craftsman and the small factory-owner (if he did not himself expand). Machines would also make many hitherto scarce skills redundant, and make men into unskilled machine minders. With labour increasingly homogeneous, its strength in the market would decrease. The reserve army of the unemployed, any member of which could do a job as well as the unskilled labourer then in employment, would bid down wage rates, leading to mass pauperization. Furthermore, Marx accepted the view of the competitive process advanced by Ricardo and the English classical economists. Competition between entrepreneurs would be so fierce that profit margins would leave little room for the indulgence of humanitarian delusions; an employer who paid more than the market wage would soon be driven into bankruptcy. (Twentieth-century economists have suggested that the growth of economic units and the emergence of oligopolistic markets makes such strict market discipline unlikely.)

Suffering itself would assist the emergence of class-consciousness, and make evident the advantages of solidarity, of collective action to multiply the industrial bargaining power of the workers, and eventually to overthrow the capitalist system. Militancy would be especially likely to emerge, for example in mining villages, where the workers share a common lot in a homogeneous community. In contrast, difficulties of communication would prevent the emergence of the peasantry, who are scattered across the countryside, as a self-conscious class (Marx–Engels 1968: 171–2). The extent to which external leadership is necessary to catalyse working-class consciousness has been in dispute among Marxists at least since Lenin and Rosa Luxemburg (see Coser 1972). Marx, however, firmly predicted increasing organization along class lines for collective action, at first in trade unions for industrial objectives, later broadening to concerted political action for the overthrow of capitalism.

Weber

In discussing the distribution of power in political communities, Weber (1968: II, 927–39) concentrated on the organization of three kinds of power resource – economic, honorific and politico-legal. Weber did *not* write about 'class, status and power', as if power were a separate dimension of stratification. And in spite of Runciman's efforts (1970: 102–40) to prove Weber's medieval preoccupation with the number three, I can see no evidence that Weber intended these three prominent kinds of power resource (economic, honorific and legal) to be exhaustive of all possibilities. Indeed, elsewhere, he spoke of military and religious power resources and corresponding social organizations, without any implication that these could be reduced to other more basic power resources. Nevertheless, he did give special attention to three kinds of social organization which emerged on the basis of these three kinds of power resource: he spoke of classes, status-groups (or estates: the German word is *Stände*), and parties.

Though he did not reject by any means all of Marx's analysis of class, Weber saw nothing inevitable in the emergence of class consciousness and collective class action. A category of people could be said to have a common class position in so far as the life chances of its members were determined by their similar position in the market. Nevertheless:

> The class situation and other circumstances remaining the same, the direction in which the individual worker, for instance, is likely to pursue his interests may vary widely.... In the same way, the direction of interests may vary according to whether or not social action of a larger or smaller portion of those commonly affected by a class situation, or even an association among them, e.g. a trade union, has grown out of the class situation, from which the individual may expect promising results for himself. The emergence of an association or even of mere social action from a common class situation is by no means a universal phenomenon. (1968: ii, 929)

The common situation may not be recognized at all. Or it may produce nothing more than similar *individual* reactions, taking the form of low morale, unorganized and perhaps semi-conscious go-slows, or at most sporadic individual acts of sabotage. Whether anything more substantial results – 'class actions' such as wildcat strikes, or the more permanent organizations of associations with class objectives – hinges on historical and cultural circumstances. Most important, the connection between the causes and consequences of the class situation must be 'transparent'. In Chapter 2 (pp. 54 ff. above), it was noted that as social networks increase in complexity, they become 'opaque' – the individual finds it more difficult to put together a mental picture of all the interconnections involved. No matter how great the disparities between the life chances of different groups, no great discontent or conflict need result as long as their causes and consequences remain unrecognizable and unexplained to the people involved.[9] Since Weber did not suppose there were only two class situations in society – the market would continue to differentiate the life chances of those with different kinds of property and various kinds of skills – he saw little reason why causes and consequences of life chances should necessarily become more transparent.

Moreover, Weber recognized that common economic situations were not the only bases for collective social action. Categories of people who shared a common status, religion, ethnic background or political outlook could also enter as units in social conflict. Of particular interest were people who shared a common 'status situation'.

> In contrast to the purely economically determined 'class situation', we wish to designate as *status situation* every typical component of the life of men that is determined by a specific, positive or negative social estimation of *honour*. (1968: ii, 932, his italics)

Sharing a common 'style of life', status-groups are normally conscious of their common status situation. Such groups as the Boston Brahmins would be examples of status-groups in modern society, but the caste system in which the original Brahmins figure illustrates the most extreme form of status-group stratification. Status distinctions are of course most often correlated with economic inequality, but 'the notion of honour peculiar to status absolutely abhors that which is essential to the market: hard bargaining' (1968: II, 937).

It is particularly dangerous to stop the time machine and treat Weber's discussion of classes, status-groups and parties as if he were concerned with three mutually exclusive principles of static ranking. What are in fact at issue are the dynamic connections between the social organization of power and the distribution and redistribution of power resources – historical processes in fact. Weber suggests, for example, that where there is little economic change, an established pattern of domination and distribution may congeal into a hierarchy of status-groups, which will tend to impede the development of free markets and further contain endogenous forces for change. On the other hand, where the economy is rapidly changing (and this can stem from the impact of change emanating outside the society in question), status will tend to be undermined by the market. These and other transformations of power structure can only be studied historically. Class organization expressing the economic interests of rising classes can normally be expected to give rise to class based political parties, political domination reinforcing the control of economic resources. Conversely, military or political power may provide stepping stones to control of economic resources, as today in many Third World countries or in the past (as Merton's discussion of political machines reminds us) in the U.S.A. The wealthy may or may not also acquire social honour with ease; the English aristocracy, for instance, was never so closed to *nouveaux riches* as the nobility of many other countries. Broadly speaking, it is to be expected that in relatively stable and static societies there will be a high degree of correlation between the distribution of ownership, wealth, social honour, political power and other forms of resource. Where there are marked discrepancies – where for example a class growing in economic power is excluded from political power – we should expect to observe tensions and conflicts. Violent historical episodes like the French Revolution, or less violent ones like the Great Reform Act of 1832 in Britain, can be interpreted as means by which such tensions were in part resolved.

Changes since Marx
On the whole, Weber's discussion of power and stratification produces fewer bold historical predictions than Marx's, and suggests reasons why patterns of social conflict have remained more complex and less neatly dichotomous than Marx anticipated. Weber had the advantage of writing several decades later, and of observing the beginnings

of several social trends which seem so far to have frustrated Marx's predictions. These include the following:

(1) First, there have been several developments in industrial economies which have tended to fragment and diversify the distribution of interests and, it is argued, to create more quasi-groups rather than fewer.

For one thing, though it is true that in some industries technology has reduced the worker to an unskilled machine minder, the broader trend of the division of labour has been to make labour more heterogeneous rather than homogeneous. This is the trend which Dahrendorf (1959: 48) refers to as 'the decomposition of labour'. More workers have skills which cannot quickly be learned, and so they cannot easily be replaced and are able to command high wages. Even relatively unskilled groups may occupy such strategic points in the division of labour that, if well organized, they have immense bargaining power. In short, there are many groups of employees who have an advantageous position in the labour market, and this differentiation does not facilitate class solidarity.

A related development has been the emergence of the so-called 'new middle class' – the salaried occupations ranging from high bureaucrats to lowly clerks. They now form a much larger proportion of the labour force than in Marx's day, and in some technologically most advanced industries actually outnumber the manual workers. Some of them earn less than some manual workers, others much more. To which class do they belong? If they earn their living entirely by selling their labour, they might be considered objectively 'working class'. But we know that this fails to coincide with the subjective identification of most of them. David Lockwood (1958) made the point that the 'work situation' of particular groups – the 'significant others' they encounter in their work – influences their group identification. We should not, for example, expect domestic servants to form a hotbed of militancy.

On the opposite side of the market has taken place a corresponding 'decomposition of capital' (Dahrendorf 1959: 41). This is the frequently discussed 'separation of ownership and control' which has occurred since Marx's day, made possible by the spread of the joint-stock, limited liability company. Economic units have become larger, yet their ownership has become more dispersed through shareholdings, while practical control has passed to salaried bureaucrats. There is a large literature in sociology and economics on the extent of this development and its implications for economic motivation and social relations (see Nichols, 1969). For his part, Dahrendorf argued that Marx's view of ownership and non-ownership of capital as the great divide in society was excessively legalistic. What is now important, said Dahrendorf, is not whether people legally own capital, but their relationship to authority and control. In any 'imperatively co-ordinated association' (1959: 167), there was a 'command class' and an 'obey class'. It is not very clear how, in a multi-tier chain of command, one decides the zero-point dividing those in authority from those in subordination. Within a complex division of labour, few people escape a considerable degree of constraint. In any case, Dahrendorf's view would give much weaker predictions about the lines of conflict in society as a whole than did Marx's. Since, in a pluralistic society, a man may belong to many groups, being in authority in one and taking orders in another, the 'theory' gives no guidance as to whether certain lines of conflict will become more salient than others, or how groups will coalesce in alliances for common objectives. If there are n 'imperatively co-ordinated associations' in a society, Dahrendorf said in effect, it may contain an indeterminate number of classes up to $2n$. Perhaps this is the only general assertion which a cautious man might make.[10]

(2) A second group of factors have impeded the crystallization of quasi-groups as self-conscious entities capable of collective action in conflict with others.

A sense of society-wide consensus, even if it be only a limited sense of common membership in one society, is said to impede the emergence of full class consciousness. T. H. Marshall (1950) traced the growth of what he called rights of citizenship in Britain from the seventeenth century. 'Civil' rights of citizenship – equality before the law – were followed by the gradual extension of political rights to all adults, and more recently by 'social' rights of citizenship as embodied in the provisions of the Welfare State. As a whole, it is argued, this process has achieved the 'civic re-incorporation' of the working classes, who no longer feel themselves 'outside' a system which exists for the benefit of others. Affluence too has often been said to dampen down discontent and discourage class conflict, though as Goldthorpe, Lockwood *et al.* (1969) have argued at length, the relationship between economic prosperity and political outlook is far from simple. Other sociologists have noted an increasing tendency towards the institutionalization of class conflict. Lipset (1960: 220) speaks of 'the democratic class struggle', and Dahrendorf remarks that:

> Instead of a battlefield, the scene of group conflict has become a kind of market in which relatively autonomous forces contend according to certain rules of the game, according to which nobody is a permanent winner or loser. (1959: 67)

Free collective bargaining between trade unions and employers used to be taken as the illustration *par excellence* of institutionalized class conflict. For about a quarter of a century after the Second World

War, it seemed to serve in most of the advanced industrial countries to prevent the conflict of interests in the industrial sphere from spilling over into the serious political conflict Marx predicted. But increasingly, governments in Britain, America and elsewhere have intervened in collective bargaining to impose incomes policies aimed at controlling inflation (see Hirsch and Goldthorpe 1978). In these circumstances, a strike more easily becomes a strike against the government, and it may well prove that the insulation of the industrial from the political sphere of conflict was only transitory.

(3) Finally, individual social mobility may in some ways be seen as an alternative to inter-group conflict. Seeking to explain why there was no strong socialist party in the U.S.A., Sombart (1976, orig. 1906) suggested that abundant opportunities for individuals to make good by individual effort – to use the system – would reduce demands for changing the system. In other words, opportunities for individual social mobility act as a safety valve for collective conflicts. Dahrendorf suggests that 'individual competition and collective action are in principle mutually convertible, that they are basically equivalent expressions of the same great social force, contest' (1967: 19). Whether or not opportunities for success by individual effort are actually abundant, a widespread *belief* that they exist may have the same effects. In practice, opportunities are unequally distributed, and this fact is reflected in the finding that members of different classes tend to have somewhat different images of their society. British middle class people, for example, are more likely to see society as a ladder of individual opportunity than members of the working class, who tend to see it more in terms of 'Them and Us' and of the need for collective action (see Lockwood 1966). Those images have some basis in the different objective situations of the two categories of people.

On the whole, non-Marxist writers see the structure of conflicts in contemporary industrial societies as becoming more and more muted and complex rather than more pronounced and clear-cut. Dahrendorf concludes that 'the social structure of interests no longer guides us directly to the parties and platforms of political conflict; interests seem to get "lost", or perhaps satisfied, before they ever appear in the arena of group antagonism' (1967: 14–15). But the evidence can be interpreted in more than one way. What to Marshall shows the growth of citizenship and to Dahrendorf and Lipset indicates the institutionalization of class conflict may look to Althusser like the power of ideology to make citizens acquiesce in their state of subjection. These problems of interpretation are pointed up very clearly in the controversy about empirical studies of power in communities.

Power in Three Dimensions

Robert Dahl's *Who Governs?* (1961), a study of politics in New Haven, Connecticut, has become a pivot in the controversy about the nature and distribution of power in local communities and, by extension, in capitalist societies generally. In the background of Dahl's research stood C. Wright Mills's celebrated book *The Power Elite* (1956), an attempt to demonstrate the coalescence of a single (albeit loosely co-ordinated) military-industrial-political complex at the pinnacle of power in America. There had also been a whole series of earlier studies of power in American towns, whose authors had in the main expected to find single local ruling élites, and found what they expected. Dahl argued that a sounder research strategy was to start from the hypothesis that no single group monopolized power in a community, and then to see whether this hypothesis could be disproved.

Dahl began his search for power in New Haven by looking at two obvious power resources, trying to identify the Social and Economic Notables. These he defined by criteria quite independent of political activity – those who attended annual 'high society' coming-out celebrations, and the directors of the largest businesses. It immediately emerged that these two categories hardly overlapped at all; the big businessmen did not include many of the New Haven patricians. Nor did many members of either group hold political offices; indeed the patricians seemed to have little contact with decision-making at all, and disappear from the study. Status was evidently not much of a power resource in New Haven politics.

Was it possible, however, that economic magnates had great influence on decisions behind the scenes? Dahl next looked at who was involved, officially and unofficially, in decision-making in three separate areas of public concern: political nominations, public education (siting and quality of schools, teachers' salaries and so on), and urban renewal (city centre redevelopment). Interestingly, different groups of people were involved in each of these three areas, so there appeared to be no single power élite. The crucial issue, however, was urban renewal. This was the question which most dramatically affected the distribution of economic resources, which hit most people in the pocket.

Urban renewal had been an issue in New Haven since the 1940s, but it had made little progress. Too many people were likely to be adversely affected, and piecemeal redevelopment seemed the only possibility. Then a new mayor, Mr Lee, came to power with urban renewal as the lynchpin of his programme. At first businessmen refused to co-operate. But Lee drew their attention to the large-scale

Federal aid available for urban renewal, and succeeded in pressurizing one businessman to head an Urban Renewal Commission. Others joined him and eventually the Commission came to include representatives of all the big interests likely to be affected – business, trade unions, Yale University. Lee invented the Commission to approve his development plans and to 'sell' them to the groups involved – its members were to act as opinion-leaders. Dahl asserts that Lee and his top aides took all the decisions, and that the Commission never challenged his plans in any major detail. Dahl therefore infers that there was no single power élite in New Haven, nor any veto-group (to use Riesman's term) which could block initiatives inimical to its interests. That had not always been the case. From colonial days until into the nineteenth century, New Haven had been dominated by the patricians of the Congregational church – 'the elect were also invariably the elected'. Later, with industrialization, entrepreneurs had been very powerful. Later still, various immigrant or ethnic groups had become interests to be reckoned with. Successive new interest groups had progressively fragmented the structure of power. By the middle of the twentieth century, according to Dahl, a movement 'from cumulative to dispersed inequalities' had produced a highly pluralistic pattern of power in New Haven. The Mayor and his assistants were the most powerful people, and they owed their power to having been democratically elected, and to their skill in persuasion and in putting together coalitions of interested groups to get things done.

One weakness of Dahl's study is that he did not fully succeed in coming to terms with the problem of 'covert power'. Unfortunately, the evidence that the Commission of leading citizens never overruled Mayor Lee is ambiguous. It *could* indeed mean that Lee always persuaded them that his policies were in their interests. It could also mean that Lee never submitted to them decisions which he thought they would reject. In other words, did he trim his policies in advance to suit their anticipated wishes? And what else might have edged them towards acquiescence? Dahl himself records that the prospect of massive Federal aid flowing into the town helped to sweeten local economic interests. Finally, why was it so vital to recruit the representatives of economic interests in the first place? The Mayor, of course, was working within an established power structure, to which concessions probably had to be made.

This leads us to a still more fundamental criticism of Dahl's study. Lukes (1974) has described Dahl's conception of power as 'one-dimensional', because his method of investigation involved studying only those political interests which find overt expression through active involvement in politics and in the making of decisions. People who are politically passive are implicitly assumed to be content with the workings of the political system – otherwise they would be involved in pursuing the issues which concern them. But, as Bachrach and Baratz (1970) argue, some issues find their way onto the political agenda more easily than others. Some groups, with certain interests, can make their voices heard more easily in the political market-place than others. The structure of power may be such that certain issues do *not* reach the political agenda. By selecting *salient* political issues, Dahl systematically rules this possibility out of consideration. Bachrach and Baratz argue that other issues exist, of which people are aware, and which yet do not find expression in political debate. The best empirical investigation of such non-decisions is Crenson's study (1971) of the 'un-politics' of air pollution in Gary, Indiana. Gary is a steel town whose air was among the most polluted in America, yet where pure air was for a long time not a political issue although it was in many other towns. Crenson contends that U.S. Steel, the town's major employer, was able to keep the issue out of the public arena. Lukes describes the work of Bachrach and Baratz and of Crenson as embodying a 'two-dimensional' view of power, because it takes account both of decisions and non-decisions. But it is still 'behavioural' in focus, in the sense that non-decisions are viewed as a form of decision-making: someone is specifically observed to do something on a specific issue. It still involves *intentional* action in pursuit of conscious interests.

Lukes, however, is still dissatisfied with the two-dimensional view of power, and advances a 'three-dimensional' one inspired mainly by the ideas of several 'Western Marxist' thinkers. Lukes is concerned to take into account circumstances where there is no conflict, no overt political issue, and not even latent discontent – situations where an issue does not reach the political agenda because no-one even thinks of it. The prevailing political and social assumptions make the thought unthinkable. This idea can be traced back to Marx's famous observation that 'the ideas of the ruling class are in every epoch the ruling ideas' (Marx–Engels 1947).[11] We have already noted Althusser's view that all societies 'secrete ideology', and that in a capitalist society ideological state apparatuses function to inculcate 'respect for the socio-technical division of labour'. An earlier but more subtle version of this is the discussion of 'hegemony' which Antonio Gramsci (1971) wrote in Mussolini's prisons. Gramsci defined hegemonic domination by the mass consent which reduced the level of coercion necessary for its maintenance, and he too stressed the role of the whole network of cultural institutions in securing this popular support. T. W. Adorno took a similar view: in his view, society and social consciousness had become increasingly or even completely reified.

> To say that society is 'completely reified' is to say that the domination of
> the exchange process has increased to the point where it controls institu-
> tions, behaviour and class formation in such a way that it prevents the
> formation of any independent and critical consciousness (Rose 1978: 48)

It is thus rather apparent that the 'three-dimensional' conception
of power is less concerned with power as Weber defined it – the probability that one actor will be in a position to carry out his *will* despite
resistance – than with what he called domination. It is less a matter
of contest or trials of strength in social relationships than of impersonal, unplanned and unwilled constraint imposed by the way the
system is structured. The most extreme version of this view is that
propounded by Poulantzas in his controversy with Miliband (see
Miliband 1969, 1970, 1973; Poulantzas 1969, 1973). Poulantzas
argued that in studying power in capitalist states, it was irrelevant
to examine the social backgrounds of élites. That could change without in any way changing the way the machine worked. As a good
Althusserian, Poulantzas contended that it was beside the point even
to study the interests which people in powerful positions consider
themselves to be pursuing. Whatever their subjective illusions, their
actions were structurally determined, and objectively the social
formation impersonally served the interests of the reproduction of
capitalism.[12]

Subjective and Objective Interests

The 'three-dimensional' view of power is inseparable from the view
that it is possible to define the objective interests of a person or class
of people independently of whether they themselves are subjectively
conscious of these interests. But does it make sense to say that members
of a social class may have a 'false consciousness', as Engels termed
it, of their 'true' interests?

The pluralist school of thought in which Dahl stands, rooted as it
is in the liberal democratic tradition, firmly answers no. People are
themselves the best judges of their own interests, and their interests
are synonymous with what they *want*. In other words, they themselves
define subjectively what their interests are. One can study objectively
only how they go about pursuing through the social and political process their interests as they see them. The tradition of Marxism and
of the sociology of knowledge, on the other hand, asks *why* people
want what they want, and recognizes that subjective wants are shaped
by social experience, by people's position in the division of labour,
by their social interdependence and the constraints it imposes upon
them. Herbert Marcuse (1964: 6) draws a fairly typical conclusion
from this line of inquiry:

In the last analysis, the question of what are true and false needs must be answered by the individuals themselves, but only in the last analysis; that is, if and when they are free to give their own answer. As long as they are kept incapable of being autonomous, as long as they are indoctrinated (down to their very instincts), their answer to this question cannot be taken as their own.

Broadly speaking, in the Marxist tradition interests are understood not as wants but as *advantages* (see Runciman 1970: 212–23). A person may be said to have an interest in something if he can be shown to 'have a stake in it', or to be affected by it. In that sense, interest can be defined objectively, because the effects of social interdependence on a person or a class can in principle be discovered by an external observer independently of whether the person or members of the class in question are aware of it. But is it logically possible to define something as being to a person's advantage even if he himself actually disagrees? Certainly it may be possible to show that the strategy adopted by a person or a class of people is objectively not furthering the ends they have in view. It may be having contrary consequences. That can easily happen where the structure of interdependence is highly complicated and opaque. But this begs the question: it brings us back to subjective ends in view. The problem of false consciousness has always been understood not to be a matter simply of the unforeseen consequences of purposive social action, important as *they* are.

There is no denying that wants are shaped within structures of social interdependence. How that occurs is a legitimate and enormously important subject for sociological investigation.[13] That is enough to underline the significance of the 'three-dimensional' view of power. Yet anyone who goes further and imputes 'false consciousness' to those he is studying has always been extremely vulnerable to the allegation that he is arbitrarily intruding his own values. James D. Stolzman (1975: 111) has suggested one possible defence:

> the delineation of advantages in a given society can normally be accomplished by reference to *its own collective standards*. The viability of this strategy derives from the fact that the various dimensions (wealth, power, prestige) comprising the structure of inequality in any society – the sum of which might be referred to as 'social goods' – owe much of their invidiousness to collectively shared definitions of what is 'worth striving for' in social life. This being the case, the observer need not adopt his own personal criteria for establishing what constitutes an 'advantage' or 'disadvantage'; suitable criteria are already embodied within a society's system of stratification.

At first glance, Stolzman's solution is very plausible. It seems to work for wealth, prestige and political power precisely because there is widespread agreement that these are resources worth contesting. It becomes much more problematic if one attempts to use it to sustain the imputation of false consciousness in the cultural domain (see Mennell 1979). On closer inspection, Stolzman's argument seems circular. What constitute scarce resources in a society – the 'things worth striving for' – are scarce precisely because people strive for them, and they strive for them because they *subjectively* see that as in their interest. And their subjective conception of their interests is, one assumes, exactly what we are attempting to define as objectively false. The problem is compounded by the appeal to the society's 'own collective standards'; if such a consensual system of common value exists that must be, one again assumes, just what a number of Marxist theorists would wish to see as ideologically distorted consciousness.

In the absence of any better defence of objective interests and false consciousness, Marxists are left still vulnerable to the charge of epistemological self-righteousness. That, however, is a not uncommon failing among sociologists.

5 The Mind and Sociology

Among the hundreds of past and present societies known to us, the social and cultural diversity is perplexing. The variation in patterns of family and kinship, in modes of government and in economic and technological organization is relatively obvious. But the variety extends much further: to morals and beliefs – religious, mythological, and cosmological – and of course to language. Societies have not only divergent ways of organizing their practical activities, but also vastly different ways of expressing their thoughts about themselves and their world.

Confronted with this diversity, sociologists and anthropologists have tried to draw inferences about human mental processes. Either they have inferred that social and cultural differences are the expression of inherently different forms of mental process. Or, on the other hand, they have tried to discern, underlying the superficial dissimilarities, universal and constant principles of the mind or of society.

Bases of Cultural Diversity

No matter how strange to our eyes are primitive societies' conceptions of reality – their explanations of natural processes and the supernatural, for example – they apparently organized their lives successfully on these assumptions. So how very different are they from the assumptions on which Western industrial man bases his way of life? This question has inevitably led to closer examination of the cognitive foundations of all societies.[1] It has also led to the disturbing question of whether Western science, and social science in particular, is not just another way of organizing a conception of reality, no more and no less valid than any other socially accepted construction of reality.

Such doubts rarely troubled Victorian social theorists like Spencer, when fairly detailed reports of the tribal societies of Africa, Australasia, North and South America were first becoming available. There was a good deal of speculation about the nature of 'the primitive mind', as compared with the mind of modern, scientific, rational, Western man. It was widely inferred that there were fundamental, probably biological, differences between the races. With the benefit of hindsight, it is possible to see how such speculations assisted the altogether nastier political racialism of the twentieth century. Yet as early as 1911, the great American anthropologist Franz Boas (1854–1942) had shown with the aid of massive evidence that there was no correlation whatsoever between the distribution of cultural traits and race in the biological sense. The evolution and development of human societies over the 50 millennia that *Homo sapiens* has existed owes nothing to biological changes in mankind.

It could still be argued, all the same, that differences in culture and social organization, though not the *result* of mental differences, would – no matter how they themselves came to develop – be *reflected* in different mental processes. Reasoning in this way, Lucien Lévy-Bruhl (1857–1939), a member of Durkheim's circle, distinguished between 'pre-logical' and 'logical' mental operations (1926). This might be described as a socially rather than biologically deterministic variant of the earlier argument, but like that it has been shown to rest on the selective or careless use of evidence.

The strongest and most subtle version of the hypothesis that there are fundamental, cognitive differences between various cultures is, however, that put forward by the anthropologist Edward Sapir (1884–1939) and his student Benjamin Lee Whorf (1897–1941). Their argument is not marked by the European ethnocentrism of the Victorians. Quite the opposite: it is a form of cultural relativism. They argued that differences in the world-views of different cultures were grounded in different linguistic structures. They suggested that the vocabularies and grammars of the languages people learn actually determine the way they perceive the world.

Sapir and Whorf were writing long before the work of Chomsky, which seems to show that the 'deep structure' of all languages is the same, and that this is so because all human minds process language in the same basic ways. If Chomsky is right, it can be argued that 'Since there are no qualitative differences in the nature of language rules, it is impossible to conceive of more "simple" or more "advanced" cognitive levels.' (Cole and Scribner, 1974: 27–28.) On the other hand, it is certainly true that languages differ greatly both in the vocabulary they apply to similar sets of phenomena, and in their *surface* structure and grammar. Words frequently do not have exact equivalents in other languages, because cultures 'group' phenomena in different ways. For example, in English we use the one word 'uncle' to designate mother's brother, father's brother, mother's sister's husband and father's sister's husband. Other societies have a distinct word for each of these four relations, while others group them differently under two or three words. Nor is this confined only to social categories of which kinship terms are a most prominent manifestation. The taxonomies used for natural phenomena such as flora, fauna and even colours vary widely indeed. Distinctions which find expression in one language fail to do so in another; similarities apparently significant in one culture seem not to be so in another. Why? The problem was brilliantly stated, though not solved, by Durkheim and Mauss in a pioneering study (1963: 7–8, orig. 1903).

> A class is a group of things; and things do not present themselves to observation grouped in such a way. We may well perceive, more or less vaguely, their resemblances. But the simple fact of these resemblances is not enough to explain how we are led to group things which thus resemble each other, to bring them together in a sort of ideal sphere, enclosed by definite limits, which we call a class, a species, etc. We have no justification for supposing that our mind bears within it at birth, completely formed, the prototype of this elementary framework of all classification. Certainly, the word can help to give a greater unity and consistency to the assemblage thus formed; but though the word is a means of realizing this grouping the better once its possibility has been conceived, it could not by itself suggest the idea of it.

The sheer variety of cultures justifies Durkheim and Mauss in their assumption that categories of thought must be learned, not innate. If concepts are learned, however, there still remain three ways in which this might take place. These are, in Roger Brown's words, that

(1) Concepts are learned from direct commerce with the physical world without any social mediation;
(2) concepts are socially mediated but the mediation is non-linguistic;
(3) concepts are socially mediated and the mediation is linguistic. (Brown 1965: 314)

If either the first hypothesis or the second (that favoured by Durkheim and Mauss) were true, then language would be merely a 'cloak' covering what is in some sense 'essentially' the same underlying patterns of thought and perception of reality in all cultures. If the third were correct, then language would rather be a 'mould' which shaped the way in which those who speak a given language perceived and thought about the world.

Probably all three kinds of learning do occur. Some of Piaget's studies give support to hypothesis(1). In the first eighteen months of life, the child learns to conceive of the existence of objects in space and time, independent of himself and his own volition, and this learning seems to be achieved by manipulating the objects and observing the results. Later on, the child learns the principles of 'conservation' of quantity, number, area and volume – that for example liquid poured from a short fat glass into a tall thin glass remains the same in volume. Speech is needed to express the understanding that it is 'the same', but in this case words seem only to label an extra-linguistic conception. But then it is unlikely that there are any societies in which the principle of conservation is not recognized. What of domains of meaning less likely to be cultural universals – kinship, moral codes, botanical and colour terminology? These are 'mapped out' by languages in many different ways; even the colour spectrum, which in physical terms is a continuum, is 'cut' at different points by different languages.

Now it is fairly obvious why the Eskimos should have words for many different kinds of snow (Whorf 1956: 216), where the one word 'snow' suffices for most purposes in English, or why rice-eating tribes are reported to be able to distinguish by name several dozen forms of rice. But it is not so obvious that this abundance of vocabulary indicates anything more profound than that their ways of life make fine distinctions necessary and give opportunities for practice in making them. An English speaker who takes to skiing or Indian cookery is also likely to become able to identify at least a few different kinds of snow or rice. Likewise, English may have only one word for four kinds of uncle, but the distinctions can be drawn, albeit clumsily, if need arises. A great deal of the evidence with which Whorf supported his hypothesis is of this kind of superficial lexical variation, and is therefore inconclusive. There is some evidence that the ability to distinguish colours is related to the 'codability' of particular colours in one's native language; but though this suggests that words play a part in the process of memorizing, it scarcely proves that people are led by their vocabulary to quite different views of the world.

Of much greater interest to the sociologist is Whorf's assertion that 'users of markedly different *grammars* are pointed by their grammars toward different types of observations and different evaluations of externally similar acts of observation, and *hence are not equivalent as observers* but must arrive at some different views of the world' (1956: 221, my italics). Whorf thought that Western science had been markedly coloured by European languages (1956: 221–2), the characteristics of which were perhaps a necessary, though certainly not a sufficient condition for the development of science. The languages which Whorf grouped together as 'Standard Average European' tended to represent even abstract ideas as a series of distinct entities and events. Similarly 'SAE' objectifies time, representing it as a linear scale marked off in equal units, a conception alien to many other languages, such as that of the Hopi which Whorf studied. 'Newtonian space, time and matter are no intuitions. They are recepts from culture and language. That is where Newton got them.' (1956: 153.)

Interesting and plausible as it may be that language flavours the way members of different societies think about the world, there is no substantial reason to suppose that there are insuperable linguistic barriers to making the world view of one society intelligible to another. The fact of successful translation shows that languages do not define incommensurable cultural universes. As Lewis Feuer (1953) pointed out, Aristotle's philosophy was translated from Greek into Arabic and Hebrew, and reached Western Europe by retranslation from the Semitic languages. Though there were obstacles to the expression of certain key ideas of Aristotelian metaphysics in Arabic and Hebrew, the misrepresentations resulting from the double translation were relatively minor. More generally, Feuer argued that

> how the relativist has escaped his own linguistic a priori to know, for example, the details of the Hopi a priori is incomprehensible. For he does manage to state the Hopi perspective in English, and this, if his doctrine were true, he should be unable to do.'

This is not to deny that the 'translation' of another culture's world view is a considerable intellectual achievement, and only possible by prolonged study or fieldwork. In the past, the effect of poor 'translation' has often been to make natives of other societies seem illogical or even childish. Yet, in the end, it is inevitable that such translations are made, no matter how circuitously, for the subject-matter of exotic societies only becomes social scientific data when it is made communicable to fellow scholars.

Lévi-Strauss and Structuralism

Is it, then, more plausible that though members of different cultures may have difficulty in understanding the way each other thinks, the basic operations of human thought are universal? One of the most fascinating attempts to demonstrate that they are is presented in the work of Claude Lévi-Strauss.

Unlike most anthropologists, Lévi-Strauss's ultimate concern is not the explanation of the organization of particular societies, but with the discovery of fundamental structures of the human mind. For him,

> Ethnographic analysis tries to arrive at invariants beyond the empirical diversity of human societies ... Rousseau foresaw this with his usual acumen: 'One needs to look near at hand if one wants to study men, but to study man one must learn to look from afar ...' (Lévi-Strauss 1968a: 247)

Ethnographic evidence, of which Lévi-Strauss makes abundant use, is in the end of interest to him only in so far as it can be used as evidence of mental processes valid for all human minds.

The recurrence of a detail of custom in two different parts of the map is not a matter to which Lévi-Strauss attaches any particular importance. In his view, the universals of human culture exist only at the level of structure, never at the level of manifest fact.

Lévi-Strauss, like Durkheim and Mauss before him, sees it as a universal requirement of the human mind to divide, to categorize and to classify phenomena. Even the colour spectrum, which physicists know to be a continuum, is universally divided up, though by different cultures in different ways. Lévi-Strauss argues that the fundamental form of our categorization is binary. Our minds process what we observe in the form Red/not-Red, Tree/not-Tree, most generally X/not-X. His inspiration for this assumption is drawn from the world of computers, which carry out complex operations entirely on the basis of binary logic, and particularly from Roman Jakobsen and the Prague school of linguistics. Jakobsen and his colleagues showed that the recognizable phonemes which constitute the units of meaning in each language are constructed by the binary opposition of contrasting phonetic sounds. We discriminate between phonemes in terms of opposed 'distinctive features' of consonant and vowel sounds, such as compact/diffuse, grave/acute, nasal/oral. Lévi-Strauss seems merely to assume that if our minds process sounds in this fashion, they must process everything else that way too (1963, chapters 2–4); his debt to linguistics is limited to an analogy, and analogies are always suspect. Moreover, the Prague school is not the latest thing in linguistics. Chomsky's work makes it appear

not necessarily false but ... certainly inadequate. Where speech is concerned, the ultimate objective of research is to discover not merely how children learn to distinguish noise contrasts as significant but how they acquire the generative rules which allow them to formulate meaningful patterns of sound in the first place and what sort of rules these may be. By comparison, the manifest cultural data with which Lévi-Strauss is playing are very superficial. (Leach, 1970: 113)

But let us now look at what Lévi-Strauss does with his cultural data. Primitive man, as much as civilized man, says Lévi-Strauss, thinks about his society, seeking to understand himself and his environment, and mentally manipulating what he perceives. Men everywhere develop semi-coherent schemes by which they give meaning to their activities. But these 'conscious models' or 'informants' models' are incomplete, contradictory and distorted. Lévi-Strauss believes it possible for the anthropologist to discern an underlying structural truth, which native explanations reflect but do not expose.

Now discrepancies between native accounts and observable social realities have been exposed by other than structuralist methods. Both Redfield (1930) and Lewis (1951) studied the village of Tepoztlan in Mexico, and the anthropological world was disturbed by the radical disagreement between their two accounts. Redfield painted a picture of a close-knit, harmonious community and went so far as to base an ideal-type of peasant or 'folk' society on his findings (1947). Lewis, however, discovered conflict, distrust and social isolation in the same society. A great controversy raged, but the most plausible reconciliation seems to be that each portrayed part of the truth, each equally essential to the other (Murphy 1971: 104). Redfield recorded the accepted 'conscious model' of the society – the ideology by which the natives represent the situation to themselves and others; Lewis recorded the action – the way things worked in practice. Lévi-Strauss has pointed to a number of similar, if superficially less dramatic, contradictions. For instance, the Sherente, Bororo and other Brazilian Indians depict their own societies as organized in two exogamous moieties. But do such 'dual organizations' actually exist? Lévi-Strauss contends that the conscious model simply cannot explain the actual pattern of marriages which takes place: 'this image amounts to a theory or rather a transmutation of reality, itself of an entirely different nature' (Lévi-Strauss, 1963: 121). The conscious model is an essential clue to reality but does not itself explain it. To explain it, it is necessary for the anthropologist to construct by inference the 'unconscious model', which is often obscured both for him and for his informant by the conscious model. In the case of the Sherente, the latent reality seems to involve three, not two descent groups, and in practice they seem to prefer to marry their patrilineal cross-cousin, while expressing preference for the matrilineal one (1963, chapter 7).[2]

None of this, however, does more than hint at the use Lévi-Strauss makes of his assumptions about the binary organization of the mind. For this it is best to turn to his more recent works on myths. These include *The Savage Mind* (1968a) and the four volume *Mythologiques* (1969, 1971, 1973, 1978). The latter title is significant – 'mytho-logic'. Lévi-Strauss is not concerned, as an earlier writer like Sir James Frazer was in his celebrated book *The Golden Bough* (1890), with the manifest meaning of myths. Rather he is concerned with their 'logic' and transmutations.

> Mythological analysis has not, and cannot have, as its aim to show how men think. . . . I therefore claim to show, not how men think in myths, but how myths operate in men's minds without their being aware of the fact. (1969: 12)[3]

The manifest meaning of myths is often obscure, even to those who tell them and hear them. And as they are passed on, they are changed and transformed. There are many variations on similar themes, and in different versions some elements are omitted or inverted. Contradiction abounds.

Lévi-Strauss believes that the structure can best be discovered by considering a whole complex of myths together and rearranging the elements. He compares a complex of myths to a musical score, which can be read simultaneously for the melodic sequence (horizontally) and for the harmonic structure (vertically). The counterparts to melody and harmony in the study of myth he calls the syntagmatic and paradigmatic dimensions. (These terms are again borrowed from linguistics, where syntagmatic refers to the sequence of words in a sentence, while the paradigmatic dimension is the stock of alternative nouns, verbs and so on which might alternatively have been used in the sentence.) The syntagmatic chain refers to the actual sequence of elements in a particular myth, while the paradigmatic dimension links the similar elements in alternative and related versions of the myth. Lévi-Strauss does not ask which is the earliest or 'true' version of a myth – never an easy question to answer, especially in pre-literate societies. 'On the contrary, we define the myth as consisting of all its versions; or to put it otherwise, a myth remains the same as long as it is felt as such.' (1963: 216–17.) So the different versions are arranged along the paradigmatic axis.

How this works out can be seen in reference to one of the most famous of all complexes of myths, that centering on Oedipus. In Fig. 7 (derived from Lévi-Strauss 1963: 214) these themes are set out. Normally the story would be read from left to right and top to bottom. But apart from the syntagmatic chains (the stories, left to right) it can be seen that certain similarities emerge in the elements as arranged in the vertical (paradigmatic) columns. Now where do binary oppositions come in? This hinges on the interpretation of the four paradigmatic themes. To explain Lévi-Strauss's interpretation would involve following him through a long argument. But briefly, the theme of Column I is blood relations which are more intimate than they should be – 'the overrating of blood relations'. Column II expresses the opposite – fratricide and patricide are 'the underrating of blood relations'. Column III relates to the slaying of monsters, and Column IV to difficulties in walking straight and standing upright. By a spectacularly speculative route, Lévi-Strauss then reasons that the third and fourth columns symbolize respectively the *denial* and the *persistence of* the autocthonous origin of man (1963: 215–16). (Autocthonous means 'sprung from the soil', incidentally – the Greeks claimed to have originated in this way.) Like the first two, the third

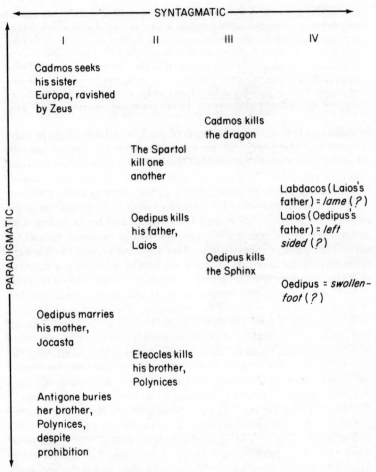

Figure 7 (from Lévi-Strauss 1963: 214)

and fourth columns are contradictory. We have two binary oppositions. At this juncture it is advisable to let Lévi-Strauss take over the
story himself:

> It follows that column four is to column three as column one is to column
> two. The inability to connect two kinds of relationships is overcome (or
> rather replaced) by the assertion that contradictory relationships are
> identical inasmuch as they are both self-contradictory in a similar way....
> The myth has to do with the inability, for the culture which holds the
> belief that man is autocthonous, ... to find a satisfactory transition between
> this theory and the knowledge that human beings are actually born from

the union of man and woman. Although the problem obviously cannot be solved, the Oedipus myth provides a kind of logical tool which relates the original problem – born from one or born from two? – to the derivative problem: born from different or born from same? By a correlation of this type, the overrating of blood relations is to the underrating of blood relations as the attempt to escape autochthony is to the impossibility to succeed in it. Although experience contradicts theory, social life validates cosmology by its similarity of structure. Hence cosmology is true. (1963: 216)

Lévi-Strauss believes that the units of myth invariably come in pairs of opposites. More recently, he has argued that the opposition self/ other is a prototypical category of thought, and that nature/culture, which he relates to our categorization of foods as raw and cooked, is another frequently recurring theme in the myths of many cultures.

The grand conclusion of Lévi-Strauss's work is the refutation of the view associated with Frazer and Lévy-Bruhl (and by extension with Sartre – see Lévi-Strauss 1963, chapter 9) that primitive thought is naïve, childish and superstitious. 'One deprives oneself of all means of understanding magical thought if one tries to reduce it to a moment or stage in technical or scientific evolution.' (1968a: 13) The principles of human thought are universal. If primitives appear childish to us, Lévi-Strauss ingeniously argues, we also appear childish to them. Children appear 'childish' because their abundant imagination and patterns of thought are as yet undisciplined, fanciful and freely expressed. Cultural training imposes mental discipline, overlaying the universal patterns of thought and selecting those suited to a particular social environment. Primitives appear childish to us because their thought is ill-suited to our technological society; but we also appear childish to them, for *our* logics are ill-adapted to *their* environment.

This outline, however bald it is,[4] should suffice to suggest the fascination of Lévi-Strauss's ideas, and a fundamental doubt: is this social science? Tracing paradigmatic themes seems often to rest on a poetic sensibility rather than on anything reducible to logic. Are Lévi-Strauss's analyses replicable – could any two anthropologists hope to come up with the same interpretation of the same raw myths, even if they were familiar with structuralist methods? Furthermore, Lévi-Strauss has often been accused of selecting data to *illustrate* his theories rather than to test them. Are the, indeed, testable? Since any contradiction seems to be grist to Lévi-Strauss's mill, perhaps they are irrefutable and therefore mean little. Yet, while making all these points, Edmund Leach still feels able to conclude:

And even if his argument eventually has to be repudiated in certain details, we simply must accept certain fundamental parts of it. Any knowledge that the individual has about the external world is derived from structured messages which are received through the senses ... patterned sound through the ears, patterned light through the eyes, patterned smell through the nose, and so on. But since we are aware of a *single* total experience ... *not* a sound world plus a light world plus a smell world ... it must be because the coding of the various sensory signal systems can be made consistent – so that hearing *and* sight *and* smell *and* taste *and* touch etc. seem all to be giving the *same* message. The problem then is simply to devise a means of breaking the code. Lévi-Strauss thinks he has solved this problem; even those who have doubts can hardly fail to be astonished by the ingenuity of the exercise. (Leach 1970: 93, italics and ellipsis marks in original)

Ethnomethodology

Certain parallels to the concerns of anthropological structuralists can be observed within sociology in the work of the ethnomethodologists. Although very different in origins and style, both movements search for constants beneath the flux and diversity of social life. That, at any rate, seems to have been the basic intention of Harold Garfinkel, who is the generally acknowledged founder of ethnomethodology and who gave it its name. The word ethnomethodology implies an attempt to discover the general and universal *methods* by which people make sense of the world – a concern not unlike Lévi-Strauss's attempt to break the code of knowledge. But the most powerful influence on Garfinkel was Alfred Schutz (see pages 19–23 above).[5] Not surprisingly, therefore, Garfinkel's preoccupation is with how people interacting together construct and maintain the *appearance* of order in social life, how they establish the *impression* that they share rules and a common life-world in which reciprocity of perspectives is possible. The semblance of order is seen as extremely fragile and, as a variety of phenomenological sociology, ethnomethodology studies the manipulation of subjective perceptions of social reality to the exclusion of any statements about the social order as an external, objective reality in itself.

Ethnomethodology has often been misinterpreted as just another variety of micro-sociology, and Garfinkel seen as simply a more radical Goffman. But whereas Goffman, Blumer, Becker and other interactionists always remained clearly within the church of sociology, ethnomethodology always constituted a radical criticism of the methods and assumptions of 'conventional' or 'positivistic' sociology. That point is sometimes lost, however, because at first glance the methods of research employed by Garfinkel and his associates do not appear very different from those of other sociologists. They have always shown a suspicion of statistical methods – but that is not enough to set them apart from many other sociologists. They have tended to rely greatly on participant observation. A notable example is Sudnow's study (1968) of the handling of death in hospitals. His perceptive account of how nurses count the deaths they have witnessed and when they stop doing so is worthy of Goffman himself. A more distinctive interest, however, has emerged in ethnomethodologists' studies of behaviour within organizational settings, especially organizations dealing with people – as patients, delinquents, as recipients of welfare payments, and so on. They have studied particularly the use and construction of official records and the way in which clients are categorized 'for good organizational reasons' as delinquent, mentally ill, or whatever. (Garfinkel 1967: 186–207; Cicourel 1968.)

Another distinctive ethnomethodological technique was Garfinkel's stratagem in his early studies of disrupting everyday situations in order to expose the background assumptions and expectations, the stock of knowledge and 'methods' which participants unconsciously use and take for granted.

> Procedurally it is my preference to start with familiar scenes and ask what can be done to make trouble. The operations that one would have to perform in order to multiply the senseless features of perceived environments; to produce and sustain bewilderment, consternation and confusion; to produce the socially structured affects of anxiety, shame, guilt and indignation; and to produce disorganized interaction should tell us something about how the structure of everyday activities are ordinarily and routinely produced and maintained.

> ... my studies are not properly speaking experimental. They are demonstrations, designed ... as 'aids to a sluggish imagination'. I have found that they produce reflections through which the strangeness of an obstinately familiar world can be detected. (Garfinkel 1967: 37–38)

In one such 'demonstration', students were asked to act out the part of a lodger in their own homes, to the bewilderment and often anger of the rest of the family, to whom the unprecedented courtesy was confusingly unexpected (Garfinkel 1967: 41–44). On another occasion, similar results were produced when students were instructed to ask their friends 'stupid' questions:

> Subject: Hi, Ray. How is your girl friend feeling?
> Experimenter: What do you mean, 'How is she feeling?' Do you mean physical or mental?
> Subject: I mean how is she feeling? What's the matter with you? (He looked peeved.)
> Experimenter: Nothing. Just explain a little clearer what do you mean?
> Subject: Skip it. How are your Med. School applications coming?
> Experimenter: What do you mean, 'How are they?'
> Subject: You know what I mean.

Experimenter: I really don't.
Subject: What's the matter with you? Are you sick?

(Garfinkel 1967: 42–43)

Garfinkel's early interest in the conventions underlying ordinary conversations was later developed under the leadership of Harvey Sacks into a whole specialist branch of socio-linguistics. Good examples of his work are his studies of 'turn-taking' in conversations (Sacks, Schegloff and Jefferson, 1974), and of how people manage the difficult business of bringing conversations to a close (Schegloff and Sacks, 1974).

If the goal of ethnomethology is to discover the universal 'practices' which make possible the creation and maintenance of an appearance of sense and order in social life, its results have not been very spectacular. Some ethnomethodologists (for example Cicourel, 1973) have shown a fascination for the work of Chomsky which implies a desire to establish a sort of socio-semantics analogous to the 'deep structures' Chomsky discovers in language. But we have already quoted Leach's remark that, compared with linguistic structures, 'the manifest cultural data with which Lévi-Strauss is playing are very superficial', and much the same could be said of the ethnomethodologists' evidence. One example of the universal practices which they claim to have identified is the 'et cetera principle', one of several kinds of 'ad hocing' procedure (Garfinkel 1967: 20–24; Cicourel, 1973: 85–88). In all conversations, a great deal is left unsaid. People are expected to fill in the information from their background knowledge or, if that is not possible, at least not to disrupt the interaction by inopportunely demanding the missing information. The 'how is your girl-friend feeling?' episode quoted above demonstrates what happens when ac hocing procedures are not employed.

That the discovery of such universal procedures is the general goal of all ethnomethodologists is, however, not clear. The movement is no longer, if it ever was, a unified school of thought. For example, Sacks's followers often now do not use the label 'ethnomethodology' for themselves, preferring to describe their activity as 'conversational analysis'. Aaron Cicourel describes his approach as 'cognitive sociology' and his work is in large part directed to the reform of sociological methods. McHugh, Blum and their associates (1974), on the other hand, have adopted a radically relativist view not just of conventional sociology but of their own work too. Jack D. Douglas, author of, among other things, *The Social Meanings of Suicide* (1967), who was once closely identified with the ethnomethodologists, would see himself as simply a phenomenological sociologist in a more general sense. What chiefly remains to unite these various authors is their criticism of conventional sociology.

The Ethnomethodological Critique of Conventional Sociology

In view of Garfinkel's original objective of discovering the general and universal practices by which people produce the appearance of an objective and stable order, it may seem paradoxical that the *Leitmotiv* of their criticism of conventional sociology is its pursuit of generalization. But it must be remembered that for ethnomethodologists, meaning in social situations is always fragile and ephemeral, and has constantly to be explored renegotiated. For them – or at least for Garfinkel and his more orthodox associates – generalization is to be sought not about the content of social situations, but only about the techniques by which situations are produced and maintained.

Conventional sociology is accused of conceptual reification, of committing the 'fallacy of misplaced concreteness' (see for instance Filmer *et al.* 1972: 62–66 *et passim*). Thus, having abstracted a concept like 'role', sociologists frequently proceed to treat roles a little too literally as things, as if they were bits of Meccano which make up a static social structure.

Related to this is the allegation that social scientists have a tendency to portray their subjects as 'judgemental dopes', or more narrowly as 'cultural dopes'. A 'cultural dope' is a man who produces 'the stable features of the society by acting in compliance with pre-established and legitimate alternatives of action that the common culture provides' (Garfinkel 1967: 68). This is reminiscent of Wrong's argument (see above, p. 34) but it goes further. Garfinkel put it like this:

> A favoured solution is to portray what the member's actions will have come to by using the stable structures – i.e. what they *came* to – as a point of departure from which to portray the necessary character of the pathways whereby the end result is assembled. (1967: 68, his italics)

This procedure, it is argued, leads to the confusion of commonsense and sociological interpretations of social situations.

In his *Method and Measurement in Sociology* (1964), Aaron Cicourel launched a thoroughgoing critique of the whole paraphernalia of sociological research methods. On the first page, he wrote:

> My basic assumption is that the clarification of sociological language is important because linguistic structure and use affects the way people interpret and describe the world. Since sociologists have evolved their own theoretical terminologies and frequently discuss, on the one hand, in these varying terms the language and substance of each other's theories and on the other hand the language of persons in everyday life whose behaviour they are interested in explaining and predicting, it is quite likely that the syntax and meaning of these languages will become entangled.

For their view of what would constitute acceptable sociological theorizing, the ethnomethodologists rely on Schutz's distinction between first and second degree constructs (see pages 22–23 above). Shutz contended that the social scientist has to construct, for scientific purposes typifications of the typifications subjects make for their practical purposes – by building 'constructs of the second degree'.

The ethnomethodologists, however, argue that 'conventional' sociology generally fails to carry out this procedure. As they put it, it tends 'to use common sense knowledge of social structures as *both* a topic and resource of inquiry' (Garfinkel, 1967: 31). Many of the 'facts' which sociologists tend to accept as data have been created in everyday situations for practical purposes. They are not facts but 'accomplishments'. As Zimmerman and Pollner (1971 : 82) express this argument:

> Sociology's acceptance of lay member's [*sic*] formulation of the formal and substantive features of sociology's topical concerns makes sociology into an eminently *folk* discipline ... Insofar as the social structures are treated as a given rather than as an accomplishment, one is subscribing to a lay inquirer's version of those structures.

To this extent, it is argued, 'conventional' sociology is merely on a par with any person's understanding of his everyday situation – a 'first degree' corpus of knowledge 'competitive' with everyday practical knowledge.

The thrust of this view can be seen in repeated criticisms of the use of official statistics in sociology (Cicourel 1968, Douglas 1967). Douglas takes a case of classic concern to sociology, that of suicide rates, and argues that they reflect the *interpretation* of deaths by coroners. Their judgements cannot be reduced merely to a formal rule of categorization – the rules are always interpreted, and Douglas purports to show that the interpretations of different coroners are inconsistent with each other. Cicourel extends similar reasoning to the field of delinquency, showing how the unconscious background assumptions of probation officers and police lead them to find delinquency where they expect to find it and to be more ready to categorize acts by certain types of people than others as delinquent. The conclusions are similar: aggregate statistics are meaningless, or at most reflect only the operations of the official bureaucracy, because identical 'real world events' may be placed in different categories, while quite different 'events' may be placed in one and the same category.

Sociologists have no doubt frequently used official statistics too uncritically. As Hindess (1973) argues, it is disastrous to impose alien categories and then to reify the resulting statistics, as he shows to have happened dramatically in the classification of the agrarian population in the Indian Census of 1951. Categories are theoretical constructs, the choice of which must be justified as appropriate. Given this, however, a great deal can be done by the framing of detailed instructions and training of enumerators, interviewers and officials to minimize the inconsistent application of categories. But, as Hindess points out, the ethnomethodologists do not show much interest in the possibility of estimating the degree of error present in statistics or in that of substantially improving them.

Why these possibilities do not interest them may become a little clearer in the light of Pollner's critique (1974) of Becker's version of the labelling theory of social deviance. The theory is summed up in Becker's statement that 'The deviant is one to whom that label has successfully been applied; deviant behaviour is behaviour that people so label' (Becker, 1963: 9). Pollner, however, accuses Becker of not following this principle consistently, and thereby confusing the commonsense actor's model of deviance with a sociological one. For the commonsense actor, deviance is an objective quality of another's action which causes and justifies an appropriate reaction to it by the community. On the other hand, Pollner writes, 'Viewed sociologically, the deviant character of the act is not intrinsic to the act but depends upon or, more emphatically, is constituted by the *subsequent* response of the community' (1974: 29), my italics). Becker employs both of these perspectives to produce his cross-classification of types of deviant (Fig. 8).

	Obedient Behaviour	Rule-breaking Behaviour
Perceived as deviant	Falsely Accused	Pure Deviant
Not perceived as deviant	Conforming	Secret Deviant

Figure 8. Types of Deviant Behaviour (Becker, 1963: 20)

Pollner, on the other hand, draws on his study of an American traffic court – where, as he points out, many of the convicted feel aggrieved because their commonsense knowledge tells them that the same offence is continually being committed without the offenders being apprehended.

... not all those who violate rules are categorized as deviant and not all those who are categorized as deviant have violated a rule. Presumably (i.e.

in perfect conformity with the criterion of rule violation), if all the faults of police and judicial processing were removed so as to provide for homogeneous categories, then labelling whould be superfluous. Rule violation and application of the label 'deviant' would coincide and the deviant would in effect be he who has violated a rule and only incidentally he who has been labelled deviant. (Pollner, 1974: 30)

Since this condition is not met, Pollner rejects the idea of 'real deviance' as a matter of no relevance for sociologists, as being in effect an unknowable *Ding an Sich*. Becker's classification is just the same as that employed by judges (who for this purpose count as laymen using commonsense practical reasoning): 'conforming' and 'pure deviant' behaviour correspond to a just acquittal and a just conviction.

The deeper roots of the ethnomethodologists' crique of 'conventional' sociology lie in their views on the nature of social interaction and the use of language within it. Underlying most sociology they see what Wilson (1971) calls 'the normative paradigm'. This involves two related ideas, that interaction is rule-governed, and that deductive explanation is appropriate to sociology. Deductive explanation involves logically deducing the facts to be explained from a number of theoretical premises and given empirical conditions. This necessitates that 'each description entering into deductive explanation must be treated as having a stable meaning that is independent of the circumstances in which it is produced' (Wilson 1971: 71). For this to be true in the explanation of social interaction, behaviour has to be seen as governed by rules, which Wilson defines as 'a stable linkage between the situation of an actor and his action in that situation' (1971: 60). What this really amounts to, he contends, is that in order to treat various instances as examples of the same category of social situation, sociologists have to assume a degree of 'cognitive consensus' – to assume that actors agree in recognizing situations at different times and in different places as being instances of 'the same kind' of situation, and therefore behave similarly.

In contrast, underlying the work of phenomenological sociologists is 'the principle of the contextual determination of meaning' (Douglas, 1971: 37). Of course, 'conventional' sociologists recognize that the same item of behaviour (a lie, for instance) can have different meanings in different contexts. Ethnomethodologists, however, take an unusually radical view of the interpretative nature of the process of social interaction. They see actors as continually groping towards a definition of the situation at hand, and situations are subject to continuous redefinition. In particular, all conversations contain numerous expressions which are not explicitly defined in a particular situation, and participants have to achieve 'operational' or working definitions of all such 'indexical' expressions which are valid only in the situation at hand.

'Indexicality' is a key term in ethnomethodology. Garfinkel (1967: 25–26, 38 ff.), illustrates his view of indexicality with an excerpt from a highly elliptical conversation between a husband and wife, together with their much longer expansion needed to make it intelligible to an outside observer. Yet 'conventional' sociologists remain unconvinced that this is a matter of vast importance. They take it as a commonplace that people in close relationships anticipate a large stock of relevant knowledge on the part of the other, making possible elliptical conversation, but that participants could explain the reference of their conversation to an outside observer if necessary and thereby make its meaning manifest, and *that this is sufficient for purposes of sociology*.

Nonetheless, the ethnomethodologists stand by their view that meaning is utterly dependent on unique situational contexts.

> It is apparent that in the interpretive [*sic*] view of social interaction, in contrast with the normative paradigm, definitions of situations and actions are not explicitly or implicitly assumed to be settled once and for all by literal application of a pre-existing, culturally established system of symbols. Rather, the meanings of situations and actions are interpretations formulated on particular occasions by the participants in the interaction and are subject to reformulation on subsequent occasions. (Wilson, 1971: 69)

Similarly, Zimmerman and Pollner (1971: 97) argue that the features of social situations are 'unique to the particular settings' and therefore 'may not be generalized *by the analyst* to other settings'. Bauman (1973b: 34) succinctly comments that those who argue for the uniqueness of socio-cultural events are:

> convinced that the 'uniqueness' of what they see and describe is an attribute of the phenomenon described and not of the very low level of particularity they have deliberately chosen or unknowingly inherited.

But given their insistence on the 'irremediability' of indexicality, they consider the interpretative view of social interaction incompatible with the logic of deductive explanation. McHugh *et al.* (1974: 3) go so far as to say that 'Speech never "solves" this problem, if by solve is meant to remedy, because any imaginable solution (any new speech) is itself a new version of the same old problem'. It is difficult to see how this extreme position is compatible with Schutz's views on the use of second degree constructs, ambiguous though those views are in certain respects.

Schutz argued that because social reality already has meaning for those living within it, the social scientist must work with constructs founded upon the constructs of the daily world. But this notion of constructs of the second degree is the source of great difficulty. For one thing, it is not entirely clear whether Schutz thought that all or only *some* of sociologists' constructs must be second order. The ethnomethodologists certainly believe that all of them must be. On the other hand, Schutz remarked that 'all scientific explanations of the social world can, *and for certain purposes must,* refer to the subjective meaning of the actions of human beings from which social reality originates' (1962: 62, my italics). This seems to imply that Schutz would agree with Gellner (1960) that, for example, 'to understand the class structure of a society one must not only know what rank, etc., mean in it, but also how many people occupy each grade, and this is a matter of counting, not understanding.' We have already noted the ethnomethodologists' objections to counting.

Schutz also argued that 'constructs of the second degree' must conform to the 'postulate of adequacy', by which he meant

> that each term in a scientific model of human action must be constructed in such a way that a human act performed within the real world by an individual actor as indicated by the typical construct would be understandable to the actor himself as well as to his fellow men in terms of commonsense interpretation of everyday life. (1962: 64)

But this statement is deeply ambiguous. If Schutz means only that social scientists' theories must be able logically to subsume the practical 'recipes' of commonsense, and so to relate generalizing propositions to descriptions of how actual people behave in actual situations, then this is nothing exceptionable. On the other hand:

> if what he means entails that the commonsense view of the social world must be immune from correction and modification by the discoveries of social science, then what he asserts is not only false but deprives the social sciences of part of their genuine importance. Our commonsense beliefs about society are not only often false, but are also sometimes incorrigible at the level of commonsense. (Emmet and MacIntyre, 1970: xiv)

The ethnomethodologists opt for the second of these two interpretations, for that is the burden of their criticism that 'conventional' sociology is merely a first degree or 'folk' sociology and that its vocabulary and theories seek to 'remedy the indexical properties of members' talk and conduct' (Garfinkel 1967: 11). Schutz, on the other hand, I believe to have intended his remarks in the contrary sense, the sense which is 'true and obviously true'. He accepted such concepts as roles and goals, often criticized by the ethnomethodologists, and spoke appreciatively of the progress of economic theory (1962: 64–65; 1972: 244–6) which claims great generality and is poles apart from the ethnomethodologists' style of investigation. He admitted that a great part of social science can be performed 'at a level which legitimately abstracts from all that happens in the individual actor' (1964: 84–85), though he regards it as a kind of intellectual shorthand. Where 'real scientific work' is done, however, the scientist will always have the option of shifting to the level of the individual actor. This condition is met even in so apparently 'abstract' a branch of social science as macroeconomic theory, and it is all that is required to meet the postulate of adequacy – nothing so sweeping as the ethnomethodologists seem to require.

Whether the ethnomethodologists are correct in their interpretation of Schutz is, however, a secondary issue. The whole distinction between 'everyday' and 'social scientific' knowledge is a source of great difficulty and ought to be treated with extreme scepticism. We may concede that many sociological concepts are 'constructs of the second degree'. Or, as Giddens (1976) expresses it, sociology involves a 'double hermeneutic', because it has to build interpretations on the interpretations already made by the subjects who consitute its field of study. But that is not enough to make it possible to draw a rigid line of demarcation between 'everyday' and sociological knowledge. So-called 'everyday' knowledge is wholly lacking neither in clarity nor in the use of 'second-degree constructs'. It is true that Schutz contended, notably in his paper 'The Problem of Rationality in the Social World' (1964: 64–88), that while scientific knowledge could attain coherence and consistency, the corpus of everyday knowledge *taken as a whole* remained inconsistent and unclear. This was restated more dogmatically by Garfinkel (1967: chapter 8). But Schutz did not rule out *parts of* the corpus of everyday knowledge being consistent and clear, especially in areas of expertise – expertise of the kind which many if not most people acquire in some field in their everyday lives. People working in organizations – or even the much maligned coroner! – may be subject to the same kind of social controls guiding them towards consistency of judgement and application of criteria as are sociologists and other social scientists. Moreover, the business of everyday life often necessitates the use of constructs of the second degree. So it may be more accurate to think of sociology as involving not necessarily always a double hermeneutic, but sometimes a single, more often a double and frequently a multiple hermeneutic. And the relationship between sociological and 'everyday' knowledge, if we must retain that term, should be seen as a continuum, not a clear-cut dichotomy.

In fact, the ethnomethodologists' acceptance of that dichotomy produces an interesting paradox.[6] They see indexicality as all-pervasive, and people's interpretations of social situations as extremely context-dependent. Yet they fail to explain satisfactorily why, if that is so, the interpretations made by social scientists are not equally context-dependent. And unless they do so, it is not easy to see how they can claim to be discovering the *universal* practices which make possible the illusion of order in social life. This paradox seems to explain why some ethnomethodologists have adopted an extreme relativism, while others have on the contrary moved towards an almost behaviouristic study of conversation.

Conclusions

If the phenomenological distinction between everyday and scientific knowledge reminds one of the confident contrasts once drawn between the mentality of primitive and modern men, then ethnomethodology and structuralism may appear very dissimilar. Yet ethnomethodology as practised by Garfinkel and structuralism as practised by Lévi-Strauss have one broad objective in common: to demonstrate to constants beneath the change and flux of human communication and social life. Garfinkel and his followers believe they can demonstrate certain rather general 'methods' or 'practices' by which people create and maintain the appearance of stability in their transactions with each other; Lévi-Strauss claims to have revealed certain principles of the workings of the mind itself. In both cases, their work consists largely of the repetitive demonstration of the same constant principles. Indeed, to many 'conventional' sociologists, the work of ethnomethodologists has often seemed simply boring. All the same, if such constant principles existed, it would be of some interest to know what they were.

On the other hand, that would hardly eliminate the inexhaustible task of understanding and explaining the development of diverse patterns of thought in diverse human societies. As Jack Goody has cogently argued, the adoption of a developmental perspective makes it unnecessary to choose between the relativisitic view that all cultures are manifestations of the same principles of thought and the absolutist view that there are fundamental mental differences. Even if some basic mental operations do not change, changes of immense consequence stem from developments in 'the modes of communication by which man interacts with man and, more especially, transmits his culture, his learned behaviour, from generation to generation' (Goody 1977: 37). Goody emphasizes in particular the consequences of literacy:

literacy made it possible to scrutinize discourse in a different form; this scrutiny favoured the increase in scope of critical activity, and hence of rationality, scepticism, and logic, to resurrect memories of those questionable dichotomies. It increased the potentialities of criticism because writing laid out discourse before one's eyes in a different kind of way; at the same time it increased the potentiality for cumulative knowledge, especially knowledge of an abstract kind, because it changed the nature of communication beyond that of face-to-face contact as well as the system for the storage of information; in this way a wider range of 'thought was made available to the reading public. No longer did the problem of memory storage dominate man's intellectual life; the human mind was free to study static 'text' (rather than be limited by participation in the dynamic 'utterance'), a process that enabled man to stand back from his creation and examine it in a more abstract, generalized, and 'rational' way.

In short, literacy accelerates the growth of knowledge. And it is the growth of knowledge through the transmission of culture which sets man apart from other animals: the constant principles which determine behaviour are a more pressing concern for the zoologist and ethologist than the sociologist.

6 The Growth of Knowledge

Knowledge grows over many generations. Individual people do not have to solve all problems anew and think everything out afresh for themselves. Most of what they learn has been discovered or thought out by people before them, but every generation learns new things, creates and solves new problems, and formulates new ideas, so that the corpus of knowledge is both developed and modified over long periods. That is as true of political ideologies and social belief systems as it is of scientific knowledge of the natural and social worlds. Today, however, the processes by which knowledge grows seem more problematic than they did in the eighteenth and nineteenth centuries when a confident belief in 'progress' reigned in the intellectual world. From that more confident period, what in their very different ways Auguste Comte (1798–1857) and Karl Marx said about the growth of knowledge has left its mark on sociology to the present day.

Comte (1830) suggested that with the development of human society, each of the principal fields of knowledge had been or would be dominated by three different principles of thought in succession. In what he called the 'theological stage', men thought about both natural and social forces in very personal terms, as gods and supernatural beings. In the 'metaphysical' stage, such personified beings were supplanted by abstract principles such as 'Reason' and 'Nature'. In the third and last stage, events in the physical, animate and even social domains could be explained in terms of law-like regularities which could be discovered by empirical and experimental study. This Comte described as the 'positive' stage, and at this time positive was simply a synonym for scientific.

Comte's three principles of thought appear to be modelled closely on those dominant in and before the medieval period, in post-Renaissance Europe, and in the nineteenth century. In other words, the theological stage corresponds loosely speaking to feudal social organization, the metaphysical thought associated with the seventeenth- and eighteenth-century philosophers to the development of a commercial economy, and the scientific stage to the emerging industrial society. But Comte recognized that the various branches of knowledge had not moved together in close harness. Mathematics, which in common with his contemporaries Comte believed to be an empirical science rather than a branch of logic, had entered the scientific stage in antiquity, as had astronomy. Physics and chemistry had been placed on a scientific footing much more recently, and the biological sciences were undergoing rapid development in Comte's own lifetime. Progress in the disciplines higher in his 'hierarchy of the sciences' was dependent on that previously made in the lower ones. At the pinnacle of the hierarchy was the study of human society, for which Comte eventually invented the name of sociology. In industrial society, when sociology had attained the scientific stage, social affairs too would be studied and then regulated scientifically. For each advance up the hierarchy of the sciences represented an increase not only in mankind's understanding of, but also in its control first over physical, then over organic and finally over social forces. Comte encapsulated this in a famous motto: *savoir pour prévoir, prévoir pour pouvoir.* As his sanity waned, he came to envisage the regulation of industrial society being entrusted to a sort of priestly élite of social scientists.

Comte's ideas were anathema to Marx. But Marx, like Comte, perceived a correlation between the structure of societies as they had developed through history and the type of knowledge and beliefs dominant within them. One of the few other points they had in common was a belief that society was developing in a definite direction. Even though their conceptions of the goal towards which it was developing were very different, that they both perceived its development as an ordered sequence had important implications for their understanding of the growth of knowledge.

Marx's assertion that it is men's 'social being' which determines their 'consciousness' and not their consciousness which determines their being is well-known. The terminology which Marx followed from the German philosophical tradition makes that a confusing statement. Consciousness and social relations in their ordinary senses are not separable things which can determine each other. Consciousness is part of all human activity – it is an element in all the concerns of everyday life. But Marx was not anticipating in any detail the ideas of G. H. Mead; he was not much preoccupied with exactly how individuals' thinking and self-conceptions are produced within intimate face-to-face social relations. His interest was more in the relation between patterns of social organization and systems of more abstract knowledge embodied in social and political philosophies. Marx and Engels have often been read, both by Marxists and non-Marxists, as 'economic determinists', though it is possible to cite remarks by them in which they acknowledge that social beliefs may in certain instances influence in turn the organization of social relations. But certainly what struck them most forcibly was the way that the interests of a dominant or exploiting class could distort its vision of social reality. The example pre-eminently before their eyes in mid-nine-teenth-century Britain was the connection between the new class of capitalist entrepreneurs and liberal political and economic theory. The larger part of Marx's mature work is a critique of political economy. The political economists conceptualized economic pro-cesses as impersonal, self-regulating mechanisms, and the state and economy as self-contained and separate 'spheres' of society. They were able to use their theories to show to their satisfaction that state inter-vention in economic life could only impede the attainment of the col-lective good which the unfettered workings of economic forces would otherwise beneficently produce. Liberal economic theory was valu-able in resisting the regulation by the state of such matters as hours and conditions of work – reforms sponsored not just by radicals but by paternalist aristocrats in opposition to the newer capitalist class. That kind of distortion of social reality by interests was inevitable, Marx considered, for any class in a dominant and exploiting position within society. On the other hand, he did not doubt the existence of a true social reality beneath the distorted perception. Moreover, non-ideological or scientific knowledge of that true reality was poss-ible, not by an élite of social scientists but by the proletarian class (and those intellectuals who identified with them). Their very state of propertylessness meant that they had no interests to distort their social vision; and since, according to Marx, the proletariat was des-tined to be victorious in class struggles and to establish a classless society, true knowledge of society would eventually be established.

Marx's work provided the foundations for the sociology of know-ledge in the twentieth century. But this century has not retained the previous one's confident belief in progress, nor indeed has the very idea of any structured processes of social development been univers-ally accepted. As we have seen, for both Comte and Marx in their different ways, it was the inexorable processes of social development which promised the growth of non-ideological or scientific knowledge about society. By and large, modern sociology of knowledge has aban-doned any very definite theory of history, and knowledge has in con-sequence seemed even more problematic.[1] This can be seen in the work of Karl Mannheim (1893–1947). Mannheim strove to avoid an out-and-out relativism, and in *Ideology and Utopia* (1936) took a posi-tion which he described as 'relationism'. Roughly speaking, that seems to mean that though social reality does in some sense exist, no social class can obtain more than a partial and distorted, historically determined perspective on it. The working class has no more privileged a view than the bourgeoisie, landed aristocracy or any other class. The nearest approach to non-ideological knowledge, Mannheim suggested, might be attained by the 'socially unattached intelligentsia' – a term he borrowed from Alfred Weber, but which also perhaps faintly recalls Comte.

Mannheim's sociology of knowledge was not exactly ahistorical in the ordinary sense. His notable essay on conservative thought (1953), for example, demonstrates subtly how German conservatism was the product of a specific historical situation after the French revolution. But for Mannheim it was questionable whether social belief-systems could be said to grow and develop towards a more adequate description and explanation of social reality. In a sense, rival political ideologies remained relative in almost the same way that Sapir and Whorf saw the Hopi and European world-views as incommensurable. And that is not satisfactory, for social and political belief-systems are always complex and far from static blends of theoretical explanation and emotionally-laden evaluation of society.

This can be seen if we look briefly once more at liberalism. Liberal economic theory certainly served class interests, and could be said to have been consciously formulated in large part as a weapon in political struggles. Even today economic theories play a prominent part in politics; there are still emotionally-charged debates about the economic role of the state. But economic theory even in Marx's time was not *just* ideology; it had considerable truth content. Marx himself was well aware of that. He himself borrowed a great deal from Smith, Malthus and Ricardo – more perhaps than with the benefit of our hindsight he would have been wise to borrow. For economic theory today is not the same as it was in the mid-nineteenth century. It has developed and grown, become infinitely more complex and refined, and is capable of explaining a much more diverse range of economic processes. Within modern economics there are many schools of thought – including Marxian – but they form together a community of arguments. Modern refinements of theories first formulated as weapons for the bourgeoisie now form part of the intellectual heritage and armoury of the most radical economists.

Science and Non-Science

For a long time, philosophers have attempted to pass human knowledge through a logical centrifuge to separate the scientific wheat from the chaff of fantasy, myth and emotion. The physical sciences in particular have served as a model of the steadily cumulative growth of knowledge through the dispassionate study of the 'facts' of nature. By following the logic of the physical sciences, the social sciences too might be purified of their admixture of irrational and historically transient religious or political ideological beliefs.

According to the traditional view, what distinguished scientific knowledge from the rest was the logical method by which it was obtained. Science began with the systematic observation and accumulation of factual evidence. From many particular observations, a hypothetical *generalization* – a general explanation for what was observed – was derived by a process of *induction*. The hypothesis would then be tested by further observation including, preferably, controlled experiments. If the hypothesis withstood test, the result was the permanent addition of a *verified* scientific theory to the corpus of knowledge.

Something like this view of science was expressed by Francis Bacon in his *Novum Organum* (1960; orig. 1620) and was prevalent, though in increasingly sophisticated forms, until well into the present century. The 'logical positivist' philosophers of the Vienna Circle – whose influence was at its peak between 1930 and 1960 – argued that only statements which were either logico-mathematical tautologies or empirically verifiable could be said to be meaningful. In other words, they used the traditional model of science as a criterion of sense and nonsense.

But that model is open to serious objections. Its first and fundamental weakness is that it represents the scientific process as starting from the patient observation and description of discrete 'facts' about heat, light, society, or whatever. That cannot be the starting point, because without some question or hypothesis already in mind it is impossible to know what to observe. All observation is selective. One cannot just 'observe'; one always observes *something* – something selected for observation. So observation is not prior to the formation of concepts and hypotheses. Without a hypothesis in mind one does not know what to observe or what experiments to conduct, and without concepts one cannot describe what one observes. Comte made exactly this point when he wrote:

> ... if on the one hand any scientific theory must necessarily be based on observation, it is equally true on the other that, in order to make observations, our minds require a theory of some sort. If, in considering phenomena, we did not relate them immediately to some principles, not only would it be impossible for us to connect these isolated observations and in consequence to make any sense of them, but we should be quite incapable of remembering them; and, most often, the facts would remain unperceived. (Comte, 1830)

I quote Comte, the founder of philosophical positivism, with paradoxical intent, because the crude 'fact-gathering' conception of science which he here rebuts has often been described as 'positivism'. A better term to describe it is 'inductivism', because its key feature is that general statements were seen as derived from accumulated masses of specific instances by the process of induction. Yet as early as the eighteenth century the philosopher David Hume rigorously questioned this view of scientific knowledge. He showed that the process of induction, unlike that of deduction, could not be represented in terms of logic. No generalization could ever be logically derived from any number of discrete facts. That the sun had been observed to rise every day for thousands of years did not *logically* justify the statement that it would always do so in the future – and so the hypothesis that its course is invariable cannot be verified. Hume argued that prediction on the basis of repeated observation was a matter of human psychology, not logic, and so were judgements of causality.

Hume's argument underlies the views of Sir Karl Popper (b. 1902), whose work has been widely read by contemporary social scientists.[2] From early in his career, Popper was a critic of the Vienna Circle, rejecting their idea that the goal of science was to verify its hypotheses by finding empirical evidence which confirmed them. According to Popper, it is quite mistaken to attempt to prove a theory to be correct or true, because that is simply impossible. All knowledge remains provisional, and indeed many theories important in the history of science have eventually turned out not to be true. But, argues Popper, if nothing can be finally verified, the same is not true of falsification. No matter how many observations seem to confirm a theory, it always remains provisional; but if we make just one absolutely indisputable observation to the contrary, then the theory is conclusively refuted. That means that though theories are unprovable, they are testable, and the aim of science must be to test them by attempting to refute them.

According to Popper, it is the potential falsifiability of scientific knowledge which distinguishes it from non-scientific. He uses this criterion to argue that such immensely influential bodies of thought as Freudian psychoanalysis and Marxism do not count as science. Psychoanalytic theory is not scientific, he contends, because it is not possible to deduce falsifiable statements from it. So many psychological observations are, for instance, interpreted as manifestations of 'displacement', 'repression' or 'sublimation' that it is difficult to see how propositions sufficiently precise to be testable can be derived from theories involving these concepts. In the case of Marxism, Popper maintains that falsifiable predictions can be derived, but that Marxists refuse to accept falsification by continually reformulating the theory and reinterpreting the evidence. There is a prescriptive or normative element in Popper's account of science: any theory can be 'immunized' in this way, but the scientist ought to be prepared eventually to abandon his theory in the face of contradictory evidence.

Popper does not, however, regard Freudianism or Marxism as meaningless. Unlike the Vienna Circle, he is concerned to distinguish not between sense and nonsense, but between science and non-science. And of psychoanalysis he writes,

> These theories describe some facts, but in the manner of myths. They contain most interesting psychological suggestions, but not in testable form. At the same time, I realized that such myths may be developed, and become testable; that historically speaking all – or very nearly all – scientific theories originate from myths, and that a myth may contain important anticipations of scientific theories. (1963: 37–38)

The problem, then, is to explain how scientific, potentially falsifiable, theories develop out of non-scientific, untestable thinking. For the traditional model of the scientific process, Popper substitutes one in which the central activity is problem-solving. The process begins from a problem, usually a rebuff to an existing theory or expectations. This stimulates a solution to the problem in the form of a new theory. From the new theory are deduced specific propositions which can be tested by observation and experiment, as a result of which preference is established among competing theories. Popper summarizes the process in the sequence

$$P_1 \rightarrow TS \rightarrow EE \rightarrow P_2$$

where P_1 is an initial problem, TS stands for a trial solution, EE for the process of error elimination, and P_2 for a resulting situation and new problem. The cycle is endlessly repeated. Knowledge moves forward by successive approximations. For example, Copernicus, Kepler, Newton and Einstein present successively more accurate accounts of planetary motion (among other things). But Einstein cannot be said to be finally 'true'; truth is analogous to the idea of accuracy in engineering – we can only say that a theory is true to within narrower tolerances than an earlier theory. Popper's is an evolutionary model of science in which knowledge, by analogy with biological adaptation to an environment, always remains knowledge for practical purposes, and it can always be thrown in doubt as new problems arise. To ask where P_1 in a cycle of scientific conjecture comes from is to risk entering another chicken-and-egg debate. P_1 in a later cycle is simply the P_2 of an earlier cycle. The ancestry of the current state of problematics in any field can in principle be traced back to the most primitive and mythical interpretations of the world. There is no starting point, nor any final state.

But is the falsifiability principle strong enough to bear the enormous weight which Popper places on it? Certain serious problems are inherent within it. Since, as Popper remarks, all observation is theory-impregnated, a theory cannot be falsified by an untheoretical observation statement, but only by observations interpreted in terms of a theory.[3] A new theory is therefore a prerequisite for the overthrow of an old one. And an accepted theory may prevent scientists from recognizing evidence which is incompatible with it. Perhaps the most famous historical case is the discovery of oxygen by Priestley and/or Lavoisier. Priestley first succeeded in filling a jar with the gas which we call oxygen, but he thought of it as 'dephlogisticated air' and tried to place it within the existing framework of the 'phlogiston' theory of combustion. He probably communicated his findings to Lavoisier, who repeated his experiments; but it was Lavoisier who realized that the existence of the gas was incompatible with the phlogiston theory and who formulated an entirely new framework for the chemistry of combustion. Priestley never accepted the new theory which his own work had helped to initiate (Kuhn 1962: 53–56).

The weakness of the simple falsification principle was exposed particularly by Thomas S. Kuhn's *The Structure of Scientific Revolutions* (1962), a study in the history of the physical sciences which has had an immense influence on philosophers and sociologists of science. As the title of his book implied, Kuhn presented (more emphatically in the first edition than in the second) a revolutionary rather than evolutionary view of scientific progress.

Kuhn calls in question whether scientists do in practice set out to test and falsify the theories with which they are working. Most of the time, when their particular area of science is passing through a period of what Kuhn calls 'normal science', scientists work *within* the assumptions of a paradigm. A paradigm is an example of scientific practice – practice including theory, applications and instrumentation – which establishes a whole tradition of research. In order to function as a paradigm, a scientific achievement must in itself be sufficiently impressive to attract researchers away from all rival theories in the field. But its achievement must not be final; while establishing the basic assumptions, it leaves numerous puzzles for later scientists to solve, by extending and articulating the paradigm. Normal science, according to Kuhn, consists of puzzle-solving, not paradigm-refuting. The greatest historical example of a paradigm – so great as to be misleadingly exceptional in its scope – was Newton's laws of motion. From these, Newton himself was able to derive Kepler's laws of planetary motion (and also to explain certain discrepancies from Kepler's predictions), together with theories about pendulums and tides. With a few more assumptions, he could explain Boyle's Law relating the volume and pressure of gases, and derive a formula for the speed of sound through air. That is an impressive list, but it is short when one considers the generality of Newton's propositions, and during the following two centuries, scientists came to be able to derive dozens of further important theories from the same general laws. Not all paradigms are so general, or affect so wide a terrain of science as did Newton's. Some establish a tradition of research in quite a narrow field – say, for instance, in the chemistry of benzene (Schofield 1974) – and would not be familiar to non-specialists. Other examples of works sufficiently wide in scope to make them famous to non-specialists are Benjamin Franklin's *Electricity*, Lyell's *Geology*, and Lavoisier's *Chemistry*. Each of these unified a field of research and established a period of 'normal science'. Normal science is eminently productive and cumulative, but it 'does not aim at novelties of fact or theory and, when successful, finds none' (Kuhn 1962: 52). Normal science, according to Kuhn, consists of pushing new observations into an accepted framework, and it has failed if they will not fit in.

But what of science before the establishment of a first paradigm in the field? The first paradigms in mathematics (Euclid) and astronomy (Ptolemy) date from antiquity – as, in different vocabulary, Comte remarked. But in most other fields of science, for example optics, heat and electricity, they are of much more recent origin. Before the end of the seventeenth century there was never a generally accepted view about the nature of light. There were a number of competing schools of thought. One group thought that light consisted of particles emitted from material bodies, a second that it was a modification of the medium which intervened between the observed body and the eye, and a third considered that something emanated (like radar) from the eye. Each school had supported its view with its own metaphysics, and each could account for certain phenomena in terms of its theory. Kuhn writes

> Any definition of the scientist that excludes at least the more creative members of these various schools will exclude their modern successors as well. These men were scientists. Yet anyone examining a survey of physical optics before Newton may well conclude that, though the field's practitioners were scientists, the net result of their activity was something less than science. (1962: 13)

It was less than science notably because it was scarcely cumulative: being able to take no accepted general principles for granted, every writer on optics felt the need to build the subject up from the foundations. Another consequence of the absence of a paradigm, or some candidate for a paradigm, is that all facts about a subject seem at this stage to be equally relevant. Kuhn remarks of Francis Bacon's writings on heat

. . . they juxtapose facts that will later prove revealing (e.g. heating by mixture) with others (e.g. the warmth of dung heaps) that will for some time remain too complex to be integrated in a theory at all. In addition, since any description must be partial, the typical natural history often omits from its immensely circumstantial accounts just those details that later scientists will find sources of important illumination. (1962: 16)

Thus hardly any of the early writers on static electricity record the fact that chaff, attracted to a rubbed glass rod, bounces off again – that seemed an irrelevant intrusion of gravity.

With the establishment of agreement on fundamental assumptions, scientists set to work on remaining problems and begin to make rapid progress. But paradigms do not last for ever. Physical optics, for example, has seen three full paradigms in succession – Newton's corpuscular theory, then the wave theory of Young and Fresnel, and most recently Planck's quantum theory. During the period of corpuscular optics, scientists unsuccessfully conducted experiments to measure the force of light falling on objects. These experiments were of course dropped when the wave theory gained ascendancy. The transition from one paradigm to another, and therefore from one period of normal science to another, takes place, in Kuhn's view, by means of 'scientific revolutions'. These begin with the discovery of 'anomalies', findings which persist in not conforming to the predictions of the paradigm. These anomalies may be quite esoteric, but in relation to the basic assumptions of the field they are not puzzles but problems. One of the anomalies in relation to Newtonian physics which emerged in the nineteenth century was that of certain discrepancies in the orbit of Mercury – not a matter of any practical importance but sufficient to cause earthquakes in physical theory. Anomalies are eventually resolved by the emergence of a new paradigm – in this case Einstein's theory of relativity, in which bent space takes care of the troublesome planet. But at first, and possibly for long afterwards, there will be far more observational evidence in favour of the old paradigm than the new.

The history of science thus plainly shows that in the past, the corpus of scientific knowledge has included many ideas which are now known to be false. It also reveals the extreme difficulty of distinguishing on logical or epistemological grounds between what is now thought to be scientific fact and previously held theories which were once considered scientific fact yet are now considered quite false. As Kuhn writes,

If these out-of-date beliefs are to be called myths, then myths can be produced by the same sorts of methods and held for the same sorts of reasons that now lead to scientific knowledge. If, on the other hand, they are to be called science, then science has included bodies of belief quite incompatible with the ones we held today. Given these alternatives, the historian must choose the latter. Out-of-date theories are not in principle unscientific because they have been discarded. (1962: 2–3)

Kuhn's work posed a considerable challenge to the traditional philosophy of science. At best it seemed to embody a 'great man' conception of scientific history, in which giants overthrow paradigms while dwarfs slave away in the Nibelheim of normal science. At worst it incorporated an irrational or arbitrary element in what had hitherto seemed the most rational of processes, the growth of scientific knowledge. That was partly acknowledged by Kuhn:

> Observation and experience can and must drastically restrict the range of admissible scientific belief, else there would be no science. But they cannot alone determine the particular body of such belief. An apparently arbitrary element compounded of personal and historical accident is always a formative ingredient of the beliefs espoused by a given scientific community at a given time. (1962: 4)

It was this irrational element to which Popper and his followers most objected.[4] For them, the engine of scientific progress is rational criticism. They recognize that the contents of science are a social product. Scientists have to state their theories, methods and evidence publicly, so that fellow members of the scientific community may subject them to replication, test and criticism. But, in their view, the rules of rationality are pre-social. There is one single and eternal 'logic of scientific discovery'. It is the failure to identify any such single and indisputable scientific method which has led some writers to go much further than Kuhn in depicting science as essentially an irrational process. Feyerabend (1975) contends that in preferring a new theory to an old one, even though the new theory for the time being contradicts may well-established facts, scientists have no general standards or norms of science on which to base their preference. They proceed, and science progresses, on the irrational expectation that the new theory will win in the long run. Feyerabend depicts science as a system of dogmatic beliefs much like any other; in effect, in rejecting the Popperian assumption that there is an eternal and absolute logic of scientific method, he goes to the opposite extreme, accepting a relativistic view of science as simply one more world-view. But it is then difficult to see how it is still possible to speak of scientific progress, and to judge a later theory to be superior to an earlier. And that seems contrary to common sense. As one commentator remarks,

> If Feyerabend contends that natural science is irrational, a belief-system just like any other, there are atomic bombs and journeys to the moon as counter-evidence. Any philosophy of science which neglects this reality is defective. It has to explain why it is that abstract scientific constructions can have such powerful applications. It has to pay attention to the fact

that, for many laymen and for many scientists too, these applications are the most convincing proof of the relative superiority of scientific knowledge ... (Wilterdink 1977: 121)

Many of these difficulties in defining the nature of scientific knowledge stem from the assumption that there is *one* universal logic of scientific method, and that this is what distinguishes science from nonscience. Usually it is further assumed that this method is to be found in the procedures of the natural sciences, and that it finds its most perfect expression in physics. When philosophers of science discuss the social sciences, they tend either to depict them as weakly developed imitations of the natural sciences, in which the pure and eternal scientific logic is adulterated by unscientific, socially determined, ideological influences; or they concentrate on defining how *the* logic of the social sciences differs from *the* logic of the natural sciences. Norbert Elias (1956; 1978a) has suggested that none of these assumptions is particularly helpful. If we study how scientists in various disciplines actually proceed, rather than trying to legislate about how they ought to proceed, we shall find that the logic and methods of different branches of science vary quite considerably. Elias notes in particular that had biology rather than physics been taken as the model, our view of scientific method would have been rather different. Biologists have worked in a much more inductive way than physicists: description and classification have played a more prominent part in the development of the biological sciences, and there has been less emphasis on the discovery of universal, timeless generalizations of the sort for which Newton's or Boyle's or Einstein's famous equations stand as archetypes in physics. The difference between physics and biology is explained by the degree of integration or complexity found in their respective subject-matters. Each level of science, Elias argues, must develop a logic, method and type of explanation appropriate to its subject-matter. The pursuit of universal, timeless, 'law-like' theories is appropriate and successful in the physical sciences only because of the relatively loose-connectedness of the objects they investigate. Theories involving precise, fixed relationships between two or more variables only work when the variables can be isolated. Biology, in contrast, has developed by describing 'pluriform' life processes and their development; and, *pace* Popper and Kuhn, it has depended to a large extent on the amassing of great quantities of empirical observations. The subject-matter of the social sciences forms still more highly integrated patterns of organization, and the atomistic method is still less appropriate here. That is one of the many implications of Elias's game models (see pages 51–56 above). What are needed in sociology, Elias suggests, are not theories emulating those of physics, but 'process theories', which depict the interdependencies between the parts of very complex wholes or figurations, and the processes by which those figurations develop. These theories may in consequence apply to relatively limited and specific historical situations.

Elias further suggests that we do not only see the content of science as a social product, but the rise of the sciences themselves as one example of a long-term developmental process. The sciences did not spring like Athene from the brain of Zeus, fully formed and fully armed with a pure scientific logic untainted by social influences. The investigation even of physical phenomena was for many centuries entangled with theological and other dominant social beliefs; early research into physical and chemical processes ran the risk of being seen as heresy and a threat to social order. Galileo's troubles with the church are perhaps remembered so well because they happened when it was already beginning to appear absurd that the church should express opinions on matters of scientific discovery. Yet it was not simply a question of enlightened and rational scientists battling against ignorance and religion; even Newton's papers reveal him to have been deeply involved in theological fantasies and speculations, and some of even his scientific work was not so far removed from alchemy. Only from the time of the Reformation onwards did physical scientists very gradually begin to acquire for their investigations a measure of relative autonomy with respect to dominant social beliefs. This slowly growing relative autonomy was associated with the gradual formation of relatively autonomous scientific communities. Again, the establishment of the Royal Society in Britain in the mid-seventeenth century is a famous episode and symptom of a more general process. Merton (1970) has noted the religious motivation behind the scientific work of many of the Royal Society's early members. But while the growth of socially relatively autonomous scientific communities increasingly shielded scientists from dominant religious and political authorities meddling in their work, it also increasingly exposed their work to control and criticism by their fellow scientists. Elias sees a corollary of the more general civilizing process (see pages 57–60 above) in the way that the increasing interdependence of scientists within scientific communities increasingly imposed limits on the extent to which 'magico-mythical' thinking could intrude in scientific theories. Scientists were forced by their increasing interdependence with each other to develop greater self-control in the expression of individual fantasy and affect in their scientific work, just as the more general growth of social interdependence brought about the civilizing of social behaviour in general.

The biological sciences gained the relative autonomy necessary for the pursuit of their investigations much later than did the physical sciences. One has only to think of the bitter controversies in the mid-nineteenth century about the theory of evolution or the practice of vivisection. Of course, their autonomy, like that of the physical sciences remains only relative; non-scientists feel entitled to some say in matters such as the applications of nuclear physics or genetic engineering which may have profound consequences for human society at large. It is not surprising that the social sciences are still very much in the throes of establishing a measure of relative autonomy. They are still quite highly involved with social beliefs and ideologies, and the scope for the expression of individual affect, fantasy or magico-mythical thinking is still relatively large in the social sciences. But the difference between the sciences is one of degree. Elias protests that

> Both philosophical and sociological theories of knowledge, in their hand-ling of the problems of knowledge, reduce all that people know to two diametrically opposite states – to a state of absolute independence of knowledge from the conditions of the groups where it is produced, and to a state of absolute dependence on these conditions; to a state of total autonomy on the one hand and to a state of total heteronomy, of absolute relativity, on the other. (Elias 1971: 364)

Elias's complaint may no longer be justified against all philosophers and sociologists. But a developmental perspective on the sciences helps to explain why it is impossible to classify a body of knowledge such as economics as *either* 'science' *or* 'ideology'. It can only be located on a continuum between the two poles. *All* knowledge is created in social processes; it is all shared, learned and developed in social figurations over many generations. Magico-mythical thought has in every case preceded the development of relatively more 'object-centred' knowledge (if we may use Elias's rather provocative phrase). The thinking of children and of primitive peoples is relatively spontaneous, undisciplined and involved. But the degree of detachment possible even for adults in the most advanced scientific and industrial societies varies from field to field of knowledge. People have gradually learned – and become socially organized – to view with relative detachment first physical processes, then later biological processes, and they still have to struggle to view social processes in a more detached way.

The Controversy about Positivism

The prestige and authority of the natural sciences in the modern world has deeply influenced the development of the discipline of sociology. Especially during the middle decades of the twentieth century when American sociology held a dominating position, few of the standard textbooks in the subject expressed doubt that sociology should be an empiricist, fact-finding discipline, and that the facts it discovered about contemporary society would and should be useful for the improvement, reform or better control of society. In both senses the ancestry of this conception of sociology could be traced back through Durkheim to Comte's ideas, and could therefore reasonably be labelled 'positivist'.[5]

Among the earliest critics of this tendency were the members of the Frankfurt School, including Max Horkheimer, Theodor W. Adorno and Herbert Marcuse, who came into close contact with American sociology after their emigration to the United States in the 1930s.[6] Indeed Adorno collaborated for a time with Paul Lazarsfeld who, though a fellow émigré from Europe, had rapidly become one of the leaders in the development of opinion surveys and other quantitative research methods in America. Adorno and his Frankfurt colleagues did not object to the use of such methods in themselves. They were a useful means of discovering the surface 'facts' of contemporary society. But such 'facts' could be only the beginning of sociological interpretation. 'Positivist' sociology tended to represent them as fixed and invariant features of society, rather then proceeding to the more important and interesting task of discovering how these 'facts' had been created through social processes. The Frankfurt theorists made particularly incisive criticisms of opinion research, which most clearly represents methodological atomism in sociology.[7] Individuals are plucked by random sample out of the networks of interdependence in which they are enmeshed. Their 'individual' responses or attitudes are then frequently represented as the properties of social atoms, the elementary units which combine to produce the properties of society as a whole. The reality, as the Frankfurters pointed out, is more nearly the opposite: individual beliefs and attitudes are themselves derived from and mediated by historical experience in society. We have to ask *why* people believe what they believe, and where possible to compare subjective opinion with objective reality. But in order to do that, it is necessary to take a developmental view, not to rely on the snapshot method of the opinion survey.

Something of what Adorno and his colleagues criticized in 'positivist' sociology lingers on in more recent works. One example from among many is Herbert Gans's *Popular Culture and High Culture* (1974). Gans sees 'high culture' and the various forms of popular culture which exist in contemporary America as 'taste-cultures' of equal worth.

> low culture is as valid for poorly educated Americans as high culture is for well-educated ones, even if the higher cultures are in the abstract better or more comprehensive than the lower cultures. (1974: ix)

He defines 'taste-culture' as 'the culture which results from choice; it has to do with those values and products about which people have some choice'. He contrasts this with political attitudes and activities, which

'cannot properly be classified as taste culture, although taste does play a role, for in many respects one's politics is not a matter of choice. Insofar as people's political values are determined by economic position, occupation, or religion, choice is restricted. (1974: 12–13)

The distinction between political and cultural attitudes expressed here is extraordinarily naïve; cultural atitudes and choices are at least as much shaped and restricted by economic position, occupation, education and so on as are political opinions. More important, Gans demonstrates particularly vividly that the liberal notion of 'taste' rests on the idea of the fully autonomous individual subject, and Adorno and his colleagues argued that in modern society individuals were no longer autonomous: their preferences were 'totally manipulated'. That view is as exaggerated as Gans's is naïve. What is perfectly clear, however, is that it is impossible to establish the degree to which preferences are shaped by social experience and to which individuals retain a measure of autonomy merely by studying a snapshot of the state of society and culture at one moment in time.

The controversy over 'positivism' in sociology became acute following a debate between Popper and Adorno at a meeting of the German Sociological Association in 1961. Over the next few years, several other prominent sociologists and philosophers continued the discussion,[8] during which the lines of disagreement became more closely defined. Popper considered it inappropriate that his position be described as positivist, since he had throughout his career opposed the philosophy of the Logical Positivists. Certainly, in view of his repeated statements that all observation is 'theory-impregnated', it was incorrect to represent him as a positivist if that means someone who holds a crudely empiricist respect for raw, uninterpreted facts. Adorno consequently made it clear that his central objection was to Popper's 'scientism', by which he meant his representation of the logic of the natural sciences as the supreme form of rationality.

The implications of the charge of scientism were more fully worked out by Jürgen Habermas (1972), who became Adorno's champion and successor in the later stages of the *Positivismusstreit*. Habermas contends that the pursuit of nomothetic theories – law-like generalizations about universal regularities in nature or society – is associated with a *technical* interest in prediction and control. It helps to understand why this is so if one considers why it was that natural scientists first borrowed the word 'law' from the social realm to describe their theories.[9] A 'law' was first, as it still is, a rule enforced by the power of the state or by other forms of community sanction. In other words, laws are one of the means by which rulers can control their subjects. In an analogous way, the establishment of 'laws' in the physical sciences led quite directly to increasing human control over nature. 'Laws of nature' in fact presuppose men as active agents; they can only be demonstrated and tested through certain operations such as laboratory experiments or observation. A scientific law is usually described as a statement of the form 'if A, then B', but that really means 'if you do A (under such and such conditions), then B will occur'. So, logically it is a short step from the discovery of universal regularities by pure scientists to their use by applied scientists – such as engineers building dams or bridges or steam-engines – to increase human control over the forces of nature.

Comte and his successors in the positivist tradition have believed that if 'laws' similar to those of the natural sciences could be found operating in human societies, then society and social forces could also be subjected to greater control for the benefit of mankind. Radcliffe-Brown quite explicitly saw the connection between the development of general theories in structural-functional anthropology and their application for the better government of British colonies. He seems to have fairly uncritically equated increasing the effectiveness and control of colonial administrators with the improvement of human welfare. Another example can be found in the field of industrial sociology. Leon Baritz (1960) has convincingly shown how the theories of the American 'human relations' school – stemming from the work of Elton Mayo and the Hawthorne experiments with their demonstration of apparently 'law-like' regularities in the dynamics of work-groups – came to be used as a tool to further the interests and enhance the control of industrial managers.

Habermas does not, however, argue that the discovery of nomothetic theories in the social sciences is either impossible or inherently undesirable. He does not seek to eradicate the technical interest, but to put it in its proper and limited place. He objects not to technical reason as such but to its universalization, to the representation of scientific and rational thought as the supreme form of rationality appropriate to all aspects of life. He speaks of 'technology and science as ideology' (1971: 81–122), and of the 'scientification of politics', which places the discussion of technical means above the more broadly rational discussion of human ends. History and the social sciences can play a part in making possible a more comprehensive form of rationality. Through the hermeneutic or interpretative process which is essential to their methodology, they have what Habermas calls a *practical* interest in making possible distortion-free communication within society. During the 1970s, in fact, Habermas was exploring the conditions for the creation of rational consensus, though many sociologists are sceptical about the value of these speculations.

Finally, in addition to the technical and practical, Habermas identifies a third 'knowledge-constitutive interest', which he calls *emancipatory*. A critical social science will not remain satisfied with the production of law-like theories, but will seek to go beyond that in order

> to determine when theoretical statements grasp invariant regularities of social action as such and when they express ideologically frozen relations of dependence that can in principle be transformed. To the extent that this is the case, [it will] take into account that information about lawlike connections sets off a process of reflection in the consciousness of those whom the laws are about. Thus the level of unreflected consciousness, which is one of the initial conditions of such laws, can be transformed. Of course, to this end a critically mediated knowledge of laws cannot through reflection alone render a law itself inoperative, but it can render it inapplicable. (Habermas 1972: 310)

Habermas looks to psychoanalysis and the Marxist critique of ideology – precisely to two bodies of thought whose status as science is disputed by Popper – for the beginnings of such a critical social science. Those were two of the principal ingredients of the kind of 'critical theory' associated with Adorno, Horkheimer and the first generation of the Frankfurt School. They described their critical theory as operating in the 'force-field' between concept and object.

> Adorno ... *presents a dialectic:* he shows how various modes of cognition, Marxist and non-Marxist, are inadequate and distorting when taken in isolation; and how by confronting them with each other precisely on the basis of their individual limitations, they may nevertheless yield insight into social processes. This approach, the analysis of reified theories and concepts, Adorno calls the 'immanent method'. (Rose 1978: 51)

For example, the relationship between culture industries and cultural consumers in modern society can be seen both in terms of the operation of iron laws of supply and demand and in terms of the manipulation of popular tastes. Through their cultural criticism, Adorno and his associates aspired to demonstrate that mass culture was not an inevitable fact but a human creation which, it was possible to conceive, could be changed by human will.

Habermas's theory of knowledge-constitutive interests goes far beyond Popper in exploring the kinds of knowledge which are not derived by the methods of the natural sciences. Yet there remains a similarity in aims between Popper and Habermas. Habermas too is concerned to identify the *a priori* conditions of possible knowledge, and if he does not find one single logic for the acquisition of knowledge, he is still looking for the eternal logics of various intellectual disciplines. So our reservations about the fruitfulness of Popper's enterprise may also be applied to Habermas's.

It is simpler to say that though the complexity of the ties of interdependence will always render social processes less than perfectly transparent to those enmeshed in them, one aim and result of social scientific investigations should always be to reduce the degree of opacity which people experience, to improve their means of orientation. Social investigations can in particular increase people's knowledge and awareness of the consequences of their actions, which in opaque social processes are frequently imperfectly foreseen and possibly unintended.

Irony and Sociology

One of the principal ingredients of great literature is irony. Characters in both tragedy and comedy fail to perceive the full significance of the situations in which they are caught up, and find themselves perversely mocked by – as it seems – fate. Their good deeds precipitate disaster, or evil intent is frustrated by circumstance. We savour irony because we, as observers, are granted greater knowledge of the situation than have the actors in it.

If the plots of real life lack the elegance of literature, they frequently abound in irony. More often than not, people's knowledge of the structure of the social processes in which they are entangled is imperfect. The situation may be incompletely known to any of the participants; even if they pool their partial knowledge, they may still not possess every piece of the jigsaw puzzle. There may be links and interdependencies unrecognized by anyone, and the figuration may play tricks on those enmeshed in it. The frequent inadequacy of the stock of knowledge at a person's disposal means that social actions very often have consequences which he has not foreseen. It may be that, had he foreseen these consequences, he would have considered them desirable, and would have intentionally committed the action nonetheless. It may be that he would have considered them undesirable and therefore, if they outweighed the benefits of any desirable consequences, refrained from the deed. There is also a large class of unforeseen consequences to which the actor would have been quite indifferent even had he anticipated them. As long as they do not foresee them, however, all three kinds of consequence remain, in Merton's famous phrase (1936), 'unanticipated consequences of purposive social action'. (As an entirely separate matter, if any of these three types of unintended consequence help to maintain the social *status quo*, the functionalist could call them latent functions; and if they undermine it, latent dysfunctions. But that is not now our concern.)

The most dramatically ironic of unanticipated consequences are the special cases of self-fulfilling and self-contradicting prophecies. In both, actions initially based on false premises have paradoxical outcomes. Merton (1968: 475–90) gives several examples of the self-fulfilling prophecy. American trade unionists earlier in the century often excluded blacks from union membership, in the belief that they accepted lower wages than whites, acted as blacklegs, and would not submit to union discipline. But their exclusion from the unions made it all the more likely that blacks would undercut union rates and break strikes. Later, of course, they gained admission to the unions and proved to be just as good members as whites. A number of economic processes are self-fulfilling. A bank may be perfectly solvent and adequately liquid for normal times. Yet if the belief spreads that it is not safe, people may begin to withdraw their deposits; and if the panic is not stemmed (and if the government does not prevent it) the hitherto solvent bank may rapidly become insolvent. Or, a case more familiar in recent decades, talk of the devaluation or revaluation of a country's currency may spark off international speculative flows of money and make it altogether more likely that the exchange rate will have to be changed. An example of a self-contradicting process is the 'paradox of thrift' (see Samuelson, 1961: 270–4). In the past, thrift was considered always to be a virtue; Weber took Benjamin Franklin's homilies on thrift as the very embodiment of the spirit of capitalism. In times of depression, people were urged to save more to restore prosperity. But private prudence can be public folly, In times of unemployment, the outcome of everyone *trying* to save more and consume less can be that production falls, the depression deepens and everyone actually saves *less*. Or consider the experiment of Prohibition in America (Mennell 1969). Many Americans initially gave their support to Prohibition, not because they were bible-belt fundamentalists but because they were Progressives seeking reform, and the liquor industry was intimately linked with crime and corruption. They did not, however, allow for the tenacity of public demand for alcohol, and it is a familiar story that the demand continued to be met illegally, and that Prohibition immeasurably increased crime and corruption.

Self-fulfilling and self-contradicting prophecies are nevertheless only among the most melodramatic examples of unanticipated consequences of action. Imperfect knowledge is much more pervasive than are such perversities. The unanticipated consequences of people's actions only rarely return like boomerangs to hit them. Throwing stones into a pool is usually a better analogy: the consequences ripple outwards through society until we lose sight of them.

This is especially true where the consequences of actions only become perceptible when carried on by numerous people separately; the link between these consequences and the actions of any single individual may remain largely unperceived. Take for example the growth of private car ownership. The benefits and convenience of private transport are easy for the individual driver to see, but the social consequences to which he singly and alone contributes only imperceptibly are, in economic parlance, externalities to him and to millions of other motorists. The individual does not intend or anticipate that his own particular car will cause traffic congestion, environmental pollution, urban sprawl, hideous motorways across beautiful countryside, the decline of rural communities, the decline of city-centre shopping and burgeoning green-field shopping centres, or death, mutilation and hospital bills. Nor is any single individual buying a car much aware of his contribution to a compelling social trend which makes it difficult for others not to emulate him: as the number of private cars on the road increases, those who still do not have one increasingly find that public transport becomes less frequent or disappears, that shops are no longer nearby, and their friends live in inaccessible places. How can they then willingly remain pedestrians?

The unanticipated consequences of social action are not a whimsical footnote to sociological theory, but of central significance to both the discovery and application of sociological knowledge. In order to discover and explain them, it is necessary to make simultaneous use of two approaches to sociological theory often considered alternatives or even contradictory – to study both the subjective knowledge and assumptions on which people base their actions, and also the objective social interdependencies of which they may be wholly or partly unaware. Certainly it is necessary to discover what meaning people attach to their social situations. To quote Thomas's remark once more: if men define situations as real, they are real in their consequences. That does not mean that all their definitions are self-fulfilling. Far from it. The realities of social interdependence have a way of invalidating definitions of the situation which are ill-founded. Thomas merely meant that any sociological explanation which neglects to consider how people perceive their situations risks going sadly adrift. Whether people's definitions of situations are factual or fanciful makes a considerable difference. On the other hand, any sociology which studies *only* how people define situations is equally deficient. If the sociologist is to unravel social processes he must be able to spot the consequences of people's actions which they did not spot, and this involves identifying the links missing from participants' pictures of their social interdependencies. Indeed Murphy (1971: 147) has suggested that unintended consequences of social actions are 'the principal *raison d'être* of the social sciences; if society followed rational intent, it would be so transparent that sociologists and anthropologists would all be out of jobs'.

Unforeseen consequences are among the chief sources of the uncontrolled and unpredictable in social life, and in detecting them the social scientist helps to make society more plannable and predictable. That is why public and politicians often view sociology as an adjunct to policy-making, a responsibility which some sociologists assume with greater alacrity than others. For social investigations, like any other social activity, frequently have unanticipated consequences. We cannot always be sure beforehand whether the growth of knowledge will serve to increase the compellingness of social processes or to enable people to bring them under rational control. But even those who view with disquiet some of the uses to which social scientific knowledge can be put would not for that reason seek to discourage the pursuit of that knowledge.

Notes

Chapter 1

1. Cf. the views advanced by Jürgen Habermas in *Zur Logik der Sozialwissenschaften* (1970). For an extensive discussion in English of Habermas's thinking, see McCarthy (1978), especially in this context pages 160–2.

2. A first-class and readable account of Chomsky's work is Lyons (1970).

3. Probably some imperfectly understood process of physiological maturation is involved; this question is examined in detail by Lenneberg (1967). He argues that 'cognitive function is species-specific'. That is not to deny, of course, that exposure to the use of language is essential at crucial stages of maturation.

4. The text of this quotation is based on the translations given by Outhwaite (1975: 85) and by McCarthy (1978: 152).

5. See C. Wright Mills (1964) for a relevant discussion of philosophy and social thought in America at that period.

6. The city is the largest social unit on which they focused. The 'Chicago school' between the wars is often thought of as a school of urban sociology, although as Rose (1962: viii) notes, urban sociology as such was not considered by members of the Chicago faculty themselves to be more than a minor sub-field. The urban ecology developed by Park, Burgess and McKenzie (1925) is perhaps the most macroscopic theoretical product of the Chicago interactionist tradition. But most of the classic texts of Chicago urban sociology – such as Nels Anderson's *The Hobo* (1923), H. W. Zorbaugh's *The Gold Coast and the Slum* (1929), E. Franklin Frazier's *The Negro Family in Chicago* (1932), and Louis Wirth's *The Ghetto* (1938) – deal with the ways of life of relatively small and specific groups found within the city. For a recent defence of symbolic interactionism as a general perspective in sociology, see Rock (1978).

7. This is emphasized by Daniel Glaser (1962), on whose article I have drawn here.

8. 'Attention' always played a key part in the pragmatists' arguments against behaviourism. See particularly John Dewey's influential paper originally published in 1896, 'The Unit of Behaviour' (1931). Dewey argued that the stimulus was neither completely prior to behaviour nor completely external to the mind; behaviour was therefore to be understood in terms not of a 'reflex arc' but of a 'circuit' – what would now be called a cybernetic relationship.

9. I am indebted for this phrase to an article (1971) by my colleague Robert Witkin.

10. This perhaps applies most emphatically to the 'Culture and Personality' school of anthropologists. For an interesting discussion of that, see Harris (1968), chapters 15–17.

11. See the collection of papers on phenomenological philosophy and sociology edited by Luckmann (1978).

12. Doubt has been cast on Schutz's fidelity to Husserl's method – see Bauman (1973a) and Hindess (1972). A few sociologists have also been influenced by the more romantic phenomenology of Maurice Merleau-Ponty. See Merleau-Ponty (1974), O'Neill (1970, 1972), and Filmer *et al.* (1972: 123 ff.) For an interpretation of earlier sociologists in the light of existential phenomenology, see Tiryakian (1965).

13. See also Schutz and Luckmann, *The Structures of the Life-World* (1974), a book completed by Luckmann from notes left by Schutz at his death.

14. The resemblances to Cooley's idea of 'the looking-glass self' is striking; indeed Laing conjures up a whole hall of mirrors.

15. The standard translation is clumsy at this point, and I have taken the improved wording from Giddens (1971: 79).

16. See R. C. Hinkle's essay 'Durkheim in American Sociology' (1960).

17. A particularly judicious and well-translated selection of Weber's work is that edited by Runciman (1978).

18. References in this book to *Wirtschaft und Gesellschaft* are to the three-volume complete translation of 1968. In this one case, however, I have quoted Talcott Parsons's original translation which conveys the meaning slightly more fully.

19. On this point, cf. Schutz (1962: 56).

20. These two terms pose such problems of translation that they are generally used in the German. Literally they mean 'purpose-rationality' and 'value-rationality' respectively. *Zweckrationalität* is sometimes rendered as 'instrumental rationality' or even 'economic rationality'. The best rendering of *Wertrationalität* I have come across is Fletcher's (1971: II,443) 'Social Action employing Rational Means in the services of an Accepted End'.

21. It also discusses Pareto and, to a lesser extent, the classical economists,

especially Alfred Marshall. For reasons of space I cannot discuss these authors. In any case, Pareto's influence on contemporary sociology is now very minor.

22. See especially Parsons's essay 'The Super-ego and the theory of Social Systems' (Parsons, Bales and Shils 1953, chapter 1).

23. Bershady (1973) argues that from the early years of his academic life Parsons was haunted by the problem of relativism – the view that absolutely certain and objective knowledge is, at least in the social sciences, impossible. In order to rebut relativism, according to Bershady, Parsons adopted an essentially Kantian strategy, seeking to determine the immutable *a priori* categories of thought indispensable to any scientific knowledge. Indeed, in *The Structure of Social Action*, Parsons did compare his social action framework to the space-time categories of (Newtonian) physics, which Kant saw as the fundamental forms of all perception. For Parsons's own revealing account of his intellectual development, see Parsons (1977a).

24. Parsons normally mentions the organism as a fourth level of organization. Though sociologists rarely need to refer to biological processes, Parsons is right to mention them, as it is known that hormonal disturbances or drugs, for instance, can have temporary or even permanent effects on behaviour. More generally, in Parsons's schema, the body is among the conditions which limit action. For a discussion of cybernetics, see pages 80–82.

25. To be fair to Parsons, this point is expressed in his distinction between the function of 'pattern-maintenance' and the function of 'integration' (see pages 71–73), but he often seemed to underemphasize it.

Chapter 2

1. This last variable seems even more obviously continuous (as opposed to dichotomous) than the rest. The majority of actions are 'collectivity orientated'. But how broad is the collectivity in question in each case – one's family, one's country, or humanity in general? Parsons's answer would be that it depends on the 'system of reference' under discussion; and indeed this fifth pattern variable was later absorbed into the AGIL schema as the distinction between internal and external functions (see pages 71–73.

2. See Robert Dubin's article (1960) and Parsons's reply, 'Pattern Variables Revisited' (1960); and also McCarthy (1978: 220).

3. Amongst an extensive literature on this, see Bales (1950); Parsons, Bales and Shils (1953); Parsons and Bales (1955).

4. Simmel's influence can be clearly seen in later theoretical and empirical studies of the formation of coalitions in three-person groups. See in particular Caplow (1968).

5. Schutz described this from the phenomenological point of view in terms of 'consociates' and others who are typified in various degrees of abstraction. See page 21 above.

6. Elias does not use game models in quite the same way as von Neumann and Morgenstern (1944) and their numerous followers. They tend to use *relatively* simple models as the basis of a rigorous decision-theory, to demonstrate rational courses of action and winning strategies. Elias uses his models heuristically to demonstrate, among other things, how in progressively more complex situations, rational courses of action and winning strategies become steadily less easy to discern and more indeterminate.

7. I have modified the published translation of this passage, drawing on the earlier, unpublished translation by Eric Dunning.

Chapter 3

1. This allusion to a long-standing discussion in sociology is phrased with caution. It is no longer safe, if ever it was, to assume that 'industrialization caused the nuclear family'. In England, the first industrial country, it is now apparent that the ties of kinship were rather loose long before the so-called Industrial Revolution. See Macfarlane (1978).

2. See Demerath and Peterson (1967) for a collection of articles which amply demonstrates the wide ramifications of the controversy over functionalism. See also Giddens's essay 'Functionalism – *après la lutte*' (1977: 96–129).

3. Harris (1968: 526) argues that this programme led to the neglect of such historical data (from earlier travellers, for example) as did exist concerning pre-literate societies.

4. This 'postulate of functional unity' is frequently contrasted with the American anthropologist Lowie's (1920: 441) description of culture as a thing of 'shreds and patches', but this remark is misleading as a guide to Lowie's views; he did not despair of finding *any* regularity in cultural data.

5. The niceties of the AGIL scheme are explained more fully in Rocher (1974: 40 ff.) For another view of the rise and fall of Parsons's functional requisites, see Sklair (1970).

6. The successive contributions to the debate are surveyed by Huaco (1966). See also Wrong (1959).

7. Just how static actually were the societies studied by anthropologists in the early twentieth century is in dispute. An unchanging 'traditional way of life' before the impact of civilization was perhaps too readily assumed. And where stasis was observed, it may have been the fairly recent product of the policies of the colonial power, especially in British Africa.

8. On functional autonomy and reciprocity, see Gouldner (1959).

9. The 'causes of another sort' do not always materialize. As Percy Cohen (1968: 41) neatly remarks, 'it could be argued that men need a way of settling all disputes without violence; but they do not have one.'

10. Functionalists have certainly seen their work as *useful* – Radcliffe-Brown for one constantly emphasized the utility of anthropology for colonial government. But they saw the functional approach itself as (in Habermas's terms) empirical-analytic, not normative-analytic.

11. Little of Luhmann's work has been translated into English. For a short summary of the main issues of his debate with Habermas, see McCarthy (1978: 219–22).

12. Althusser is normally classified as a structuralist Marxist, since it is from French structuralism that his arguments derive much of their form (see Glucksmann 1974). Lately, however, he has claimed only to have 'flirted' with structuralism (Althusser 1976: 126–31) and, taking a broad view of his writings, it is the resemblances to old-fashioned functionalism which are most striking. See Thompson's scathing critique (1978).

13. For a good discussion of rival theories about 'developing societies', see Hoogvelt (1976).

14. These brief remarks are intended to hint that neither vulgar Marxist beliefs in 'iron laws of history', nor Popper's dogmatic denial (1945, 1957) that any such 'laws' are possible, is adequate for sociological purposes. See Elias (1978a: Chapter 6).

Chapter 4

1. See for example Mishan (1960), Coleman (1966, 1972, 1973), Olson (1965), Arrow (1951, 1967).

2. Talcott Parsons (1963) used the term power in an entirely different sense; he was really concerned more with what I have called the problem of collective action than with power in Weber's or most other sociologists' sense. For critiques of this aspect of Parsons's thinking, see Coleman (1963), Rocher (1974: 63–67, 77–97) and Giddens (1977: 333–46).

3. For an explanation of the connection between power and intention, see White (1971) and Wrong (1968).

4. Marx himself spoke of alienation in several senses. For a careful analysis of these and pre-Marxian usages, see Schacht (1971, chapters 1–3); and for a full-length study of the place of alienation in Marx's thought as a whole, see Ollman (1976).

5. How this freedom of choice is to be made compatible with the degree of specialization and interdependence necessary to support the present population of the globe is not entirely evident from Marx's work.

6. This *is* too simplistic. Durkheim's treatment of altrusitic suicide makes it plain that he felt that social constraint could also be excessive. 'Durkheim argues in effect that the relations of suicide rates to social regulation is curvilinear – high rates being associated with both excessive individuation and excessive regulation.' (Coser 1971 : 134.)

7. This perspective on power has been most thoroughly explored by the 'exchange theorists', including Homans (1961), Thibaut and Kelley (1959), Emerson (1962) and Blau (1964). Their basic idea is a simple one. Where two or more people are equally interdependent, their mutual obligation may impose constraints on them, but none is 'more powerful' than the others. However, if social exchange is not fully reciprocal, if one person or group is more dependent on another than the other is on it, then unreciprocated benefits produce power differentials. Exchange theorists have borrowed the paraphernalia of economics to give their ideas a false air of precision. For critiques of exchange theory, see Ekeh (1974) and Heath (1976). See also Martin (1977).

8. For an excellent discussion of that literature, see Giddens (1973). Crompton and Gubbay (1977) present a reply in the Marxian mould to the neo-Weberian position represented by Giddens.

9. The connection between opacity and social stability has been noted by writers of various theoretical persuasions. Althusser, whose view that social formations constitute highly stable structures-in-dominance was discussed in chapter 3, argues that communist as well as capitalist societies remain opaque to the individuals living in them. That is the function of ideology, and 'all human societies secrete ideology as the very element and atmosphere indispensable to their historical respiration and life' (Althusser 1969: 232). On a more empirical plane, the connection between opacity and contentment can be seen through the idea of relative deprivation. There is considerable evidence that most people most of the time do not pay much heed to the distribution of rewards in society as a whole. They compare their lot not with groups remote from them and vastly better off than themselves, but with people known more directly who are a little better off or a little worse off. They experience deprivation not in absolute terms but in relation to particular reference groups or to accustomed standards. Runciman (1966) uses this idea of relative deprivation to explain why the British were not more discontented with social inequalities. On the other hand it is implicit in Durkheim's discussion of anomie that the deregulation of people's customary aspirations by rapid social or economic change can increase their sense of relative deprivation. J. C. Davis (1962) used this insight to explain the incidence of revolutions.

10. Dahrendorf later (1967) rejected this approach. Though it is not easy to test the hypothesis that relationships to authority are the prime determinant of group consciousness, Lopreato (1968) did attempt to do so. His findings were not favourable to Dahrendorf's original thesis.

11. Karl Mannheim's (1936) conception of 'total ideology' should also be noted among the antecedents of the idea.

12. See also Therborn (1978).

13. In Elias's investigation of the civilizing process (summarized on pages 57–60), we have already seen one example of such a study which does not involve the altogether more problematic ideas of true or false consciousness.

Chapter 5

1. A first-class account of research into the relationship between culture and thought and its ramifications is Cole and Scribner (1974).

2. These remarks touch upon the controversy surrounding Lévi-Strauss's *Elementary Structures of Kinship* (1968b, orig. 1949), but there is no space to discuss that here. A very clear (brutally clear) account of this confused debate can be found in Harris (1968: 487–513); alternatively, see Leach (1970: 95–111), or (briefer and more sympathetic) Murphy (1972: 197–205).

3. The last sentence is obscure in the French: '*Nous ne prétendons donc pas montrer comment les hommes pensent dans les mythes mais comment les mythes se pensent dans les hommes et à leur insu.*' Two published English translations are somewhat at odds.

4. For a more general exposition of structuralist analysis in social anthropology, see Leach (1976). An interesting and specifically sociological view of Lévi-Strauss is presented by Badcock (1975), who relates his thinking to that of Comte, Durkheim, Mauss, Parsons and Freud.

5. Wittgensteinian philosophy has also been a notable influence on ethonomethodology, although it may have been used to give *post facto* support to a stance which had already evolved. For some remarks on the connection between Wittgensteinian philosophy and ethnomethodology, see Mennell (1975), on which the present discussion is partly based, and Hughes (1977).

6. See Habermas (1976b) and McCarthy (1978: 410–12).

Chapter 6

1. These remarks about the sociology of knowledge are necessarily brief. See Curtis and Petras (1970) for an excellent introduction to the field, and the stimulating essay by Barnes (1977).

2. Popper's views on science are set out principally in *The Logic of Scientific*

Discovery (1959), *Conjectures and Refutations* (1963) and *Objective Knowledge: An Evolutionary Approach* (1972). Magee (1973) give a lucid overall account of Popper's ideas, though understating the criticisms which have been levelled at them. In *Unended Quest* (1976), Popper gives a fascinating and readable picture of his own intellectual development.

3. This argument is pushed to an extreme by Althusser and his followers who, paradoxically for self-styled Marxists, adopt a form of old-fashioned philosophical idealism. See Althusser and Balibar (1970) and Hindess and Hirst (1975: 308–23).

4. See Lakatos and Musgrave (1970) for a discussion of Kuhn's work, chiefly by Popperians. Lakatos's article in that volume is particularly important as an attempt to retain the main principles of Popper's philosophy of science while incorporating many of Kuhn's insights. In his reply to his critics, Kuhn concedes a good deal of ground to the Popperians, and this is also evident in the second edition of his own book.

5. For a careful analysis of this ancestry and of the several varieties of positivism, see Giddens (1977: 29–89).

6. Martin Jay (1973) provides a history of the work of the Frankfurt School from its foundation in 1923 and the development of its members' thought up to its return to Germany in 1950.

7. See particularly Pollock (1976) and Adorno (1976).

8. The main papers are collected in Adorno *et al.* (1976).

9. For this point and the exposition which immediately follows I am indebted to an unpublished paper on 'The improvement of orientation as a primary task of the social sciences' by my friend Godfried van Benthem van den Bergh.

Bibliography

Aberle, D. F., A. K. Cohen, A. K. Davis, M. J. Levy, Jr and F. X. Sutton, 1950: The Functional Prerequisites of a Society. *Ethics*, **60**, 2, 100–11.

Adorno, Theodor W., 1976 (orig. 1957): Sociology and Empirical Research. In *Critical Sociology* (P. Connerton, ed.), pp. 237–57. Penguin, Harmondsworth. Also in T. W. Adorno *et al.*, *The Positivist Dispute in German Sociology*, pp. 68–86. Heinemann, London, 1976.

Adorno, Theodor W., H. Albert, R. Dahrendorf, J. Habermas, H. Pilot and K. R. Popper, 1976: *The Positivist Dispute in German Sociology*. Heinemann, London.

Althusser, Louis, 1969: *For Marx*. Allen Lane, London.

Althusser, Louis, 1971: Ideology and Ideological State Apparatuses. In *Lenin and Philosophy and other Essays*, pp. 121–73. New Left Books, London.

Althusser, Louis, 1976: *Essays in Self-Criticism*. New Left Books, London.

Althusser, Louis and Etienne Balibar, 1970: *Reading Capital*. New Left Books, London.

Anderson, Nels, 1923: *The Hobo*. University of Chicago Press, Chicago.

Anderson, Perry, 1976: *Considerations on Western Marxism*. New Left Books, London.

Aristotle, 1905: *Aristotle's Politics* (trans. by Benjamin Jowett). Clarendon Press, Oxford.

Arrow, Kenneth J., 1951: *Social Choice and Individual Values*. Wiley, New York.

Arrow, Kenneth J., 1967: Values and Collective Decision-Making. In *Philosophy, Politics and Society*, 3rd series (P. Laslett and W. G. Runciman, eds.), pp. 215–32. Basil Blackwell, Oxford.

Bachrach, P. and M. S. Baratz, 1970: *Power and Poverty: Theory and Practice*. Oxford University Press, New York.

Bacon, Francis, 1960 (orig. 1620): *Novum Organum*. Bobbs-Merrill, Indianapolis.

Badcock, C. R., 1975: *Lévi-Strauss, Structuralism and Sociological Theory*. Hutchinson, London.

Bales, Robert F., 1950: *Interaction Process Analysis*. Addison-Wesley, Cambridge, Mass.

Baritz, Leon, 1960: *The Servants of Power: A History of the Use of Social Science in American Industry.* Wesleyan University Press, Middletown, Conn.

Barnes, Barry, 1977: *Interests and the Growth of Knowledge.* Routledge and Kegan Paul, London.

Bauman, Z. A., 1973a: On the Philosophical Status of Ethnomethodology. *Sociological Review,* ns, **21**, 1, 5–23.

Bauman, Z. A., 1973b: *Culture as Praxis.* Routledge and Kegan Paul, London.

Becker, Howard S., 1963: *Outsiders.* Free Press, New York.

Berger, Peter, 1973: *The Social Reality of Religion.* Penguin Books, Harmondsworth. (Published in U.S.A. under the title *The Sacred Canopy.* Doubleday, Garden City, N.Y., 1967.)

Berger, Peter and Thomas Luckmann, 1967: *The Social Construction of Reality.* Allen Lane, London.

Bershady, Harold J., 1973: *Ideology and Social Knowledge.* Basil Blackwell, Oxford.

Bierstedt, Robert, 1950: An Analysis of Social Power. *American Sociological Review,* **15**, 6, 730–38. Reprinted in *Power and Progress,* pp. 220–41. McGraw-Hill, New York, 1974.

Blalock, Hubert M., Jr, 1964: *Causal Inference in Non-experimental Research.* University of North Carolina Press, Chapel Hill.

Blalock, Hubert M., Jr, 1967: *Toward a Theory of Minority Group Relations.* Wiley, New York.

Blalock, Hubert M., Jr, 1970: The Formalization of Sociological Theory. In *Theoretical Sociology* (J. C. McKinney and E. A. Tiryakian, eds.), pp. 272–300. Appleton-Century-Crofts, New York.

Blau, Peter M., 1955: *The Dynamics of Bureaucracy.* University of Chicago Press, Chicago.

Blau, Peter M., 1964: *Exchange and Power in Social Life.* Wiley, New York.

Blauner, Robert, 1964: *Alienation and Freedom.* University of Chicago Press, Chicago.

Blumer, Herbert, 1969: *Symbolic Interactionism: Perspective and Method.* Prentice-Hall, Englewood Cliffs, N.J.

Boas, Franz, 1911: *The Mind of Primitive Man.* Macmillan, New York.

Boissevain, Jeremy, 1974: *Friends of Friends.* Basil Blackwell, Oxford.

Bott, Elizabeth, 1955: Urban Families: Conjugal Roles and Social Networks. *Human Relations,* **8**, 4, 345–84.

Bott, Elizabeth, 1957: *Family and Social Network.* Tavistock Publications, London.

Brown, A. R. Radcliffe-, 1952: *Structure and Function in Primitive Society.* Cohen and West, London.

Brown, Roger, 1965: *Social Psychology.* Free Press, New York.

Buckley, Walter, 1967: *Sociology and Modern Systems Theory.* Prentice-Hall, Englewood Cliffs, N.J.

Burgess, R. L. and D. Bushell, eds., 1969: *Behavioural Sociology: The Experimental Analysis of Behaviour.* Columbia University Press, New York.

Caplow, Theodore, 1968: *Two Against One: Coalitions in Triads.* Prentice-Hall, Englewood Cliffs, N.J.

Catton, William R., Jr, 1964: The Development of Sociological Thought. In *Handbook of Modern Sociology* (R. E. L. Faris, ed.), pp. 912–50. Rand McNally, Chicago.

Chomsky, Noam, 1959: Review of Skinner's *Verbal Behaviour*. *Language*, **35**, 1, 26–58. Reprinted in *The Structure of Language* (J. A. Fodor and J. J. Katz, eds.), pp. 547–78. Prentice-Hall, Englewood Cliffs, N.J., 1964.

Chomsky, Noam, 1967: The Formal Nature of Language. Appendix A to E. H. Lenneberg, *Biological Foundations of Language*. Wiley, New York.

Cicourel, Aaron V., 1964: *Method and Measurement in Sociology*. Free Press, New York.

Cicourel, Aaron V., 1968: *The Social Organization of Juvenile Justice*. Wiley, New York.

Cicourel, Aaron V., 1973: *Cognitive Sociology*. Penguin, Harmondsworth.

Cloward, R. A. and L. E. Ohlin, 1960: *Delinquency and Opportunity*. Free Press, New York.

Cohen, Percy S., 1968: *Modern Social Theory*. Heinemann, London.

Cole, Michael and Sylvia Scribner, 1974: *Culture and Thought: A Psychological Introduction*. Wiley, New York.

Coleman, James S., 1963: Comment on 'On the Concept of Influence'. *Public Opinion Quarterly*, **27**, 1, 63–82.

Coleman, James S., 1966: Foundations for a Theory of Collective Decisions. *American Journal of Sociology*, **71**, 6, 615–27.

Coleman, James S., 1972: Collective Decisions and Collective Action. In *Philosophy, Politics and Society*, 4th series (P. Laslett, W. G. Runciman, and Q. Skinner, eds.), pp. 208–19. Basil Blackwell, Oxford.

Coleman, James S., 1973: *The Mathematics of Collective Action*. Aldine Books, Chicago.

Comte, Auguste, 1830: *Cours de philosophie positive*, Vol. I. Bachelier, Paris.

Coser, Lewis A., 1956: *The Functions of Social Conflict*. Routledge and Kegan Paul, London.

Coser, Lewis A., 1971: *Masters of Sociological Thought*. Harcourt Brace Jovanovitch, New York.

Coser, Lewis A., 1972: Marxist Thought in the First Quarter of the Twentieth Century. *American Journal of Sociology*, **78**, 1, 173–201.

Crenson, Matthew A., 1971: *The Un-Politics of Air Pollution*. John Hopkins Press, Baltimore.

Crompton, Rosemary and Jon Gubbay, 1977: *Economy and Class Structure*. Macmillan, London.

Curtis, J. E. and Petras, J. W., 1970: *The Sociology of Knowledge: A Reader*. Duckworth, London.

Dahl, Robert A., 1961: *Who Governs?* Yale University Press, New Haven.

Dahrendorf, Ralf, 1959: *Class and Class Conflict in Industrial Society*. Stanford University Press, Stanford, Cal.

Dahrendorf, Ralf, 1967: *Conflict after Class: New Perspectives on the Theory of Social and Political Conflict*. Longmans, London.

Davis, James C., 1962: Toward a Theory of Revolution. *American Sociological Review*, **27**, 1, 5–19.

Davis, Kingsley, 1959: The Myth of Functional Analysis as a Special Method in Sociology and Anthropology. *American Sociological Review*, **24,** 6, 757–72.

Davis, Kingsley and Wilbert E. Moore, 1945: Some Principles of Stratification. *American Sociological Review*, **10,** 2, 242–9.

Dawe, Alan, 1970: The Two Sociologies. *British Sociological Review*, **21,** 2, 207–18.

Demerath, N. J., III, and R. A. Peterson, eds., 1967: *System, Change and Conflict*. Free Press, New York.

Deutsch, Karl W., 1961: Social Mobilization and Political Development. *American Political Science Review*, **60,** 3, 493–514.

Dewey, John, 1931 (orig. 1896): The Unit of Behaviour. In *Philosophy and Civilization*. G. P. Putnam's Sons, New York.

Douglas, Jack D., 1967: *The Social Meanings of Suicide*. Princeton University Press, Princeton, N.J.

Douglas, Jack D., ed., 1971: *Understanding Everyday Life*. Routledge and Kegan Paul, London.

Dubin, Robert, 1960: Parsons's Actor: Continuities in Social Theory. *American Sociological Review*, **25,** 4, 457–66.

Durkheim, Emile, 1933 (orig. 1893): *The Division of Labour in Society*. Macmillan, New York.

Durkheim, Emile, 1938 (orig. 1895): *The Rules of Sociological Method*. University of Chicago Press, Chicago.

Durkheim, Emile, 1951 (orig. 1897): *Suicide*. Free Press, Glencoe, Ill.

Durkheim, Emile, 1953 (orig. 1898): Individual and Collective Representations. In *Sociology and Philosophy*, pp. 1–34. Cohen and West, London.

Durkheim, Emile, 1960: Pragmatism and Sociology. In *Essays on Sociology and Philosophy by Emile Durkheim et al.*, pp. 386–436. Harper and Row, New York.

Durkheim, Emile, 1965 (orig. 1912): *The Elementary Forms of the Religious Life*. Free Press, New York.

Durkheim, Emile and Marcel Mauss, 1963 (orig. 1903): *Primitive Classification*. Cohen and West, London.

Ekeh, Peter P., 1974: *Social Exchange Theory: The Two Traditions*. Heinemann, London.

Elias, Norbert, 1956: Problems of Involvement and Detachment. *British Journal of Sociology*, **7,** 3, 226–52.

Elias, Norbert, 1971: Sociology of Knowledge – New Perspectives. *Sociology* **5,** 2–3, 149–68, 355–70.

Elias, Norbert, 1978a: *What is Sociology?* Hutchinson, London.

Elias, Norbert, 1978b (orig. 1939): *The Civilizing Process: The History of Manners*. Basil Blackwell, Oxford, and Urizen, New York.

Elias, Norbert, forthcoming (orig. 1939): *The Civilizing Process: The Dynamics of the State*. Basil Blackwell, Oxford, and Urizen, New York.

Emerson, Richard M., 1962: Power-Dependence Relations. *American Sociological Review*, **27,** 1, 31–41.

Emmet, Dorothy, and Alasdair MacIntyre, eds., 1970: *Sociological Theory and Philosophical Analysis*. Macmillan, London.

Etzioni, Amitai, 1968: *The Active Society*. Free Press, New York.

Faris, R. E. L., 1967: *Chicago Sociology 1920–32*. Chandler, San Francisco.

Feuer, Lewis S., 1953: Sociological Aspects of the Relation between Language and Philosophy. *Philosophy of Science*, **20,** 2, 85–100.

Feyerabend, Paul K., 1975: *Against Method*. New Left Books, London.

Filmer, Paul, Michael Phillipson, David Silverman and David Walsh, 1972: *New Directions in Sociological Theory*. Collier-Macmillan, London.

Fletcher, Ronald, 1971: *The Making of Sociology*, vols. I and II. Michael Joseph, London.

Frank, André Gunder, 1967: *Capitalism and Underdevelopment in Latin America*. Monthly Review Press, New York.

Frank, André Gunder, 1971: *Sociology of Development and the Underdevelopment of Sociology*. Pluto Press, London.

Frazer, Sir James, 1890: *The Golden Bough*. Macmillan, London.

Frazier, E. Franklin, 1932: *The Negro Family in Chicago*. University of Chicago Press, Chicago.

Freud, Sigmund, 1962 (orig. 1930): *Civilization and its Discontents*. W. W. Norton, New York.

Friedrichs, Robert W., 1970: *A Sociology of Sociology*. Free Press, New York.

Galbraith, John Kenneth, 1952: *American Capitalism*. Hamish Hamilton, London.

Gans, Herbert, 1974: *Popular Culture and High Culture*. Basic Books, New York.

Garfinkel, Harold, 1967: *Studies in Ethnomethodology*. Prentice-Hall, Englewood Cliffs, N.J.

Gellner, Ernest, 1960: Review of Peter Winch, *The Idea of a Social Science*. *British Journal of Sociology*, **11,** 2, 170–72.

Germani, Gino, 1968: Secularisation, Modernisation and Economic Development. In *The Protestant Ethic and Modernisation* (S. N. Eisenstadt, ed.), pp. 343–66. Basic Books, New York.

Giddens, Anthony, 1971: *Capitalism and Modern Social Theory*. Cambridge University Press, Cambridge.

Giddens, Anthony, 1973: *The Class Structure of the Advanced Societies*. Hutchinson, London.

Giddens, Anthony, 1976: *New Rules of Sociological Method*. Hutchinson, London.

Giddens, Anthony, 1977: *Studies in Social and Political Theory*. Hutchinson, London.

Glaser, Daniel, 1962: The Differential-Association Theory of Crime. In *Human Behaviour and Social Processes* (A. M. Rose, ed.), pp. 425–42. Routledge and Kegan Paul, London.

Gluckman, Max, 1955: *Custom and Conflict in Africa*. Basil Blackwell, Oxford.

Glucksman, Miriam, 1974: *Structuralist Analysis in Contemporary Social Thought*, Routledge and Kegan Paul, London.

Goffman, Erving, 1955: On Face-Work. *Psychiatry*, **18**, 3, 213–31. Reprinted in *Interaction Ritual*, pp. 5–45. Doubleday, Garden City, N.Y., 1967.

Goffman, Erving, 1959: *The Presentation of Self in Everyday Life*. Doubleday, Garden City, N.Y. (Harmondsworth, Penguin, 1971).

Goffman, Erving, 1961a: *Asylums*. Doubleday, Garden City, N.Y. (Harmondsworth, Penguin, 1968).

Goffman, Erving, 1961b: Role-distance. In *Encounters*. Bobbs-Merrill, Indianapolis. Also in *Where the Action Is*. Allen Lane, London, 1969.

Goldthorpe, John H., D. Lockwood, F. Bechofer and J. Platt, 1969: *The Affluent Worker in the Class Structure*. Cambridge University Press, Cambridge.

Goody, Jack, 1977: *The Domestication of the Savage Mind*. Cambridge University Press, Cambridge.

Gouldner, Alvin W., 1959: Reciprocity and Autonomy in Functional Theory. In *Symposium on Sociological Theory* (Llewellyn Gross, ed.), pp. 241–70. Harper and Row, New York.

Gouldner, Alvin W., 1971: *The Coming Crisis of Western Sociology*. Heinemann, London.

Gramsci, Antonio, 1971: *Selections from the Prison Notebooks*. Lawrence and Wishart, London.

Grathoff, Richard, ed., 1978: *The Theory of Social Action: The Correspondence of Alfred Schutz and Talcott Parsons*. Indiana University Press, Bloomington.

Green, R. W. ed., 1959: *Protestantism and Capitalism: The Weber Thesis and its Critics*. D. C. Heath, Lexington, Mass.

Gross, N., W. S. Mason and A. McEachern, 1958: *Explorations in Role Analysis*. Wiley, New York.

Habermas, Jürgen, 1970: *Zur Logik der Sozialwissenschaften*, 2nd ed. Suhrkamp, Frankfurt.

Habermas, Jürgen, 1971: *Toward a Rational Society*. Heinemann, London.

Habermas, Jürgen, 1972: *Knowledge and Human Interests*. Heinemann, London.

Habermas, Jürgen, 1974: *Theory and Practice*. Heinemann, London.

Habermas, Jürgen, 1976a: *Legitimation Crisis*. Heinemann, London.

Habermas, Jürgen, 1976b: On Communicative Action. Paper delivered at the Boston Colloquium for the Philosophy of Science.

Habermas, Jürgen, and Niklas Luhmann, 1971: *Theorie der Gesellschaft oder Sozialtechnologie – Was leistet die Systemforschung?* Suhrkamp, Frankfurt.

Harris, Marvin, 1968: *The Rise of Anthropological Theory*. Routledge and Kegan Paul, London.

Heath, Anthony, 1976: *Rational Choice and Social Exchange*. Cambridge University Press, Cambridge.

Hempel, C. G., 1959: The Logic of Functional Analysis. In *Symposium on Sociological Theory* (L. Gross, ed.), pp. 271–307. Harper and Row, New York.

Hindess, Barry, 1972: The 'phenomenological' sociology of Alfred Schutz. *Economy and Society*, **1**, 1, 1–27.

Hindess, Barry, 1973: *The Use of Official Statistics in Sociology: A Critique of Positivism and Ethnomethodology*. Macmillan, London.

Hindess, Barry, and Paul Q Hirst, 1975: *Pre-Capitalist Modes of Production.* .Routledge and Kegan Paul, London.

Hinkle, Roscoe C., 1960: Durkheim in American Sociology. In *Essays on Sociology and Philosophy by Emile Durkheim et al.* (K. H. Wolff, ed.), pp. 267–95. Harper and Row, New York.

Hinkle, Roscoe C., 1963: Antecedents of the Action Orientation in American Sociology before 1935. *American Sociological Review*, **28,** 5, 705–15.

Hirsch, F. and J. H. Goldthorpe, eds., 1978: *The Political Economy of Inflation.* Martin Robertson, London.

Hobbes, Thomas, 1651: *Leviathan.* Crooke, London.

Homans, George C., 1961: *Social Behaviour: Its Elementary Forms.* Routledge and Kegan Paul, London. (2nd revised edition, 1974).

Homans, George C., 1964: Bringing Men Back In. *American Sociological Review,* **29,** 6, 809–18.

Hoogvelt, Ankie M., 1976: *The Sociology of Developing Societies.* Macmillan, London.

Horton, John, 1964: The Dehumanization of Anomie and Alienation. *British Journal of Sociology*, **15,** 4, 283–300.

Hoselitz, Bert, and Wilbert E. Moore, eds., 1963: *Industrialization and Society.* Mouton, The Hague.

Huaco, George A., 1966: The Functionalist Theory of Stratification: Two Decades of Controversy. *Inquiry*, **9,** 3, 215–40.

Hughes, John A., 1977: Wittgenstein and Social Science: Some Matters of Interpretation. *Sociological Review*, NS, **25,** 4, 721–41.

Jay, Martin, 1973: *The Dialectical Imagination.* Heinemann, London.

Kerr, Clark, John T. Dunlop, Frederick H. Harbison and Charles A. Myers, 1962: *Industrialism and Industrial Man.* Heinemann, London.

Kuhn, Thomas S., 1962: *The Structure of Scientific Revolutions.* University of Chicago Press, Chicago. (Second revised edition, 1970).

Laing, R. D., 1967: *The Politics of Experience and The Bird of Paradise.* Penguin, Harmondsworth.

Lakatos, Imre and A. Musgrave, eds. 1970: *Criticism and the Growth of Knowledge.* Cambridge University Press, Cambridge.

Leach, Edmund, 1970: *Lévi-Strauss.* Fontana, London.

Leach, Edmund, 1976: *Culture and Communication.* Cambridge University Press, Cambridge.

Lenneberg, E. H., 1967: *Biological Foundations of Language.* Wiley, New York.

Lévi-Strauss, Claude, 1963: *Structural Anthropology.* Basic Books, New York.

Lévi-Strauss, Claude, 1968a: *The Savage Mind.* Weidenfeld and Nicolson, London.

Lévi-Strauss, Claude, 1968b (orig. 1949): *The Elementary Structures of Kinship.* Eyre and Spottiswoode, London.

Lévi-Strauss, Claude, 1969 (orig. 1964): *The Raw and the Cooked (Mythologiques* I) Jonathan Cape, London.

Lévi-Strauss, Claude, 1971: *L'Homme nu* (*Mythologiques* IV). Plon, Paris.

Lévi-Strauss, Claude, 1973 (orig. 1966): *From Honey to Ashes* (*Mythologiques* II) Jonathan Cape, London.

Lévi-Strauss, Claude, 1978 (orig. 1968): *The Origin of Table Manners* (*Mythologiques* III). Jonathan Cape, London.

Lévy-Bruhl, Lucien, 1926 (orig. 1910): *How Natives Think*. George Allen and Unwin, London.

Lewis, Oscar, 1951: *Life in a Mexican Village*. University of Illinois Press, Urbana, Ill.

Linton, Ralph, 1936: *The Study of Man*. Appleton, New York.

Lipset, Seymour Martin, 1960: *Political Man*. Heinemann, London.

Lockwood, David, 1958: *The Blackcoated Worker*. George Allen & Unwin, London.

Lockwood, David, 1964: Social Integration and System Integration. In *Explorations in Social Change* (G. K. Zollschan and W. Hirsch, eds.), pp. 244–57. Routledge and Kegan Paul, London.

Lockwood, David, 1966: Sources of Variation in Working-class Images of Society. *Sociological Review*, NS **14**, 3, 249–67.

Lopreato, Joseph, 1968: Authority Relations and Class Conflict. *Social Forces*, **47**, 1, 70–79.

Lorenz, Konrad, 1966: *On Aggression*. Methuen, London.

Lowie, Robert, 1920: *Primitive Society*. Boni and Liveright, New York.

Luckmann, Thomas, 1967: *The Invisible Religion*, Macmillan, New York.

Luckmann, Thomas, ed., 1978: *Phenomenology and Sociology*. Harmondsworth, Penguin.

Lukes, Steven, 1967: Alienation and Anomie. In *Philosophy, Politics and Society*, 3rd series (P. Laslett and W. G. Runciman, eds.), pp. 134–56. Basil Blackwell, Oxford.

Lukes, Steven, 1973: *Emile Durkheim: His Life and Work*. Allen Lane, London.

Lukes, Steven, 1974: *Power: A Radical View*. Macmillan, London.

Lyons, John, 1970: *Chomsky*. Fontana, London. (2nd revised edition, 1977).

McCarthy, Thomas, 1978: *The Critical Theory of Jürgen Habermas*. Hutchinson, London.

McClosky, Herbert, and John Schaar, 1965: Psychological Dimensions of Anomy. *American Sociological Review*, **30**, 1, 14–40.

Macfarlane, Alan, 1978: *The Origins of English Individualism*. Basil Blackwell, Oxford.

McHugh, Peter, S. Raffell, D. C. Foss and A. F. Blum, 1974: *On the Beginning of Social Inquiry*. Routledge and Kegan Paul, London.

Machlup, Fritz, 1958: Equilibrium and Disequilibrium: Misplaced Concreteness and Disguised Politics. *Economic Journal*, **68**, 1, 1–24.

Magee, Bryan, 1973: *Popper*. Fontana, London.

Malinowski, Bronislaw, 1944: *A Scientific Theory of Culture*. University of North Carolina Press, Chapel Hill.

Mannheim, Karl, 1936: *Ideology and Utopia*. Kegan Paul, London.

Mannheim, Karl, 1953: Conservative Thought. In *Essays on Sociology and Social Psychology*, pp. 74–164. Routledge and Kegan Paul, London.

Marcuse, Herbert, 1964: *One-Dimensional Man*. Routledge and Kegan Paul, London.

Marshall, T. H., 1950: *Citizenship and Social Class and Other Essays*. Cambridge University Press, Cambridge.

Martin, Roderick, 1977: *The Sociology of Power*. Routledge and Kegan Paul, London.

Marx, Karl, 1947 (orig. 1846): *The German Ideology*. International Publishers Co., New York.

Marx, Karl, and Frederick Engels, 1968: *Selected Works* (in 1 vol.). Lawrence and Wishart, London.

Mead, George Herbert, 1932: *The Philosophy of the Present*. Open Court Publishing Co., Chicago.

Mead, George Herbert, 1934: *Mind, Self and Society*. University of Chicago Press, Chicago.

Mead, George Herbert, 1936: *Movements of Thought in the Nineteenth Century*. University of Chicago Press, Chicago.

Mead, George Herbert, 1938: *The Philosophy of the Act*. University of Chicago Press, Chicago.

Mennell, Stephen J., 1969: Prohibition: A Sociological View. *Journal of American Studies*, **3**, 2, 159–75.

Mennell, Stephen J., 1975: Ethnomethodology and the New *Methodenstreit*. *Acta Sociologica*, **18**, 4, 287–302, and in *New Directions in Sociology* (D. C. Thorns, ed.), pp. 139–57. David and Charles, Newton Abbot, 1976.

Mennell, Stephen J., 1979: Theoretical Considerations on the Study of Cultural 'Needs'. *Sociology*, **13**, 2, 235–57.

Merleau-Ponty, Maurice, 1974: *Phenomenology, Language and Society*. Selected essays edited by John O'Neill. Heinemann, London.

Merton, Robert K., 1936: The Unanticipated Consequences of Purposive Social Action. *American Sociological Review*, **1**, 6, 894–904.

Merton, Robert K., 1957: The Role-set: Problems in Sociological Theory. *British Journal of Sociology*, **8**, 2, 106–20.

Merton, Robert K., 1968: *Social Theory and Social Structure*, enlarged edition. Free Press, New York.

Merton, Robert K., 1970 (orig. 1938): *Science, Technology and Society in Seventeenth-Century England*. Harper and Row, New York.

Miliband, Ralph, 1969: *The State in Capitalist Society*. Weidenfeld and Nicolson, London.

Miliband, Ralph, 1970: The Capitalist State: Reply to Nicos Poulantzas. *New Left Review*, **59,** 53–60. Reprinted in *Power in Britain: Sociological Readings* (J. Urry and J. Wakeford, eds.), pp. 306–14. Heinemann, London, 1973.

Miliband, Ralph, 1973: Review of Poulantzas's *Political Power and Social Classes*. *New Left Review*, **82,** 83–92.

Mills, C. Wright, 1956: *The Power Elite*. Oxford University Press, New York.

Mills, C. Wright, 1964: *Sociology and Pragmatism: The Higher Learning in America*. Oxford University Press, New York.

Mishan, E. J., 1960: A Survey of Welfare Economics, 1939–59. *Economic Journal*, **70**, 2, 197–265.

Murphy, Robert F., 1971: *The Dialectics of Social Life*. Basic Books, New York.

Nagel, Ernest, 1956: A Formalization of Functionalism. In *Logic Without Metaphysics*, pp. 247–83. Free Press, New York. Reprinted in *System, Change and Conflict* (N. J. Demerath III and R. A. Peterson, eds.), pp. 77–94. Free Press, New York, 1967.

Nettler, Gwynn, 1957: A Measure of Alienation. *American Sociological Review*, **22**, 6, 670–77.

Neumann, John von, and Oscar Morgenstern, 1944: *Theory of Games and Economic Behaviour*. Princeton University Press, Princeton, N.J.

Nichols, Theo., 1969: *Ownership, Control and Ideology*. George Allen and Unwin, London.

Ollman, Bertell, 1976: *Alienation: Marx's Conception of Man in Capitalist Society*. Second edition, Cambridge University Press, Cambridge.

Olson, Mancur, 1965: *The Logic of Collective Action*. Harvard University Press, Cambridge, Mass.

O'Neill, John, 1970: *Perception, Expression and History: The Social Phenomenology of Maurice Merleau-Ponty*. Northwestern University Press, Evanston, Ill.

O'Neill, John, 1972: *Sociology as a Skin Trade*. Heinemann, London.

Outhwaite, William, 1975: *Understanding Social Life: The Method Called Verstehen*. George Allen and Unwin, London.

Park, Robert E., E. W. Burgess, and R. D. McKenzie, 1925: *The City*. University of Chicago Press, Chicago.

Parsons, Talcott, 1937: *The Structure of Social Action*. McGraw-Hill, New York.

Parsons, Talcott, 1951: *The Social System*. Free Press, New York.

Parsons, Talcott, 1960: Pattern Variables Revisited: A Response to Robert Dubin. *American Sociological Review*, **25**, 4, 467–83.

Parsons, Talcott, 1961: An Outline of the Social System. In *Theories of Society* (T. Parsons, E. A. Shils, K. D. Naegele and J. R. Pitts, eds.), pp. 30–79. Free Press, New York.

Parsons, Talcott, 1963: On the Concept of Political Power. *Proceedings of the American Philosophical Society*, **107**, 3, 232–62. Reprinted in *Politics and Social Structure*, pp. 352–404 (Free Press, New York, 1969) and in *Sociological Theory and Modern Society*, pp. 297–354 (Free Press, New York, 1967).

Parsons, Talcott, 1964: Evolutionary Universals in Society. *American Sociological Review*, **29**, 3, 339–57.

Parsons, Talcott, 1977a: On Building Social System Theory. In *Social Systems and the Evolution of Action Theory*, pp. 22–76. Free Press, New York.

Parsons, Talcott, 1977b: *The Evolution of Societies*. Prentice-Hall, Englewood Cliffs, N.J. (Combined and revised version of *Societies: Evolutionary and Comparative Perspectives*, 1966, and *The System of Modern Societies*, 1971.)

Parsons, Talcott, and Robert F. Bales, 1955: *Family, Socialization and Interaction Process*. Free Press, Glencoe, Ill.

Parsons, Talcott, R. F. Bales and E. A. Shils, 1953: *Working Papers in the Theory of Action*. Free Press, New York.

Parsons, Talcott, and E. A. Shils, eds., 1951: *Toward a General Theory of Action*. Harvard University Press, Cambridge, Mass.

Parsons, Talcott, and Neil J. Smelser, 1956: *Economy and Society*. Free Press, New York.

Piaget, Jean, 1926: *The Language and Thought of the Child*. Kegan Paul, London.

Piaget, Jean, 1932: *The Moral Judgment of the Child*. Kegan Paul, London.

Pollner, Melvin, 1974: Sociological and Common-sense Models of the Labelling Process. In *Ethnomethodology* (Roy Turner, ed.), pp. 27–40. Harmondsworth, Penguin.

Pollock, Friedrich, 1976 (orig. 1955): Empirical Research into Public Opinion. In *Critical Sociology* (P. Connerton, ed.), pp. 225–36. Penguin, Harmondsworth.

Popper, Sir Karl R., 1945: *The Open Society and its Enemies* (2 vols.). Routledge and Kegan Paul, London.

Popper, Sir Karl R., 1957 (orig. 1944–45): *The Poverty of Historicism*. Routledge and Kegan Paul, London.

Popper, Sir Karl R., 1959: *The Logic of Scientific Discovery*. Hutchinson, London.

Popper, Sir Karl R., 1963: *Conjectures and Refutations*. Routledge and Kegan Paul, London.

Popper, Sir Karl R., 1972: *Objective Knowledge: An Evolutionary Approach*. Clarendon Press, Oxford.

Popper, Sir Karl R., 1976: *Unended Quest*. Fontana, London.

Poulantzas, Nicos, 1969: The Problem of the Capitalist State. *New Left Review*, 58, 67–78. Reprinted in *Power in Britain: Sociological Readings* (J. Urry and J. Wakeford, eds.), pp. 291–305. Heinemann, London, 1973.

Poulantzas, Nicos, 1973: *Political Power and Social Classes*. New Left Books, London.

Radcliffe Brown, A. R., 1952: *Structure and Function in Primitive Society*. Cohen and West, London.

Reddaway, W. B., 1964 (orig. 1936): Review of J. M. Keynes's *The General Theory of Employment, Interest and Money*. In *Keynes's General Theory: Reports on Three Decades* (R. Lekachman, ed.), pp. 99–108. Macmillan, London.

Redfield, Robert, 1930: *Tepoztlán, A Mexican Village*. University of Chicago Press, Chicago.

Redfield, Robert, 1947: The Folk Society. *American Journal of Sociology*, **52,** 4, 293–308. Reprinted in *Human Nature and the Study of Society* (M. P. Redfield, ed.), pp. 231–53. University of Chicago Press, Chicago.

Riesman, David, with Nathan Glazer and Reuel Denney, 1950: *The Lonely Crowd*. Yale University Press, New Haven.

Rocher, Guy, 1974: *Talcott Parsons and American Sociology*. Nelson, London.

Roethlisberger, F. J. and W. J. Dickson, 1939: *Management and the Worker*. Harvard University Press, Cambridge, Mass.

Rock, Paul, 1978: *The Making of Symbolic Interactionism*. Macmillan, London.

Rose, Arnold, M., ed., 1962: *Human Behaviour and Social Processes.* Houghton Mifflin, Boston.

Rose, Gillian, 1978: *The Melancholy Science: An Introduction to the Thought of Theodor W. Adorno.* Macmillan, London.

Rudner, Richard S., 1966: *Philosophy of Social Science.* Prentice-Hall, Englewood Cliffs, N.J.

Runciman, W. G., 1966: *Relative Deprivation and Social Justice.* Routledge and Kegan Paul, London.

Runciman, W. G., 1970: *Sociology in its Place and Other Essays.* Cambridge University Press, Cambridge.

Runciman, W. G. ed., 1978: *Max Weber: Selections in Translation.* Cambridge University Press, Cambridge.

Sacks, Harvey, E. Schegloff and G. Jefferson, 1974: A Simplest Systematics for the Organization of Turn-taking. *Language,* **50,** 4 (part 1), 696–735.

Samuelson, Paul A., 1961: *Economics: An Introductory Analysis,* 5th ed. McGraw-Hill, New York.

Schacht, Richard L., 1971: *Alienation.* George Allen and Unwin, London.

Schegloff, E. and H. Sacks, 1974: Opening Up Closings. In *Ethnomethodology* (Roy Turner, ed.) pp. 233–64. Penguin, Harmondsworth.

Schofield, Kenneth, 1974: *Benzene.* Inaugural Lecture, University of Exeter, Exeter.

Schutz, Alfred, 1962: *Collected Papers I: The Problem of Social Reality.* Martinus Nijhoff, The Hague.

Schutz, Alfred, 1964: *Collected Papers II: Studies in Social Theory.* Martinus Nijhoff, The Hague.

Schutz, Alfred, 1966: *Collected Papers III: Studies in Phenomenological Philosophy.* Martinus Nijhoff, The Hague.

Schutz, Alfred, 1972 (Orig. 1932): *The Phenomenology of the Social World.* Heinemann, London.

Schutz, Alfred, and Thomas Luckmann, 1974: *The Structures of the Life-World.* Heinemann, London.

Scott, J. Finley, 1963: The Changing Foundations of the Parsonian Action Scheme. *American Sociological Review,* **28,** 5, 716–35.

Seeman, Melvin, 1959: On the Meaning of Alienation. *Americal Sociological Review,* **24,** 6, 783–91.

Shaw, Clifford R., with the collaboration of H. D. MacKay, F. Zorbaugh and L. S. Cottrell, 1929: *Delinquency Areas.* University of Chicago Press, Chicago.

Shaw, Clifford R., 1930: *The Jack-Roller: A Delinquent Boy's Own Story.* University of Chicago Press, Chicago.

Simmel, Georg, 1950 (orig. 1908): *The Sociology of Georg Simmel.* Free Press, Glencoe, Ill.

Skinner, B. F., 1948: *Walden Two.* Macmillan, New York.

Skinner, B. F., 1953: *Science and Human Behaviour.* Macmillan, New York.

Skinner, B. F., 1957: *Verbal Behaviour.* Appleton-Century-Crofts, New York.

Skinner, B. F., 1972: *Beyond Freedom and Dignity.* Knopff, New York.

Sklair, Leslie, 1970: The Fate of the 'Functional Requisites' in Parsonian Sociology. *British Journal of Sociology*, **21**, 1, 30–42.

Smith, Adam, 1970 (orig. 1776): *An Inquiry into the Nature and Causes of The Wealth of Nations*. Penguin, Harmondsworth.

Smelser, Neil J., 1959: *Social Change in the Industrial Revolution*. Routledge and Kegan Paul, London.

Sombart, Werner, 1976 (orig. 1906): *Why is there no Socialism in the United States?* Macmillan, London.

Spencer, Herbert, 1893: *Principles of Sociology* (3 vols.) 3rd ed., Williams and Norgate, London.

Srole, Leo, 1956: Social Integration and Certain Corollaries: An Exploratory Study. *American Sociological Review*, **21**, 6, 709–16.

Stolzman, James D., 1975: Objective and Subjective Concepts of Interest in Sociological Analysis. *Sociological Analysis and Theory*, **5**, 1, 107–15.

Stone, Gregory P., and Harvey A. Farberman, 1967: On the Edge of Rapprochement: Was Durkheim moving toward the Perspective of Symbolic Interactionism? *Sociological Quarterly*, **8**, 2, 149–64.

Stouffer, Samuel A., 1949: An Analysis of Conflicting Social Norms. *American Sociological Review*, **14**, 6, 707–17.

Stouffer, Samuel A., and Jackson Toby, 1951: Role Conflict and Personality. *American Journal of Sociology*, **61**, 5, 395–406.

Sudnow, David, 1968: *Passing On: The Social Organization of Dying*. Prentice-Hall, Englewood Cliffs, N.J.

Sutherland, Edwin H., 1947: *Principles of Criminology*, 4th edition. Lippincott, Philadelphia.

Suttles, Gerald D., 1972: *The Social Construction of Communities*. University of Chicago Press, Chicago.

Sztompka, Piotr, 1974: *System and Function: Toward a Theory of Society*. Academic Press, New York.

Therborn, Göran, 1978: *What does the Ruling Class do When it Rules?* New Left Books, London.

Thibaut, J. W. and H. H. Kelley, 1959: *The Social Psychology of Groups*. Wiley, New York.

Thomas, W. I., and F. Znaniecki, 1918–20: *The Polish Peasant in Europe and America*, 5 vols. University of Chicago Press, Chicago.

Thompson, E. P., 1978: *The Poverty of Theory and Other Essays*. Merlin Press, London.

Thrasher, Frederick M., 1926: *The Gang*. University of Chicago Press, Chicago.

Tiryakian, Edward A., 1965: Existential Phenomenology and the Sociological Tradition. *American Sociological Review*, **30**, 5, 674–88.

Turner, Ralph H., 1962: Role-taking: Process versus Conformity. In *Human Behaviour and Social Processes* (A. M. Rose, ed.), pp. 20–40. Houghton Mifflin, Boston.

Wallerstein, Immanuel, 1974: *The Modern World-System*. Academic Press, New York.

Weber, Max, 1930 (orig. 1904–5): *The Protestant Ethic and the Spirit of Capitalism*. George Allen and Unwin, London.

Weber, Max, 1968 (orig. 1922): *Economy and Society*, 3 vols. Bedminster Press, New York.

White, D. M., 1971: Power and Intention. *American Political Science Review*, **65,** 3, 749–59.

Whorf, Benjamin Lee, 1956: *Language, Thought and Reality*. Wiley, New York.

Wilson, Thomas P., 1971: Normative and Interpretive Paradigms in Sociology. In *Understanding Everyday Life* (Jack D. Douglas, ed.), pp. 57–79. Routledge and Kegan Paul, London.

Wilterdink, Nico, 1977: Norbert Elias's Sociology of Knowledge and its Significance for the Study of the Sciences. In *Human Figurations: Essays for Norbert Elias* (P. R. Gleichmann, J. Goudsblom and H. Korte, eds.), pp. 110–26. Stichting Amsterdams Sociologisch Tijdschrift, Amsterdam.

Wirth, Louis, 1938: *The Ghetto*. University of Chicago Press, Chicago.

Witkin, Robert W., 1971: Social Action and Subcultural Theories: A Critique. In *Crime and Delinquency in Britain* (W. G. Carson and P. Wiles, eds.), pp. 153–63. Martin Robertson, London.

Woodward, Joan, 1958: *Management and Technology*. Her Majesty's Stationery Office, London. Excerpted in *Industrial Man* (Tom Burns, ed.), pp. 196–231. Penguin, Harmondsworth, 1969.

Wouters, Cas, 1977: Informalization and the Civilizing Process. In *Human Figurations: Essays for Norbert Elias* (P. R. Gleichmann, J. Goudsblom and H. Korte, eds.), pp. 437–53. Stichting Amsterdams Sociologisch Tijdschrift, Amsterdam.

Wrong, Dennis H., 1959: The Functional Theory of Stratification: Some Neglected Considerations. *American Sociological Review*, **24,** 6, 772–82. Reprinted in *Skeptical Sociology*, pp. 103–20, Heinemann, London, 1976.

Wrong, Dennis H., 1961: The Oversocialized Conception of Man in Modern Sociology. *American Sociological Review*, **26,** 2, 183–93. Reprinted in *Skeptical Sociology*, pp. 31–54, Heinemann, London, 1976.

Wrong, Dennis H., 1968: Some Problems in Defining Social Power. *American Journal of Sociology*, **73,** 5, 673–81. Reprinted in *Skeptical Sociology*, pp. 163–82, Heinemann, London, 1976.

Zijderveld, Anton C., 1972: *The Abstract Society: A Cultural Analysis of our Time*. Allen Lane, London.

Zimmerman, D. H. and M. Pollner, 1971: The Everyday World as a Phenomenon. In *Understanding Everyday Life* (Jack D. Douglas, ed.), pp. 80–103. Routledge and Kegan Paul, London.

Zorbaugh, H. W., 1929: *The Gold Coast and the Slum*. University of Chicago Press, Chicago.

Index